Japanese Grammar

Keiko Uesawa Chevray

Tomiko Kuwahira

Schaum's Outline Series

New York   Chicago   San Francisco   Lisbon   London   Madrid
Mexico City   Milan   New Delhi   San Juan   Seoul
Singapore   Sydney   Toronto

The McGraw·Hill Companies

Keiko Uesawa Chevray is director of the Japanese Language Program at Columbia University in New York, and full time senior lecturer in Japanese in the Department of East Asian Languages and Cultures. She is also a member of the Board of Directors of the Japanese American Association of New York.

Tomiko Kuwahira is lecturer in Japanese in the Department of East Asian Languages and Cultures at Columbia University. She has also taught Japanese at Beijing University in the People's Republic of China.

4 5 6 7 8 9 10   CUS/CUS   1 9 8 7 6 5 4 3

ISBN   978-0-07-175608-2
MHID   0-07-175608-6

Contents

Chapter *1* **COPULA**

Affirmative Non-Past.   Negative Non-Past.   Affirmative Past.   Negative Past.
Tentative Form.   *Te*-Form.

Chapter *2* **ADJECTIVES**

I-Adjective.   *Na*-Adjective.

I-Adjective.   *Na*-Adjective.

I-Adjective.   *Na*-Adjective.

I-Adjective.   *Na*-Adjective.

I-Adjective.   *Na*-Adjective.

I-Adjective.   *Na*-Adjective.

I-Adjective.   *Na*-Adjective.

V-stem + *Tai*.   V-*te* + *Hoshii*.   (*Hoshii*).   V-stem + *Yasui*.   V-stem + *Nikui*.

CONTENTS   v

Chapter *7* CONJUNCTIONS

Chapter *8* VERBS

Chapter *14* HONORIFIC EXPRESSIONS

Chapter *15* USEFUL EXPRESSIONS

Preface

Schaum's Outline of Japanese Grammar has been designed to be used as a review book for Japanese grammar at the elementary level. The book is divided into fifteen chapters. At the beginning of each chapter, basic elements of the language are introduced, pointing out their differences from English. Chapters 1 through 14, concentrate on the basic problem areas of the language: copula, adjectives, adverbs, pronouns, numbers, particles, conjunctions, verbs, conditional clauses, interrogative words, modification of a noun, nominalization, modality, and honorific expressions. The last chapter introduces several useful expressions to be learned at the elementary level.

Each grammatical or structural point is followed by a simple explanation in English and then by concrete examples for the further clarification. These are followed by exercises. An answer key appears at the end of the book.

All the examples and exercises are written first in both Japanese characters, *kana*, and Chinese characters, *kanji*, so that they will be authentic Japanese sentences. They are then followed by the same sentences in Roman letters, and then, finally, in English translations which are written in italic.

The vocabulary employed here is limited to those words which are considered to be basic. The loan words from European languages, mainly from English, are written in *katakana,* and some of them are directly followed by English translation because they are different from the originals when written in *katakana.*

Since this is a review book for basic Japanese grammar as stated above, all grammar and expressions introduced here are limited to those which are regarded to be basic.

The examples and exercises for each chapter are written so that the students can get the clear understanding of the function of each grammatical point. The students are encouraged to read all the examples after the grammatical explanation and then to work on the exercises.

This book can be used not only as a review book but also as a supplementary workbook to any textbook, or as a reference book for understanding basic Japanese grammatical points.

Keiko Uesawa Chevray
Tomiko Kuwahira

Writing System

There are three different kinds of symbols in Japanese, Hiragana, Katakana, and Kanji (Chinese characters). Katakana are used to write out loan words from other languages. Hiragana can be used to write out all the other Japanese words, but Kanji are commonly used for nouns. They are also used for verbs and adjectives except for their inflected parts. The following are the charts of Hiragana, Katakana, and the corresponding Rooma-ji (the system used for transcribing Japanese with the Latin alphabet), which we use in this book.

Hiragana Katakana Rooma-ji	あ ア a	か カ ka	さ サ sa	た タ ta	な ナ na	は ハ ha	ま マ ma	や ヤ ya	ら ラ ra	わ ワ wa	ん ン n
	い イ i	き キ ki	し シ shi	ち チ chi	に ニ ni	ひ ヒ hi	み ミ mi	い イ i	り リ ri	い イ i	
	う ウ u	く ク ku	す ス su	つ ツ tsu	ぬ ヌ nu	ふ フ fu	む ム mu	ゆ ユ yu	る ル ru	う ウ u	
	え エ e	け ケ ke	せ セ se	て テ te	ね ネ ne	へ ヘ he	め メ me	え エ e	れ レ re	え エ e	
	お オ o	こ コ ko	そ ソ so	と ト to	の ノ no	ほ ホ ho	も モ mo	よ ヨ yo	ろ ロ ro	を ヲ wo	

Hiragana Katakana Rooma-ji	が ガ ga	ざ ザ za	だ ダ da	ば バ ba	ぱ パ pa
	ぎ ギ gi	じ ジ ji	ぢ ヂ ji	び ビ bi	ぴ ピ pi
	ぐ グ gu	ず ズ zu	づ ヅ zu	ぶ ブ bu	ぷ プ pu
	げ ゲ ge	ぜ ゼ ze	で デ de	べ ベ be	ぺ ペ pe
	ご ゴ go	ぞ ゾ zo	ど ド do	ぼ ボ bo	ぽ ポ po

Hiragana Katakana Rooma-ji	きゃ キャ kya	ぎゃ ギャ gya	しゃ シャ sya	じゃ ジャ ja	ちゃ チャ cha	にゃ ニャ nya	ひゃ ヒャ hya	びゃ ビャ bya	ぴゃ ピャ pya	みゃ ミャ mya	りゃ リャ rya
	きゅ キュ kyu	ぎゅ ギュ gyu	しゅ シュ shu	じゅ ジュ ju	ちゅ チュ chu	にゅ ニュ nyu	ひゅ ヒュ hyu	びゅ ビュ byu	ぴゅ ピュ pyu	みゅ ミュ myu	りゅ リュ ryu
	きょ キョ kyo	ぎょ ギョ gyo	しょ ショ sho	じょ ジョ jo	ちょ チョ cho	にょ ニョ nyo	ひょ ヒョ hyo	びょ ビョ byo	ぴょ ピョ pyo	みょ ミョ myo	りょ リョ ryo

Some Characteristics of Japanese Grammar

WORD ORDER

I. <u>Basic Sentence Structure</u>

Japanese is different from English in the word order of a sentence. The main verb is preceded by the object, and it always comes at the end of a sentence in Japanese (the main verb precedes the object of a sentence in English).

友達が/は 時計を買いました。

<u>Tomodachi</u> ga/wa <u>tokei</u> wo <u>kaimashita</u>.　　　　My friend bought a watch.

　(friend)　　　　(watch)　(bought)　　　　Subject　Verb　Object

　　Subject　　　Object　　Verb

II. <u>Modifiers</u>

Japanese is regarded as a left-branching language, which means that all noun modifiers such as possessives, adjectives, and sentence modifiers. precede the head nouns. Also, all adverbial phrases precede their modifying verbs or adjectives.

1. これは**日本語の学生の**<u>辞書</u>だ。

   Kore wa　**nihongo no gakusei no** <u>jisho</u> da.

   (This is a dictionary of Japanese language students.)

2. **安くてきれいな**<u>アパート</u>を探しています。

   Yasukute kireina <u>apaato</u> wo sagashite imasu.

   (I am looking for an apartment that is cheap and clean.)

3. 昨日家で**友達に借りた**<u>本</u>を読んだ。

   Kinoo uch de **tomodachi ni karita** <u>hon</u> wo yonda.

   (Yesterday I read the book at home, which I borrowed from a friend.)

PARTICLES

Particles play the roles of case markers in Japanese sentences. Each of them follows a noun phrase and tells how the noun phrase is related to the predicate of a sentence. For example, the particle "**wa**" functions as a topic marker, and it marks a noun phrase as the topic of a sentence.

1. 私は日本語を話します。

   Watashi **wa** (= topic) nihon-go **wo** (= object) hanashimasu.

   (I speak Japanese.)

2. 電車でボストンに行きます。

   Densha **de** (= manner) Boston **ni** (= goal/direction) ikimasu.

   (I will go to Boston by train.)

OMISSION

A noun phrase such as a topic or an object is commonly omitted if it is understood in context.

1. A: **(あなたは)** 昨日映画を見ましたか。

   (Anata wa) kinoo eiga wo mimashita ka.

   (Did (you) see a movie yesterday?)

   B:　はい、**(私は)** **(映画を)** 見ました。

   Hai, **(watashi wa) (eiga wo)** mimashita.

   (Yes, (I) did.)

2. 父は日本に行ったから今 **(父は)** 家にいません。

   Chichi wa nihon ni itta kara ima **(chichi wa)** uchi ni imasen.

   (My father went to Japan, so (he) is not home now.)

SPEECH STYLES

There are mainly two types of speech style in Japanese, formal and informal.　Informal style is considered to be a non polite expression, and it is used among people who have intimate or close personal relationships like one's own family and friends.　On the other hand, formal style is considered to be a polite expression, and it is usually used between the people who carry on a conversation in a formal or public situation, or it is used between people who are not personally very close.　A sentence in formal style ends in "**desu**" or "**masu**."　The informal style corresponds to the plain form.

Formal speech style

    Ex. (A conversation between A and B, who are colleagues)

        A: 今日は何時に**帰ります**か。

           Kyoo wa nan-ji ni **kaerimasu** ka.

           (What time will you go home today?)

        B: 六時頃帰るつもり**です**。

           Roku-ji goro kaeru tsumori **desu**.

           (I'm going to go home around six o'clock.)

Informal speech style

    Ex. (A conversation between A and B, who are a daughter and a father)

        A: お父さん、今日何時頃**出かける**の。

           Otoosan, kyoo nan-ji goro **dekakeru** no?

           (Father, what time will you go out today?)

        B: 九時頃出かけるつもり**だ**よ。

           Ku-ji goro dekakeru tsumori **da** yo.

           (I'll go out around nine o'clock.)

HONORIFICS

    Japanese honorific expressions are highly developed and based on the hierarchy of age and status in the society. They are used to show one's respect especially to the elderly or to people of higher status than oneself. There are two kinds of honorific. One is "honorific" and the other is "humble." The honorific form refers to the person who is to be respected, and the humble form is used to talk about the speaker or the speaker's own family.

Honorific form

   Ex. 田中先生は今日学校に**いらっしゃいません**（＝いません）。

      Tanaka sensei wa kyoo gakkoo ni **irasshaimasen** (=imasen).

      (Professor Tanaka is not at school today.)

Humble form

   Ex. 父も母も今家に**おりません**（＝いません）。

      Chichi mo haha mo ima uchi ni **orimasen** (=imasen).

      (Neither my father nor my mother is home now.)

Chapter 1

Copula

FORMS

	non-past	neg. non-past	past	neg. past
Plain	だ	では/じゃ ない	だった	では/じゃ なかった
	da	dewa/ja nai	datta	dewa/ja nakatta
Polite	です	では/じゃ ありません	でした	では/じゃ ありませんでした
	desu	dewa/ja arimasen	deshita	dewa/ja arimasen deshita

Affirmative non-past

The affirmative non-past of copula is "**da**" (plain) or "**desu**" (polite) and is equivalent to "is", "am," or "are" in English. "X **wa** Y **da/desu**" means "X is Y" or "As for X, it is Y." When X is understood from context, just "Y **da/desu**" is sufficient.

1. 田中さんは大学生**です**。

   Tanaka-san wa daigakusei **desu**.

   (Ms. Tanaka is a college student.)

2. A: ピーターさん**です**か。 *

   Piitaa-san **desu** ka. *

   (Are you Peter?)

   B: はい、そう**です**。

   Hai, soo **desu**.

   (Yes, I am /Lit. it is so.)

(* **か** is added at the end of a sentence to make it into interrogative.)

1

3. 一時**です**。

Ichi-ji **desu**.

(It is one o'clock.)

4. 田中さんのアパートはきれい**です**ね。

Tanaka-san no apaato wa kirei **desu** ne.

(Miss Tanaka's apartment is pretty, isn't it?)

5. 星野さんは先生**だ**。

Hoshino-san wa sensei **da**.

(Mr. Hoshino is a teacher.)

6. コンピューターは便利**だ**。

Konpyuutaa wa benri **da**.

(A computer is convenient.)

7. 新幹線は早いですよ。

Shinkansen wa hayai desu yo.

(The bullet train is fast, you know.)

Negative non-past

The negagive non-past of copula is "**ja/dewa nai**" (plain) or "**ja/dewa arimasen**" (polite). "X **wa** Y **ja nai/arimasen**" and "(X **wa**) Y **ja nai/arimasen**" mean "X is not Y" and "It is not Y" respectively.

1. これはダイエット・コーク**じゃありません**。

Kore wa daietto kooku **ja arimasen**.

(This is not diet Coke.)

2. あれはさくら**じゃない**。

Are wa sakura **ja nai**.

(That is not a cherry tree.)

3. A: パーティーは今日ですか。

Paatii wa kyoo desu ka

(As for the party, is it today?)

B:いいえ、今日**じゃありません**。

Iie, kyoo **ja arimasen**.

(No, it is not today.)

4. この問題は簡単**じゃない**。

Kono mondai wa kantan **ja nai**.

(This problem is not simple.)

5. それは私の**じゃありません**。

Sore wa watashi no **ja arimasen**.

(That is not mine.)

Affirmative past

The affirmative past of copula is "**datta**" (plain) or "**deshita**" (polite). "X **wa** Y **datta/deshita**" and "(X **wa**) Y **datta/deshita**" mean "X was Y" and "It was Y" respectively.

1. 山本さんはパイロット**でした**。

   Yamamoto-san wa pairotto **deshita**

   (Mr. Yamamoto was a pilot.).

2. 昨日はコロンバス・デー**だった**。

   Kinoo wa Koronbasu dee (Columbus day) **datta**.

   (Yesterday it was Columbus day.)

3. A: いくら**でしたか**。

      Ikura **deshita** ka.

      (How much was it?)

   B: 五十ドル**でした**。

      Gojuu-doru **deshita**.

      (It was fifty dollars.)

4. この間行った神社は立派**だった**。

   Kono aida itta jinja wa rippa **datta**.

   (The shrine where I went the other day was splendid.)

5. 私の最初の車はホンダ**でした**。

   Watashi no saisho no kuruma wa Honda **deshita**.

   (My first car was a Honda.)

Negative past

The negative past of copula is "**ja/dewa nakatta**" (plain) or "**ja/dewa arimasen deshita**" (polite). "X **wa** Y **ja nakatta/arimasen deshita**" and "(X **wa**)Y **ja nakatta/arimasen deshita**" mean " X was not Y" and "It was not Y" respectively.

1. A: 学校は休みでしたか。

   Gakkoo wa yasumi deshita ka.

   (Was school closed?)

B: いいえ、休み**じゃありませんでした**。

    Iie, yasumi **ja arimasen deshita**.

    (No, it was not closed.)

2. 昨日シカゴは雪**じゃありませんでした**。

Kinoo Shikago wa yuki **ja arimasen deshita**.

(Yesterday it did not snow in Chicago.)

3. 私がニューヨークで泊まったホテルは静か**じゃありませんでした**。

Watashi ga Nyuu Yooku de tomatta hoteru wa shizuka **ja arimasen deshita**.

(The hotel where I stayed in New York was not quiet.)

4. 図書館にいた女の人は学生**じゃなかった**。

Toshokan ni ita onna no hito wa gakusei **ja nakatta**.

(The woman who was in the library was not a student.)

Note: "**desu**" could also be a substitution for a predicate which is obvious from context.

友子さんはいつもコーヒーを飲みますが、私はお茶**です**。

Tomoko-san wa itsumo koohii wo nomimasu ga, watashi wa o-cha **desu**.

*(Tomoko drinks always coffee, but I **drink** tea.)*

Tentative form

The tentative form of copula is "**daroo**" (plain) or "**deshoo**" (polite) and is preceded by a noun, an adjective, or a verb. It indicates the speaker's conjecture and is equivalent to "probably" in English.

1. 明日は雨**でしょう**。

Ashita wa ame **deshoo**.

(It will probably rain tomorrow.)

2. 田宮さんのアパートは高かった**でしょう**ね。

Tamiya-san no apaato wa takakatta **deshoo** ne.

(Mr. Tamiya's apartment was probably expensive, wasn't it?)

3. ヘブライ語は難しい**だろう**と思います。

Hebrai-go wa muzukashii **daroo** to omoimasu.

(I think that Hebrew is probably difficult.)

4. 良子さんはアメリカに五年いたから、英語が上手**でしょう**。

Yoshiko-san wa Amerika ni go-nen ita kara, ei-go ga joozu **deshoo**.

(Yoshiko was in the United States for five years, so she is probably fluent in English.)

5. 私の友達は今日本にいる**でしょう**。

Watashi no tomodachi wa ima Nihon ni iru **deshoo**.

(My friend is probably in Japan now.)

Te-form

The te-form of copula is "**de**" and links a sentence, "X **wa** Y **da/desu**," with another sentence. It is equivalent to "and" in English.

1. 木村さんは先生**で**、奥さんは医者です。

   Kimura-san wa sensei **de**, okusan wa isha desu.

   (Mr. Kimura is a teacher, and his wife is a doctor.)

2. これは日本のカメラ**で**、あれはドイツのです。

   Kore wa Nihon no kamera **de**, are wa Doitsu no desu.

   (This is a Japanese camera, and that is a German (one).)

3. 結婚式は三時**で**、レセプションは五時です。

   Kekkon-shiki wa san-ji **de**, resepushon wa go-ji desu.

   (The wedding is at three o'clock, and the reception is at five o'clock.)

4. スミスさんはイギリス人**で**、去年ロンドンから来ました。

   Sumisu-san wa igirisu-jin **de**, kyonen Rondon kara kimashita.

   (Mr. Sumith is English and came from London last year.)

5. 友子さんはテニスがとても上手**で**、プロになりました。

   Tomoko-san wa tenisu ga totemo joozu **de**, pro ni narimashita.

   (Tomoko plays tennis very well and has became a professional.)

1. Change the following into the required form given in the parentheses.

   Ex.   新聞だ → (polite past) <u>新聞でした</u>

   　　　shinbun da → (polite past) <u>shinbun deshita</u>

1. 母だ (plain negative) _____

   Haha da (plain negative) _____

2. 火曜日だ (polite past) _____

   Kayoobi da (polite past) _____

3. 日本人だ (polite negative past) _____

   Nihon-jin da (polite negative past) _____

4. 大きいビルだ (te-form) _____

   Ookii biru da (te-form) _____

    Ookii biru da   (te-form) _____

5. 田中さんだ   (polite negative non-past) _____

   Tanaka-san da   (polite negative non-past) _____

6. 魚だ   (plain past) _____

   Sakana da   (plain past) _____

7. イタリアの映画だ   (plain negative past) _____

   Itaria no eiga da   (plain negative past) _____

2. Fill in the blanks with an appropriate form of copula.

1. 今日は火曜日_____。

   Kyoo wa kayoobi _____.

2. A: あれはさくらですか。

     Are wa sakura desu ka.

   B: いいえ、そう _____。

     Iie, soo _____.

3. 五年前ピーターさんは先生 _____ が、今はサラリーマン _____。

   Gonen mae Piitaa-san wa sensei _____ ga, ima wa sarariiman _____.

4. 今年父は六十才 _____、母は五十五才になります。

   Kotoshi chichi wa rokujis-sai _____, haha wa gojuugo-sai ni narimasu.

5. 今日は何日 _____か。

   Kyoo wa nan nichi _____ ka.

6. 斎藤さんは車で行きますが、私はバス _____。

   Saitoo-san wa kuruma de ikimasu ga, watashi wa basu (bus)_____.

7. A: さっき来た人は吉田さんでしたか。

     Sakki kita hito wa Yoshida-san deshita ka.

   B: いいえ、吉田さん _____。

     Iie, Yoshida-san _____.

8. これは中国のお茶_____、それは日本のお茶ですよ。

   Kore wa Chuugoku no o-cha _____, sore wa nihon no o-cha desu yo.

9. この町には地下鉄がないから、不便 _____ ね。

   Kono machi ni wa chikatetsu ga nai kara, fuben _____ ne.

Chapter 2

Adjectives

There are two types of Japanese adjectives, I-adjectives and Na-adjectives. Japanese adjectives have tense, while English ones do not. The structure of the Japanese adjectival sentence is basically "X **wa** I-adjecitive/**Na**-adjective" or "X **wa** Y **ga** I-adjective/**Na**-adjective" and it corresponds to "X is/are so and so" and "Speaking of X, Y is/are so and so" respectively.

I-ADJECTIVE

	non-past	**neg. non-past**	**past**	**neg. past**
Plain	大きい	大きくない	大きかった	大きくなかった
	ookii	ookikunai	ookikatta	ookikunakatta
Polite	大きいです	大きくありません	大きかったです	大きくありませんでした
	ookii desu	ookiku arimasen	ookikatta desu	ookiku arimasen deshita

NA-ADJECTIVE

	non-past	**neg. non-past**	**past**	**neg. past**
Plain	静かだ	静かじゃ/ではない	静かだった	静かじゃ/ではなかった
	shizuka da	shizuka ja/dewa nai	shizuka datta	shizuka ja/dewa nakatta
Polite	静かです	静かじゃありません	静かでした	静かじゃありませんでした
	shizuka desu	shizuka ja arimasen	shizuka deshita	shizuka ja arimasen deshita

NON-PAST

Both I-adjectives and Na-adjectives have two forms of non-past, plain and polite non-past.

I-adjective

The plain form of an I-adjective is identical to the dictionary form. The copula "**desu**" is added to the plain form to construct the polite form.

    Ex.   plain: **ookii**   polite: **ookii desu**

1. この時計は**大きいです**ね。
   Kono tokei wa **ookii desu** ne.
   (This watch is big, isn't it?)

2. ナイルは**長い**。
   Nairu wa **nagai**.
   (The Nile is long.)

3. ダイアモンドは**高い**。
   Daiamondo wa **takai**.
   (Diamonds are expensive.)

4. 日本語は**おもしろいです**。
   Nihon-go wa **omoshiroi desu**.
   (Japanese is interesting.)

5. トムさんは背が**高い**。
   Tomu-san wa se ga **takai**.
   (Tom is tall.)

6. フランスはパンが**おいしいです**。
   Furansu wa pan ga **oishii desu**.
   (Bread is delicious in France/ Lit. Talking about France, bread is delicious.)

Na-adjective

The copula "**da**" or "**desu**" is added to the stem to construct the plain and polite form respectively.

    Ex.   plain: **heta da**   polite: **heta desu**.

1. 鈴木さんは**元気です**。
   Suzuki-san wa **genki desu**.
   (Mr. Suzuki is well/ Lit. healthy.)

2. このテストは**簡単だ**。

   Kono tesuto wa **kantan da**.

   (This test is easy/ Lit. simple.)

3. 友子さんはテニスがとても**上手です**。

   Tomoko-san wa tenisu ga totemo **joozu desu**.

   (Tomoko plays tennis very well/ Lit. Tomoko is very good at tennis.)

4. 一男さんは魚が**好きだ**。

   Kazuo-san wa sakana ga **suki da**.

   (Kazuo likes fish/ Lit. Speaking of Kazuo, he likes fish.)

NEGATIVE NON-PAST

I-adjective

In order to form the plain or polite negative non-past of I-adjective, the last vowel ("**i**") of the plain non-past is changed to "**ku**," and then "**nai**" or "**arimasen**" is added.

Ex.	**plain**	**polite**
	ookii→ ooki**ku nai**	ooki**ku arimasen**
Irregular:	**ii** → **yoku nai**	**yoku arimasen**

1. 今日は**寒くない**。

   Kyoo wa **samuku nai**.

   (It is not cold today.)

2. A: 正さんの車は赤いですか。

   Tadashi-san no kuruma wa akai desu ka.

   (Is Tadashi's car red?)

   B: いいえ、**赤くありません**。

   Iie, **akaku arimasen**.

   (No, it is not red.)

3. この部屋はあまり**広くありません**ね。

   Kono heya wa amari **hiroku arimasen** ne.

   (This room is not very spacious, is it?)

4. 父はもう**若くない**。

   Chichi wa moo **wakaku nai**.

   (My father is not young any more.)

5. あのビルは窓が**大きくない**。

   Ano biru wa mado ga **ookiku nai**.

   (The windows of that building are not large/ Lit. As for that building, the windows are not large.)

Na-adjective

   In order to form the plain or polite negative non-past of the Na-adjective, the copula "**da**" in the non-past form is changed to "**ja/dewa nai**" or "**ja/dewa arimasen**."

   Ex.   **Plain**   **Polite**
        heta **desu**→ heta **ja/dewa nai**   heta **ja/dewa arimasen**

1. あのレストランは**有名じゃありません**。

   Ano resutoran wa **yuumei ja arimasen**.

   (That restaurant is not famous.)

2. 内田さんは**正直ではない**。

   Uchida-san wa **shoojiki dewa nai**.

   (Mr. Uchida is not honest.)

3. この町は**きれいではありません**ね。

   Kono machi wa **kirei dewa arimasen** ne.

   (This town is not clean, is it?)

4. 私は歌が下手だから、カラオケは**好きじゃない**。

   Watashi wa uta ga heta da kara, karaoke wa **suki ja nai**.

   (Since I am not good at singing, I don't like karaoke.)

PAST

I-adjective

   In order to form the plain or polite past of the I-adjective, the final vowel ("**i**") of the plain non-past is changed in "**katta**" or "**katta desu**" is added.

   Ex.   **Plain**   **Polite**
            ookii → ooki**katta**   ooki**katta desu**
   Irregular: ii → **yokatta**   **yokka desu**

1. この車は**安かったです**。

   Kono kuruma wa **yasukatta desu**.

(This car was inexpensive.)

2. 昨日のコンサートはとても**よかった**。

   Kinoo no konsaato wa totemo **yokatta**.

   (Yesterday's concert was very good.)

3. 今年の冬は**暖かかったですね**。

   Kotoshi no fuyu wa **atatakakatta desu** ne.

   (This winter was warm, wasn't it?)

4. 今日見た映画は**つまらなかった**。

   Kyoo mita eiga wa **tsumaranakatta**.

   (The movie which I saw today was boring.)

5. 子供の時ジムさんは背が**低かったです**。

   Kodomo no toki Jimu-san wa se ga **hikukatta desu**.

   (Jim was short when he was a child.)

Na-adjective

In order to form the plain or polite past of the Na-adjective, the copula "**da**" is changed to "**datta**" or "**deshita**."

    Ex.   **plain**   **plain**

           heta **da** → heta **datta**   heta **deshita**

1. 田中さんのアパートは**きれいでした**か。

   Tanaka-san no apaato wa **kirei deshita** ka.

   (Was Ms. Tanaka's apartment pretty?)

2. 昨日私は**ひまでした**。

   Kinoo watashi wa **hima deshita**.

   (I was free yesterday.)

3. この店は昔**有名だった**。

   Kono mise wa mukashi yuumei **datta**.

   (This store was famous a long time ago.)

4. 大学生の時、私はロックが**好きでした**。

   Daigakusei no toki, watashi wa rokku ga **suki deshita**.

   (When I was in college (Lit. I was a college student), I liked rock music.)

NEGATIVE PAST

I-adjective

In order to form the plain or polite negative past of the I-adjective, the "**nai**" in the plain negative non-past is changed to "**nakatta** " or "**arimasen deshita.**"

Ex.	**Plain**	**Polite**
	ookiku **nai**→ookiku **nakatta**	ookiku **arimasen deshita**

1. けさ飲んだコーヒーは**おいしくなかった**。

    Kesa nonda koohii wa **oishiku nakatta**.

    (The coffee I drank this morning was not good.)

2. 昨日は**暑くありませんでした**ね。

    Kinoo wa **atsuku arimasen deshita** ne.

    (It was not hot yesterday, was it?)

3. A: 先週のオペラはよかったですか。

    Senshuu no opera wa yokatta desu ka.

    (Was last week's opera good?)

   B: いいえ、あまり**よくありませんでした**。

    Iie, amari **yoku arimasen deshita**.

    (No, it wasn't very good.)

Na-adjective

In order to form the plain or polite negative past of the Na-adjective, the "**nai**" in the plain negative non-past is changed into "**nakatta** " or "**arimasen deshita.**"

Ex.	**Plain**	**Polite**
	heta ja **nai** → heta ja **nakatta**	heta ja **arimasen deshita**

1. A: 谷さんのアパートはどうでしたか。

    Tani-san no apaato wa doo deshita ka.

    (How was Ms. Tani's apartment?)

   B: **静かじゃありませんでした**。

    Shizuka ja arimasen deshita.

    (It was not quiet.)

2. 昔この辺は**便利じゃありませんでした**。

    Mukashi kono hen wa **benri ja arimasen deshita**.

    (This neighborhood was not convenient a long time ago.)

3. 子供のころ私は野菜が**好きじゃなかった**。

Kodomo no koro watashi wa yasai ga **suki ja nakatta**.

(In my childhood I didn't like vegetables.)

1. Change the following adjectives into the negative form of its corresponding plain or polite style.

Ex.   yasui → <u>yasuku nai</u>

kantan deshita → <u>kantan ja arimasen deshita</u>

1. 大きい _____

   ookii _____

2. 暑かったです _____

   atukatta desu _____

3. きれいだった _____

   kirei datta _____

4. 若かった _____

   wakakatta _____

5. 簡単だ _____

   kantan da _____

6. 好きでした _____

   suki deshita _____

7. 寒い _____

   samui _____

8. 上手です _____

   joozu desu _____

9. 高い _____

   takai _____

10. 正直でした _____

    shoojiki deshita _____

2. Answer the following questions according to the given cue.

1. この時計は高かったですか。

   Kono tokei wa taka katta desu ka.

   はい、_____。

   Hai, _____.

2. その辞書はいいですか。

   Sono jisho wa ii desu ka.

   いいえ、＿＿＿＿＿＿＿＿＿＿＿＿＿。

   Iie, ＿＿＿＿＿＿＿＿＿＿＿＿.

3. 昨日の映画はどうでしたか。

   Kinoo no eiga wa doo deshita ka.

   ぜんぜん（interesting）＿＿＿＿＿＿＿＿＿＿＿＿＿。

   Zenzen (interesting)＿＿＿＿＿＿＿＿＿＿＿＿＿.

4. とし子さんはピアノが上手ですか。

   Toshiko-san wa piano ga joozu desu ka.

   いいえ、あまり＿＿＿＿＿＿＿＿＿＿＿＿＿＿。

   Iie, amari ＿＿＿＿＿＿＿＿＿＿＿＿＿＿.

5. どうしてそれを買ったのですか。

   Dooshite sore wo katta no desu ka.

   （pretty）＿＿＿＿＿＿＿＿＿＿＿＿からです。

   (pretty)＿＿＿＿＿＿＿＿＿＿＿＿kara desu.

ADJECTIVAL USAGE

When an I-adjective or a Na-adjective modifies a noun, it always precedes the noun.

I-adjective

The plain non-past of an I-adjective can modify a noun directly.

1. 昨日**小さい**辞書を買いました。

   Kinoo **chiisai** jisho wo kaimashita.

   (I bought a small dictionary yesterday.)

2. この**赤い**車はよくありません。

   Kono **akai** kuruma wa yoku arimasen.

   (This red car isn't good.)

3. 私の**新しい**コンピューターは高かったです。

   Watashi no **atarashii** konpyuutaa wa takakatta desu.

   (My new computer was expensive.)

Na-adjective

When a Na-adjective modifies a noun, the final "**da**" of its plain non-past is replaced by "**na**."

Ex.   heta **da** → heta **na**

1. きれいな字で書いてください。

   Kirei na ji de kaite kudasai.

   (Please write neatly/ Lit. with neat letters.)

2. これは**大事な**本です。

   Kore wa **daiji na** hon desu.

   (This is a valuable book.)

3. 静かな所へ行きましょう。

   Shizuka na tokoro e ikimashoo.

   (Let's go to a quiet place.)

ADVERBIAL USAGE

I-adjectives and Na-adjectives can modify verbs.

I-adjective

When an I-adjective modifies a verb, the final "**i**" of its plain non-past is replaced by "**ku**."

Ex.   ookii → ooki**ku**

1. 明日学校に**早く**来てください。

   Ahita gakkoo ni **hayaku** kite kudasai.

   (Please come to school early tomorrow.)

2. もっと**大きく**書きましょうか。

   Motto **ookiku** kakimashoo ka.

   (Shall I write it bigger?)

3. 昨日から**涼しく**なりましたね。

   Kinoo kara **suzushiku** narimashita ne

   (It has become cool since yesterday, hasn't it?)

Na-adjective

When a Na-adjective modifies a verb, the final "**da**" of its plain non-past is replaced by "**ni**."

Ex.   heta **da** → heta **ni**

1. 子供がねているから、**静かに**話してください。

    Kodomo ga nete iru kara, **shizuka ni** hanashite kudasai.

    (A child is sleeping, so please speak quietly.)

2. 地図を**簡単に**書きましょう。

    Chizu wo **Kantan ni** kakimashoo.

    (I will draw a simple map/ Lit. I will draw a map simply.)

3. **ひまに**なったら、ゴルフをしようと思います。

    Hima ni nattara, gorufu wo shiyoo to omoimasu.

    (I think that I will play golf when I have time.)

3. Change the given adjectives into an appropriate form.

    Ex.   Hanako-san wa <u>kirei na</u> hana wo moraimashita. **(kirei)**

           Suupu wo moo sukoshi <u>atsuku</u> shite kudasai. **(atsui)**

1. これはとても _____ 本です。(**高い**)

    Kore wa totemo _____ hon desu. **(takai)**

2. 漢字を _____ 書いてください。(**きれいだ**)

    Kanji wo _____ kaite kudasai. **(kirei da)**

3. 明日は _____ 起きましょう。(**早い**)

    Ashita wa _____ okimashoo. **(hayai)**

4. 私はいつも _____ 料理を作ります。(**簡単だ**)

    Watashi wa itsumo _____ ryoori wo tsukurimasu. **(kantan da)**

5. _____ 休みがほしいです。(**長い**)

    _____ yasumi ga hoshii desu. **(Nagai)**

6. 父の _____ ビールはアサヒ ビールです。(**好きだ**)

    Chichi no _____ biiru wa Asahi biiru desu. **(suki da)**

7. _____ なりたいと思いますか。(**有名だ**)

    _____ naritai to omoimasu ka. **(Yuumei da)**

TE-FORM

The **te**-form of an adjective links with another adjective or predicate. The meaning of the **te**-form varies depending on the context, but usually it is equivalent to "and" in English. The **te**-form itself is tenseless, and the tense of the statement is determined by the main verb or predicate of the sentence.

I-adjective

In order to form a te-form of an I-adjective, the final vowel ("**i**") of its plain non-past is replaced by "**kute.**"

  Ex. ookii → ooki**kute**

1. 札幌は**涼しくて**いい所です。

  Sappro wa **suzushikute** ii tokoro desu.

  (Sapporo is a cool and nice place.)

2. やよいさんのねこは**小さくて**かわいいですよ。

  Yayoi-san no neko wa **chiisakute** kawaii desu yo.

  (Yayoi's cat is small and cute, you know.)

3. あのレストランは**安くて**いいそうです。

  Ano resutoran wa **yasukute** ii soo desu.

  (I have heard that the restaurant is inexpensive and good.)

4. ロールスロイスはとても**高くて**買えません。

  Roorusuroisu wa totemo **takakute** kaemasen.

  (A Rolls-Royce is too expensive and I cannot buy it.)

5. この間読んだ本は**むずかしくて**分かりませんでした。

  Kono aida yonda hon wa **muzukashikute** wakarimasen deshita.

  (The book I read the other day was difficult and I did not understand it.)

Na-adjective

 In order to form the **te**-form of a Na-adjective, the "**da**" of its plain non-past is replaced by "**de.**"

  Ex. heta **da** →heta **de**

1. ジョゼさんはとても**親切で**いい人です。

  Joze-san wa totemo **shinsetsu de** ii hito desu.

  (Jose is a very kind and nice person.)

2. 電子辞書は**簡単で**便利だ。

  Denshi-jisho wa **kantan de** benri da.

  (An electronic dictionary is simple and convenient.)

3. 野田さんは歌が**上手で**カーネギーホールで歌いました。

  Noda-san wa uta ga **joozu de** kaanegii hooru de utaimashita.

  (Ms. Noda is good at singing and sang at Carnegie Hall.)

4. パリで泊まったホテルは**静かで**よかったです。

Pari de tomatta hoteru wa **shizuka de** yokatta desu.

(The hotel we stayed in Paris was quiet and nice.)

4. Translate the following sentences into Japanese.

1. This tea is very hot and I cannot drink.

2. Mr. Okada is an honest and nice (person).

3. That restaurant is famous for tempura and always crowded.

4. Yesterday I was busy and I could not go to my friend's party.

5. This camera is inexpensive and easy to use.

AUXILIARY ADJECTIVE

V-stem + tai

"V-stem + **tai**" expresses one's desire to do something and is equivalent to "**want to** (do) " in English. The conjugation of this phrase is the same as that of I-adjectives.

Ex.	**Plain**	**Polite**
non-past	ikimasu → iki-tai	iki-tai **desu**
neg. non-past	iki-ta**ku nai**	iki-ta**ku arimasen**
past	iki-ta**katta**	iki-ta**katta desu**
neg. past	iki-ta**ku nakatta**	iki-ta**ku arimasen deshita**

1. 私はいつかタヒチへ**行きたいです**。

Wtashi wa itsuka Tahichi e **iki-tai desu**.

(I want to go to Tahiti someday.)

2. 今お腹がいっぱいだから、何も**食べたくありません**。

Ima onaka ga ippai da kara, nani mo **tabe-taku arimasen**.

(I don't want to eat anything, because I am full now.)

3. 去年アルバイトが**したかった**けれど、いい仕事がありませんでした。

Kyonen arubaito ga **shi-takatta** keredo, ii shigoto ga arimasen deshita.

(I wanted to work part-time last year, but there was not a good job.)

4. 昨日は頭が痛かったので、パーティーでだれとも**話したくありませんでした**。

Kinoo wa atama ga itakatta node, paatii de dare to mo **hanashi-taku arimasen deshita**.

(I had a headache yesterday, so I did not want to talk to anyone at the party.)

5. 安子さんが今一番**会いたい**人はおばあさんです。

Yasuko-san ga ima ichiban **ai-tai** hito wa o-baasan desu.

(The person whom Yasuko wants to see the most now is her grandmother.)

6. 日本語が上手に**なりたくて**、日本に来ました。

Nihon-go ga joozu ni **nari-takute**, Nihon ni kimashita.

(I wanted to become good at Japanese, so I came to Japan.)

V-te + hoshii/morai-tai

"V-te+ **hoshii/morai-tai**" expresses one's desire and is equivalent to "want someone to do something." "Someone" is marked by the particle "**ni**" and should not be of a higher status than the subject of the expression. The conjugation of this phrase is the same as that of I-adjectives.

Ex.	**Plain**	**Polite**
non-past	iku → itte + hoshii/morai-tai	itte + hoshii/morai-tai **desu**
neg. non-past	itte hoshi**ku**/morai-ta**ku nai**	itte hoshi**ku**/morai-ta**ku arimasen**
past	itte hoshi**katta**/morai-ta**katta**	itte hoshi**katta**/morai-ta**katta desu**
neg. past	itte hoshi**ku**/morai-ta**ku nakatta**	itte hoshi**ku**/morai-ta**ku arimasen deshita**

1. 私は道子さんにパーティーに**来てほしい/もらいたい**んですが、来週の金曜日ひまですか。

Watashi wa Michiko-san ni paatii ni **kete hoshii/moraitai** n' desu ga, raishuu no kin-yoobi hima desu ka.

(I want you, michiko, to come to the party. Are you free next Friday?)

2. 新しいアパートを見て**ほしい/もらいたい**から、今晩来てください。

Atarashii apaato wo **mite hoshii/moraitai** kara, konban kite kudasai.

(I want you to look at my new apartment, so please come tonight.)

3. 兄に母と一緒に**住んでほしかった/もらいたかった**けれど、兄は仕事でイギリスへ行ってしまいました。

Ani ni haha to issho ni **sunde hoshikatta/moraitakatta** keredo, ani wa shigoto de Igirisu e itte shimaimashita.

(I wanted my older brother to live with my mother, but he had gone to England because of his work.)

Note: "**Hoshii**" without the "te-form" expresses one's desire to have something, and "X wa Y ga hoshii (desu)" is equivalent to "X wants Y" in English. The conjugation of "hoshii" is the same as that of I-adjectives.

1. 私は東京に大きいアパートが**ほしいです**。

   Watashi wa Tookyoo ni ookii apaato ga **hoshii desu**.

   (I want a large apartment in Tokyo.)

2. 弟はプレゼントを見て、「そんなものは**ほしくない**。」と言いました。

   Otooto wa purezento wo mite, "Sonna mono wa **hoshiku nai**" to iimashita.

   (My younger brother looked at the present and said, "I don't want such a thing.")

3. 子供の時赤い車が**ほしかったです**。

   Kodomo no toki akai kuruma ga **hoshikatta desu**.

   (When I was a child, I wanted a red car.)

4. こんな高い時計は**ほしくなかった**けれど、母が買ってくれたんです。

   Konna takai tokei wa **hoshiku nakatta** keredo, haha ga katte kureta n desu.

   (I did not want such an expensive watch, but my mother bought it for me.)

5. 今私が**ほしい**ものは時間です。

   Ima watashi ga **hoshii** mono wa jikan desu.

   (What I want now is time.)

6. 古い机が**ほしくて**さがしています。

   Furui tsukue ga **hoshikute** sagashite imasu.

   (I want an old desk and have been looking for it.)

Note: The third person's desire in the three expressions above, "v-stem + **tai**," "v-te + **hoshii**," and "**hoshii**," is usually expressed by "v-stem + **tagaru/tagatte iru**," "v-te + **moraitagaru/moraitagatte iru**" and "**hoshigaru/hoshigatte iru**" respectively. The conjugation of those three expressions is the same as that of "u-verb."

1. 弟は散歩に行くと電車に**乗りたがります**。

   Otooto wa sanpo ni iku to densha ni **nori-tagarimasu**.

   (Whenever we go for a walk, my younger brother wants to ride a train.)

2. 一郎さんは大学生なのに、お母さんに何でも**してもらいたがります**。

   Ichiroo-san wa daigakusei na no ni, okaa-san ni nan demo **shite morai-tagarimasu**.

   (Although Ichiroo is a college student, he wants his mother to do everything for him.)

3. 吉田さんは古い中国の絵を**ほしがっています**。

   Yoshida-san wa furui Chuugoku no e wo **hoshigatte imasu**.

   (Mr. Yoshida wants an old Chinese painting.)

V-stem + yasui

"V-stem + **yasui**" is equivalent to "something is easy to do" in English. The conjugation of this phrase is the same as that of I-adjectives.

Ex.	Plain	Polite
non-past	ikimasu → iki + yasui	iki+ yasui **desu**
neg. non-past	iki-yasu**ku nai**	iki-yasu**ku arimasen**
past	iki-yasu**katta**	iki-yasu**katta desu**
neg-past	iki-yasu**ku nakatta**	iki-yasu**ku arimasen deshita**

1. このペンは**書きやすい**。

   Kono pen wa **kaki-yasui**.

   (This pen is easy to write with.)

2. 鈴木先生の講演は**分かりやすくて**おもしろかったです。

   Suzuki sensei no kooen wa **wakari-yasukute** omoshirokatta desu.

   (Professor Suzuki's lecture was easy to understand and interesting.)

3. **作りやすい**日本料理を教えてください。

   Tsukuri-yasui nihon-ryoori wo oshiete kudasai

   (Please tell (Lit. teach) me a Japanese dish which is easy to make.)

V-stem +nikui

"**V-stem + nikui**" is equivalent to "something is difficult to do" in English. The conjugation of this phrase is the same as that of I-adjectives.

Ex.	Plain	Polite
non-past	ikimasu → iki + niku**i**	iki+niku**i desu**
neg. non-past	iki-niku**ku nai**	iki-niku**ku arimasen**
past	iki-niku**katta**	iki-niku**katta desu**
neg-past	iki-niku**ku nakatta**	iki-niku**ku arimasen deshita**

1. この本は字が小さくて**読みにくい**ですね。

   Kono hon wa ji ga chiisakute **yomi-nikui** desu ne.

   (The letters of this book are small and difficult to read, aren't they?)

2. 津田さんに理由を聞かれたけれど、**説明しにくかった**。

   Tsuda-san ni riyuu wo kikareta keredo, **setsumeishi-niku katta**.

   (I was asked the reason by Mr. Tsuda, but it was difficult to explain.)

3. オフィスの古いタイプライターは**使いにくくて**、誰も使いません。

   Ofisu no furui taipuraitaa wa **tsukai-nikukute**, dare mo tsukaimasen.

   (The old typewriter in our office is difficult to use, so nobody uses it.)

4. 白田さんはちょっと**話しにくい**人ですよ。

Shirota-san wa chotto **hanashi-nikui** hito desu yo.

(Ms. Shirota is a little difficult (Lit. difficult person) to talk to.)

5. Change the following words into the required form given in the parentheses.

    Ex.   読む yomu (difficult to read) → **読みにくい** **yomi-nikui**

           乗る noru   (wanted to ride) → **乗りたかった** **nori-takatta**

  1. 話す hanasu (want to talk) _____

  2. 行く iku (easy to go) _____

  3. 帰る kaeru (difficult to return) _____

  4. 食べる taberu (not difficult to eat) _____

  5. 来る kuru (wanted to come) _____

  6. 読む yomu (not easy to read) _____

  7. する suru (did not want to do) _____

  8. 見る miru (was not easy to look at) _____

  9. 使う tsukau (want someone to use) _____

6. Translate the following sentences into Japanese.

  1. I want a small radio.

  2. I do not want to drink sake tonight.

  3. This kanji is difficult to memorize.

  4. The shoes I bought the other day are comfortable (Lit. easy) to wear.

  5. When I was a child, I wanted to become a policeman.

  6. I wanted to talk with my mother in Japan, and I called her from the United States.

Review

7. Give the Japanese equivalent of the following English sentences and phrases.

  1. It is cold.

  2. This inexpensive pen is easy to write with.

  3. A slow train

  4. The man was not young.

  5. The place where I want to live the most

  6. A convenient shop

7. I wanted Toshiko to come to my house.

8. The building was magnificent.

9. The teacher's voice was difficult to hear.

8. Choose the most appropriate adjective from the following list, and then fill in the blanks with the te-form of the adjective.

きれいだ、したい、暑い、はきにくい、ほしい、高い、静かだ、

kirei da,   shitai,   atsui,   haki-nikui,   hoshii,   takai,   shizuka da,

Ex.   高志さんは背が<u>高くて</u>、ハンサムだ。

Takashi-san wa se ga <u>takakute</u>, hansamu (handsome) da.

1. この部屋は＿＿＿＿＿＿　ねられません。

Kono heya wa ＿＿＿＿＿＿＿ neraremasen.

2. ここは ＿＿＿＿＿＿、勉強するのにいいです。

Koko wa ＿＿＿＿＿＿＿, benkyoo suru no ni ii desu.

3. スイスの時計が＿＿＿＿＿、父に買ってもらいました。

Suisu (Swiss) no tokei ga ＿＿＿＿＿＿ chichi ni katte moraimashita.

4. 勉強が＿＿＿＿＿＿＿、大学院に入ることにしました。

Benkyoo ga ＿＿＿＿＿＿, daigakuin ni hairu koto ni shimashita.

5. 幸子さんのアパートはとても＿＿＿＿＿、大きいです。

Sachiko-san no apaato wa totemo ＿＿＿＿＿＿, ookii desu.

6. このくつは＿＿＿＿＿＿＿、足が痛くなってしまいました。

Kono kutsu wa ＿＿＿＿＿＿, ashi ga itaku natte shimaimashita.

9. Fill in the blanks with Japanese adjective according to the given cue.

Ex. <u>元気な</u>赤ちゃんですね。(healthy)

<u>Genki na</u> akachan desu ne.

1. ゆうべは＿＿＿＿＿＿＿ねました。(late)

Yuube wa ＿＿＿＿＿＿＿nemashita.

2. ルビンシュタインは＿＿＿＿＿＿＿ピアニストだった。(famous)

Rubinshutain wa ＿＿＿＿＿＿pianisuto datta.

3. 昨日の試験はあまり＿＿＿＿＿＿＿＿＿。(was not difficult)

Kinoo no shiken wa amari ＿＿＿＿＿＿＿＿.

4. 日本で＿＿＿＿＿＿＿＿＿＿＿＿人にたくさん会いました。(kind)

Nihon de ＿＿＿＿＿＿＿＿＿＿ hito ni takusan aimashtia.

5. 来年ロンドンへ＿＿＿＿＿＿＿＿＿と思います。(want to go)

Rainen Rondon (London) e ＿＿＿＿＿＿＿ to omoimasu.

6. このすしは＿＿＿＿＿＿＿＿＿できませんでした。(skillfully)

Kono sushi wa ＿＿＿＿＿＿＿＿ dekimasen deshita.

7. タバコは体に＿＿＿＿＿＿＿＿＿＿＿＿。(no good)

Tabako wa karada ni ＿＿＿＿＿＿＿＿＿.

8. 前のアパートは＿＿＿＿＿＿＿＿＿＿。(was not convenient)

Mae no apaato wa ＿＿＿＿＿＿＿＿＿.

9. ＿＿＿＿＿＿＿＿辞書を買ってください。(easy to use)

＿＿＿＿＿＿＿jisho wo katte kudasai.

10. 今日はぜんぜん仕事が＿＿＿＿＿＿＿＿＿＿＿。(do not want to do)

Kyoo wa zenzen shigoto ga ＿＿＿＿＿＿＿＿＿.

Chapter 3

Adverbs

Japanese adverbs are always placed before the words they modify. Here are frequently used adverbs.

MOO

The adverb "**moo**" means "already" in an affirmative sentence and "(not) any more" in a negative sentence.

1. あの新しい映画を**もう**見ましたか。

   Ano atarashii eiga wo **moo** mimashita ka

   (Have you already seen the new movie?)

2. 榎本さんのお子さんは**もう**三才ですか。

   Enomoto-san no o-ko-san wa **moo** san-sai desu ka.

   (Is Mr. Enomoto's child already three years old?)

3. A: 昼ご飯をたべましたか。

   Hiru-gohan wo tabemashita ka.

   (Did you eat lunch?)

   B: ええ、**もう**食べました。

   Ee, **moo** tabemashita.

   (Yes, I have already eaten.)

4. あのレストランはよくないから、**もう**行きたくありません。

   Ano resutoran wa yoku nai kara **moo** ikitaku arimasen.

   (That restaurant is not good, so I do not want to go any more.)

5. 美絵さんはタバコを**もう**吸わないそうです。

Mie-san wa tabako wo **moo** suwanai soo desu.

(I have heard that Mie does not smoke any more.)

MADA

The adverb "**mada**" means "still" or "yet" in a positive sentence and "(not) yet" in a negative sentence. A positive sentence of "**Mada desu.**" corresponds to "Not yet." in English.

1. 兄は**まだ**学生です。

   Ani wa **mada** gakusei desu.

   (My older brother is still a student.)

2. ジルさんは八十才ですが、**まだ**スキーをします。

   Jiru-san wa hachijus-sai desu ga, **mada** sukii wo shimasu.

   (Jill is eighty years old, but she still skies.)

3. A: お父さんはもうアメリカから帰って来ましたか。

   Otoo-san wa moo Amerika kara kaette kimashita ka.

   (Has your father already returned from the United States?)

   B: いいえ、**まだ**帰って来ません。/いいえ、**まだ**です。

   Iie, **mada** kaette kimasen./ Iie, **mada** desu.

   (No, he has not yet returned./No, not yet.)

4. A: このチョコレート**まだ**ありますか。

   Kono chokoreeto **mada** arimasu ka.

   (Do you still have this kind of chocolate?)

   B: すみません。もうありません。

   Sumimasen. Moo arimasen.

   (Sorry. We do not have it any more.)

5. この本を**まだ**読んでいないの。

   Kono hon wo **mada** yonde inai no.

   (Haven't you read this book yet?)

1. Fill in the blanks with either "moo" or "mada."

1. 弟は＿＿＿＿＿ヨーロッパへ行ったことがありません。

   Otooto wa ＿＿＿＿＿ Yooroppa (Europe) e itta koto ga arimasen.

2. A: スコットさんは＿＿＿＿＿＿空手を教えていますか。

       Sukotto-san wa ＿＿＿＿＿＿ karate wo oshiete imasu ka

  B: いいえ、＿＿＿＿＿＿教えていません。

      Iie, ＿＿＿＿＿＿ oshiete imasen.

3. ＿＿＿＿＿＿九時ですが、今晩は＿＿＿＿＿眠くなりました。

    ＿＿＿＿＿＿ ku-ji desu ga, konban wa ＿＿＿＿＿＿ nemuku narimashita.

4. A: クリスマス・カードを＿＿＿＿＿書きましたか。

       Kurisumasu kaado wo ＿＿＿＿＿＿ kakimashita ka.

  B: いいえ、＿＿＿＿＿一枚も書いていません。

      Iie, ＿＿＿＿＿＿ ichi-mai mo kaite imasen.

AMARI

The adverb "**amari**" is always used in a negative sentence, and it means "not so much," "not often," or "not enough" in English.

1. 肉は**あまり**食べたくありません。

    Niku wa **amari** tabetaku arimasen.

    (I do not want to eat meat.)

2. 最近**あまり**テニスはしていません。

    Saikin **amari** tenisu wa shite imasen.

    (Recently I have not been playing tennis often.)

3. お金が**あまり**ないから旅行はできません。

    O-kane ga **amar**i nai kara ryokoo wa dekimasen.

    (I do not have much money, so I cannot take a trip.)

4. この辞書は**あまり**よくありませんね。

    Kono jisho wa **amari** yoku arimasen ne.

    (This dictionary is not so good, is it?)

ZENZEN

The adverb "**zenzen**" is always used in a negative sentence, and it means "not at all" in English.

1. ゆうべは**ぜんぜん**寝られませんでした。

    Yuube wa **zenzen** neraremasen deshita.

    (I could not sleep at all last night.)

2. 中国語は分かりますが、韓国語は**ぜんぜん**分かりません。

    Cyuugoku-go wa wakarimasu ga, kankoku-go wa **zenzen** wakarimasen.

    (I understand Chinese, but I do not understand Korean at all.)

3. あの映画は**ぜんぜん**おもしろくありませんでした。

    Ano eiga wa **zenzen** omoshiroku arimasen deshita.

    (That movie was not interesting at all.)

TOKIDOKI

The adverb "**tokidoki**" is always used in an affirmative sentence, and it corresponds to "sometimes" or "now and then" in English.

1. 松田さんはいい学生ですが、**時々**クラスを休みます.

    Matsuda-san wa ii gakusei desu ga, **tokidoki** kurasu wo yasumimasu.

    (Ms. Matsuda is a good student, but she sometimes misses class.)

2. **時々**一緒に食事をしましょう。

    Tokidoki issho ni shokuji wo shimasyoo.

    (Let's eat together, now and then.)

3. **時々**変な人から姉に電話があって両親が心配しています。

    Tokidoki hen na hito kara ane ni denwa ga atte ryooshin ga shinpai shite imasu.

    (Sometimes there is a call from a strange person for my big sister and my parents are worried.)

NAKANAKA

The adverb "**nakanaka**" means "quite so and so" in English in an affirmative sentence. In a negative sentence it is used when something is not completed as easily or as soon as one expects. It is interpreted as "it takes time for something to be done" or "not easily /not soon" in English.

1. **なかなか**いい映画でしたね。

    Nakanaka ii eiga deshita ne.

(It was quite a good movie, wasn't it?)

2. ルネさんは**なかなか**上手に日本語を話しますね。

   Rune-san wa **nakanaka** joozu ni nihon-go wo hanashimasu ne.

   (Rune speaks Japanese quite well, doesn't he?)

3. 天ぷらを注文したのに、**なかなか**持ってきません。

   Tenpura wo chuumon-shita noni, **nakanaka** motte kimasen.

   (I ordered tempura, but it takes time for them to bring it.)

4. この本は漢字が多くて**なかなか**読めません。

   Kono hon wa kanji ga ookute **nakanaka** yomemsen.

   (There are many kanji in this book, and I can not read it easily.)

2. Translate the following English sentences into Japanese.

  1. I do not drink whiskey at all.

  2. I usually study at home but sometimes I study in the library.

  3. The weather is not so good today.

  4. I water this flower every day, but it takes time to bloom.

  5. Mr. Eguchi is quite good at singing.

Review

3. Choose the right adverb from the ones in parentheses.

  1. 学生の時にはバーによく行きましたが、この頃は（**なかなか、あまり、時々**）行きません。

    Gakusei no toki ni wa yoku baa (bar) ni ikimashita ga konogoro wa (**nakanaka, amari, tokidoki**) ikimasen.

  2. 三年前にドイツ語を勉強したのですが、（**もう、なかなか、まだ**）全部忘れてしまいました。

    San-nen mae ni doitsu-go wo benkyoo shita no desu ga, (**moo, nakanaka, mada**) zenbu wasurete shimaimashita.

  3. 病気だったから（**時々、ぜんぜん、なかなか**）出かけませんでした。

    Byooki datta kara (**tokidoki, zenzen, nakanaka**) dekakemasen deshita.

  4. ベストセラーを買ったけれど、（**もう、まだ、なかなか**）読んでいません。

    Besuto seraa (best seller) wo katta keredo, (**moo, mada, nakanaka**) yonde imasen.

  5. いつもお茶を飲みますが、（**なかなか、あまり、時々**）コーヒーも飲みます。

    Itsumo o-cha wo nomimasu ga, (**nakanaka, amri, tokidoki**) koohii mo nomimasu.

  6. バスを三十分も待っていますが、（**あまり、もう、なかなか**）来ませんね。

    Basu wo sanjup-pun mo matte imasu ga, (**amari, moo, nakanaka**) kimasen ne.

4. Fill in the blanks in the following sentences with the adverb "**moo**," "**mada**," "**amari**,"
"**zenzen**," "**nakanaka**," or "**tokidoki**."

   1. A: オペラを聞きに行きますか。

         Opera wo kiki ni ikimasu ka.

     B: ＿＿＿＿＿＿＿行きませんね。ニューヨークに十年も住んでいるんですが、一度も

         ＿＿＿＿＿＿＿ ikimasen ne. Nyuuyooku ni juu-nen mo sunde iru n' desu ga, ichi-do mo

         ＿＿＿＿＿＿＿聞いていません。

         ＿＿＿＿＿＿＿ kiite imasen.

   2. A: ゴルフをよくしますか。

         Gorufu wo yoku shimasu ka.

     B: ＿＿＿＿＿＿＿しません。＿＿＿＿＿＿＿するだけですね。

         ＿＿＿＿＿＿＿shimasen. ＿＿＿＿＿＿＿suru dake desu ne.

   3. 洋子さんのレポートは ＿＿＿＿＿＿＿よかったですよ。

     Yooko-san no repooto wa ＿＿＿＿＿＿＿yokatta desu yo.

   4. このマニュアルを＿＿＿＿＿＿＿三度読みましたが、＿＿＿＿＿＿＿分かりません。

     Kono manyuaru (manual) wo ＿＿＿＿＿＿＿san-do yomimashita ga,

     ＿＿＿＿＿＿＿wakarimasen.

Chapter 4

Pronouns

DEMONSTRATIVE PRONOUNS

Japanese demonstrative pronouns are represented by "ko-so-a-do" words. They have several forms each and refer to a thing, a subject, and so forth. The **ko**-group refers to a thing that is closer to the speaker than the listener. The **so**-group refers to a thing that is closer to the listener than the speaker. The **a**-group refer to a thing that is far from both the speaker and the listener. The **do**-group corresponds to the interrogative words.

Nominals

Thing	Place
Kore *(this thing)*	Koko *(here/this place)*
Sore *(that thing)*	Soko *(there/that place)*
Are *(that thing)*	Asoko *(there/that place)*
Dore *(which one)*	Doko *(where/which place)*

Noun modifers

Kono ~ *(this ~)*	Konna ~ *(this kind of ~)*
Sono ~ *(that ~)*	Sonna ~ *(that kind of ~)*
Ano ~ *(that ~)*	Anna ~ *(that kind of ~)*
Dono ~ *(which ~)*	Donna ~ *(what kind of ~)*

1. A: **これ**はいくらですか。

   Kore wa ikura desu ka.

   (How much is this?)

B: **それ**は千円です。

   Sore wa sen-en desu.

   (It/that is 1000 yen.)

2. **この**本はおもしろいですよ。

   Kono hon wa omoshiroi desu yo.

   (This book is interesting.)

3. **どんな**車を買いましたか。

   Donna kuruma wo kaimashita ka.

   (What kind of car did you buy?)

4. 今日の新聞は**ここ**にあります。

   Kyoo no shinbun wa **koko** ni arimasu.

   (Today's newspaper is here.)

"**Ko-so-a-do**" words also refer to a subject that has been already mentioned in a given context.   The **ko**-group refers to the subject that belongs to the domain of the speaker's knowledge. The

so-group refers to the subject that belongs to the domain of the listener's knowledge, and the

a-group refers to the subject that is shared by the speaker and the listener as their common knowledge.

1. A: 昨日「桜」というレストランで食べました。

      Kinoo "Sakura" to iu resutoran de tabemashita.

      (I ate at a restaurant called "Sakura" yesterday.)

   B: **その**レストランはどこにありますか。

      Sono resutoran wa doko ni arimasu ka.

      (Where is that restaurant?)

2. A: 先月京都へ行ってきました。

      Sengetsu Kyooto e itte kimashita.

      (I went to Kyoto last month.)

   B: そうですか。私も去年行きましたが、**あの**町はきれいな町ですね。

      Soo desu ka. Watashi mo kyonen ikimashita ga, **ano** machi wa kirei na machi

      Desu ne.

      (Did you? So did I last year. It is a beautiful city, isn't it?)

In item 2, speaker B refers to Kyoto as "**ano machi**" because both A and B are familiar with the city.

PERSONAL PRONOUNS

	Single		**Plural**	
1st person	Watashi	*(I)*	Watashi-tachi	*(we)*
2nd person	Anata	*(you)*	Anata-tachi	*(you)*
3rd person	Kanojo	*(she)*	Kanojo-ra/tachi	*(they)*
	Kare	*(he)*	Kare-ra/tachi	*(they)*

In general, the personal pronouns are frequently omitted if they are understood in context. Furthermore, second-person and third-person pronouns are seldom or never used, especially to address a superior, because it carries an arrogant tone. Secnd person (e.g., the listener) and third person are usually referred to by their names instead of the pronouns. They are also referred to by "**kono/sono/ano hito**."

1. お元気ですか。

   O-genki desu ka?

   *(Are **you** well? /How are **you**?)*

2. 昨日ボストンへ行きました。

   Kinoo Bosuton e ikimashita.

   *(**I** went to Boston yesterday.)*

3. 山田さんは何を食べますか。

   Yamada-san wa nani o tabemasu ka?

   *(**Mr./Ms. Yamada**, what are **you** going to eat?)*

4. あの人は今何才ですか。

   Ano hito wa ima nan-sai desu ka.

   *(How old is **he/she**?)*

PRONOUN "NO"

The pronoun "**no**" corresponds to "one" in English and refers to something which is already introduced in the given context.   In general, the thing referred to by "**no**" is tangible.

1. この辞書は私が持っている**の**と同じです。

   Kono jisho wa watashi ga motte iru **no** to onaji desu.

   (This dictionary is the same as the one I have.)

2. 赤いかばんは五千円ですが、黒い**の**は七千五百円ですよ。

Akai kaban wa gosen-en desu ga, kuroi **no** wa nanasengohyaku-en desu yo.

(The red bag is 5000 yen, and the black one is 7500 yen.)

3. このカメラは大きいですね。もっと小さい**の**がありますか。

Kono kamera wa ookii desu ne. Motto chiisai **no** ga arimasu ka.

(This camera is big.   Do you have a smaller one?)

1. Put the appropriate Japanese pronoun on each blank based on the given English word.

 Ex. <u>これ</u>は何ですか。 (this one)

  <u>Kore</u> wa nan desu ka.

 1. A: _____ かばんは六千円ですか。 (that ~)

  _____ kaban wa rokusen-en desu ka.

  B: いいえ、これは一万円です。

  Iie, kore wa ichiman-en desu.

 2. A: _____ 人はだれですか。 (that ~ over there)

  _____ hito wa dare desu ka.

  B: 山田さんです。

  Yamada-san desu.

 3. A: _____ はあなたがよく使う辞書ですか。 (this one)

  _____ wa anata ga yoku tsukau jisho desu ka.

  B: いいえ、そうじゃありません。

  Iie, soo ja arimasen..

  A: _____ はどこにありますか。 (the one that you often use)

  _____ wa doko ni arimasu ka.

  B: _____にありますよ。 (here)

  _____ ni arimasu yo.

Review

2. Fill in the blanks with the appropriate words based on the contexts.

 1. (A and B talk about the restaurant called "Hana," which both of them know.)

  A: 昨日花ですしを食べましたよ。

  Kinoo Hana de sushi wo tabemashita yo.

B: そうですか。_____ 店のすしはとてもおいしいですね。

Soo desu ka. _____ mise no sushi wa totemo oishii desu ne.

2. A: あさひ屋という本屋を知っていますか。

Asahi-ya to iu hon-ya wo shitte imasu ka.

B: いいえ、知りません。_____ はどこにありますか。

Iie, shirimasen. _____ wa doko ni arimasu ka.

A: 駅のそばに新しいビルがありますね。

Eki no soba ni atarashii biru ga arimasu ne.

B: はい。

Hai.

A: _____ビルの中にありますよ。

_____biru no naka ni arimasu yo.

3. 昨日きっさ店へ行きました。そして____で本を読みました。

Kinoo kissaten e ikimashita. Soshite _____ de hon wo yomimashita.

4. A: ハワイは_____ 所ですか。

Hawai wa _____ tokoro desu ka.

B: 暖かくて楽しい所ですよ。

Atatakakute tanoshii tokoro desu yo.

3. Translate the following English sentences into Japanese.

1. A: What is this food?

   B: It is a Japanese sweet.

2. I worked for a Japanese bank and I met my wife there.

3. A: What kind of car do you want?

   B: Mr. Shimizu has a small red one, doesn't he? I want that kind.

Chapter 5

Numbers, Time, Dates, Counters

NUMBERS

1	ichi	40	yon-juu
2	ni	50	go-juu
3	san	60	roku-juu
4	yon/shi	70	nana/shichi-juu
5	go	80	hachi-juu
6	roku	90	kyuu-juu
7	shichi/nana	100	hyaku
8	hachi	101	hyaku-ichi
9	kyuu	110	hyaku-juu
10	juu	200	ni-hyaku
11	juu-ichi	300	san-byaku
12	juu-ni	400	yon-hyaku
13	juu-san	500	go-hyaku
14	juu-yon/shi	600	rop-pyaku
15	juu-go	700	nana-hyaku
16	juu-roku	800	hap-pyaku
17	juu-shichi/nana	900	kyuu-hyaku
18	juu-hachi	1,000	sen
19	juu-kyuu	1,100	sen-hyaku
20	ni-juu	2,000	ni-sen
21	ni-juu-ichi	3,000	san-zen
30	san-juu	4,000	yon-sen

5,000	go-sen	8,000	has-sen
6,000	roku-sen	9,000	kyuu-sen
7,000	nana-sen	10,000	ichi-man

Interrogative words: nan-juu, nan-byaku, nan-zen, nan-man

1. Read the following numbers.

   Ex.   1,500   sen-go-hyaku

1. 24
2. 89
3. 198
4. 356
5. 881
6. 630
7. 9,003
8. 13,200
9. 50,000

TIME

Hours

1:00 A.M.	午前一時	gozen ichi-ji	7:00	七時	shichi-ji
2:00 P.M	午後二時	gogo ni-ji	8:00	八時	hachi-ji
3:00	三時	san-ji	9:00	九時	ku-ji
4:00	四時	yo-ji	10:00	十時	juu-ji
5:00	五時	go-ji	11:00	十一時	juuichi-ji
6:00	六時	roku-ji	12:00	十二時	juuni-ji

Interrogative word: 何時 nan-ji

Minutes

1	一分	ip-pun	6	六分	rop-pun
2	二分	ni-fun	7	七分	nana/shichi-fun
3	三分	san-pun	8	八分	hap-pun
4	四分	yon-pun	9	九分	kyuu-fun
5	五分	go-fun	10	十分	jup-pun

11	十五分	juugo-pun	35	三十五分	sanjuugo-fun
20	二十分	nijup-pun	40	四十分	yonjup-pun
25	二十五分	hap-pun	45	四十五分	yonjuugo-fun
30	三十分	kyuu-fun	50	五十分	gojup-pun

Interrogative word: 何分 nan-pun

1. A: 今何時ですか。

   Ima **nan-ji** desuka.

   (What time is it now?)

   B: 二時三十分です。/ 二時半です。

   Ni-ji sanjup-pun desu. / **Ni-ji han** desu.

   (It is two thirty.) / (It is half past two.)

2. 今七時十分前です。

   Ima **shichi-ji jup-pun** mae desu.

   (It is ten minutes before seven o'clock.)

3. もう五時五分すぎですね。

   Moo **go-ji go-fun** sugi desu ne.

   (It is already five minutes past five, isn't it?)

2. Read the following time.

   Ex.   3:20   San-ji nijup-pun

   1. <u>4:10</u>
   2. <u>5:15</u>
   3. <u>9:30</u>
   4. <u>8:50</u>
   5. <u>7:45</u>
   6. <u>2:40</u>
   7. <u>1:05</u>
   8. <u>12:20</u>

Counter of hours and minutes

   "~ **jikan**" and "~ **fun/pun** (**kan**)" are used with numerals to count the number of hours and minutes respectively.

Ex.

1 hours 二時間 ni-jikan

1 hour and half 一時間半 ichi-jikan-han

9 hours 九時間 ku-jikan

13 hours 十三時間 juusan-jikan

24 hours 二十四時間 nijuu yo-jikan

5 minutes 五分(間) go-fun-(kan)

30 minutes 三十分（間） / 半時間 sanjup-pun (-kan) / han-jikan

Interrogative word: nan-ji-kan, nan--pun (kan), dono gurai

1. ゆうべは**六時間**ぐらいしか寝ませんでした。

   Yuube wa **roku-jikan** gurai shika nemasendeshita.

   (I slept only about six hours last night.)

2. 日本語の期末試験は**三時間**ですよ。

   Nihon-go no kimatsu shiken wa **san-jikan** desu yo.

   (The Japanese final examination is three hours long, you know.)

3. Q：ここから学校までバスでどのぐらいかかりますか。

   Koko kara gakkoo made basu de **dono gurai** kakarimasu ka.

   (How long does it take to go from here to school by bus?)

   A: **二十五分**ぐらいかかります。

   Nijuugo-fun gurai kakarimasu.

   (It takes about twenty- five minutes.)

DATES

Months

January	一月	ichi-gatsu	July	七月	shichi-gatsu
February	二月	ni-gatsu	August	八月	hachi-gatsu
March	三月	san-gatsu	September	九月	ku-gatsu
April	四月	shi-gatsu	October	十月	juu-gatsu
May	五月	go-gatsu	November	十一月	juuichi-gatsu
June	六月	roku-gatsu	December	十二	juuni-gatsu

Interrogative word: 何月 nan-gatsu

Days of the month

1st	一日	tsuitachi	17th	十七日	juushichi-nichi
2nd	二日	futsuka	18th	十八日	juuhachi-nichi
3rd	三日	mik-ka	19th	十九日	juuku-nichi
4th	四日	yok-ka	20th	二十日	hatsuka
5th	五日	itsu-ka	21st	二十一日	nijuuichi-nichi
6th	六日	mui-ka	22nd	二十二日	nijuuni-nichi
7th	七日	nano-ka	23rd	二十三日	nijuusan-nichi
8th	八日	yoo-ka	24th	二十四日	nijuuyok-ka
9th	九日	kokono-ka	25th	二十五日	nijuugo-nichi
10th	十日	too-ka	26th	二十六日	nijuuroku-nichi
11th	十一日	juuichi-nichi	27th	二十七日	nijuushichi-nichi
12th	十二日	juuni-nichi	28th	二十八日	nijuuhachi-nichi
13th	十三日	juusan-nichi	29th	二十九日	nijuuku-nichi
14th	十四日	juuyok-ka	30th	三十日	sanjuu-nichi
15th	十五日	juugo-nichi	31st	三十一日	sanjuuichi-nichi
16th	十六日	juuroku-nichi			

Interrogative word: 何日 nan-nichi

1. 私の誕生日は**四月九日**です。

   Watashi no tanjoobi wa **shi-gatsu kokono-ka** desu.

   (My birthday is April 9th.)

2. **九月三日**から学校が始まります。

   Ku-gatsu mik-ka kara gakkoo ga hajimarimasu.

   (School starts on September 3rd.)

3. Read the following dates.

   Ex.   Jan. 10th   ichi-gatsu too-ka

   1. Dec. 4th   6. Feb. 28th
   2. Mar. 22nd   7. Apr. 8th
   3. Sept. 5th   8. June 2nd
   4. Nov. 20th   9. July 30th
   5. May. 14th   10. Aug. 6th

Counters of days and months

"~ **ka** (-**kan**) / **nichi** (-**kan**)" and "~ **ka-getsu** (-**kan**)" are used with numerals to count the number of days and months respectively.

Ex.

1 day	一日 （間）	ichi-nichi(-kan)	2 days	二日 （間）	futsu-ka (-kan)
3 days	三日 （間）	mik-ka (-kan)	4 days	四日 （間）	yok-ka (-kan)
6 days	六日 （間）	mui-ka (-kan)	15 days	十五日 （間）	juugo-nichi (-kan)
20 days	二十日 （間）	hatsu-ka (-kan)	24 days	二十四日 （間）	nijuu-yok-ka (-kan)

Note: "**Tsuitachi**" refers only to "the first day of a month."   It is not used to count "one day."

Interrogative word: 何日 （間） nan-nichi (-kan)

1 month	一ヶ月 （間） ik-ka-getsu (-kan)	5 months	五ヶ月 （間） go-ka-getsu (-kan)
6 months	六ヶ月 （間） rok-ka-getsu (-kan)	8 months	八ヶ月 （間） hak-ka/hachi-ka-getsu (-kan)
10 months	十ヶ月 （間） juk-ka-getsu (-kan)	12 months	十二ヶ月 （間） juuni-ka-getsu (-kan)

Interrogative word: 何ヶ月 （間） nan-ka-getsu (-kan), どのぐらい dono gurai

1. 五日前に田中さんと一緒にゴルフをしました。

   Itsu-ka mae ni Tanaka-san to issho ni gorufu wo shimashita.

   (I played golf with Mr. Tanaka five days ago.)

2. 大学の夏休みは三ヶ月ぐらいです。

   Daigaku no natsu-yasumi wa **san-ka-getsu** gurai desu.

   (The summer vacation of a university is about three months long.)

3. お腹がいたくて二日(間)何も食べられませんでした。

   O-naka ga itakute **futsu-ka(-kan)** nani mo taberaremasen deshita.

   (I had a stomach ache and I could not eat anything for two days.)

Days of the week

Monday	月曜日	getsu-yoobi	Friday	金曜日	kin-yoobi
Tuesday	火曜日	ka-yoobi	Saturday	土曜日	do-yoobi
Wednesday	水曜日	sui-yoobi	Sunday	日曜日	nichi-yoobi
Thursday	木曜日	moku-yoobi			

Interrogative word: 何曜日 nan-yoobi

1. 来週の月曜日に試験があります。

   Raisyuu no **getsu-yoobi** ni shiken ga arimasu.

   (I have an examination on next Monday.)

2. **火曜日**と**木曜日**は日本語のクラスがありません。

   Ka-yoobi to **moku-yoobi** wa nihon-go no kurasu ga arimasen.

   (There is no Japanese class on Tuesday and Thursday.

Counters of weeks

"~**shuukan**" is used with numerals to count the number of weeks.

Ex. 1 week   一週間   is-shuukan   4 weeks 四週間   yon-shuukan

    8 weeks   八週間   has-shuukan   10 weeks 十週間   jus-shuukan

    Interrogative word: nan-shuukan

1. **二週間**ぐらい旅行がしたいです。

   Ni-shuukan gurai ryokoo ga shitai desu .

   (I want to travel for about two weeks.)

2. この論文を書くのにちょうど**三週間**かかりました。

   Kono ronbun wo kaku noni choodo **san-shuukan** kakarimashita.

   (It took me exactly three weeks to write this paper.)

Years

"~**nen**" is used with numerals to name years.

Ex. The year of 2000   二千年   nisen-nen

     The year of 1900   千九百年   senkyuuhyaku-nen

     Interrogative: 何年 nan-nen

Counters of years

"~**nen (kan)**" is used to count the number of years.

Ex. 1 year   一年（間）   ichi-nen (-kan)

     10 years 十年（間）   jyuu-nen (-kan)

     Interrogative: nan-nen (-kan)

1. 私は**１９８０年**の四月に東京で生まれました。

   Watashi wa **sen-kyuuhyaku-hachijuu-nen** no shi-gatsu ni Tookyoo de umaremashita.

   (I was born in Tokyo in April of 1980.)

2. Q: **何年（間）**ぐらい日本に住んでいましたか。

   Nan-nen (-kan) gurai Nihon ni sunde imashita ka.

   (How many years did you live in Japan?)

A: 三年です。 ９５年から９８年まで日本にいました。

San-nen desu. **Kyuujuu-go-nen** kara **kyuujyuu-hachi-nen** made Nihon ni imashita.

(For three years. I was in Japan from 1995 to 1998.)

COUNTERS

There is no clear distinction between singular and plural forms in Japanese except for several words.   However, counter words are always attached to the number of the objects which are counted.   Here are some of the counters which are frequently used.

~Mai

This is used to count flat things such as paper and CDs.   The numbers before "**mai**" are the same as given in the earlier list of numbers of 1 to 10,000.

1. フロッピーディスクを**二枚**買いました。

   Furoppii disuku wo **ni-mai** kaimashita.

   (I bought two floppy disks.)
2. その紙を**四枚**ください。

   Sono kami wo **yon-mai** kudasai.

   (Please give me four sheets of the papers.)

~Hon (Pon/Bon)

This is used to count long, shaped things such as pencils, bottles, and trees.

1	ip-pon	11	juuip-pon
2	ni-hon	12	juuni-hon
3	san-bon	20	nijup-pon
4	yon-hon	30	sanjup-pon
5	go-hon	50	gojup-pon
6	rop-pon	100	hyap-pon
7	nana/shichi-hon	110	hyakujup-pon
8	hap-pon	120	hyakunijup-pon
9	kyuu-hon	1000	sen-bon
10	jup-pon		

Interrogative word: 何本   nan-bon

1. 昨日ビールを**三本**飲みました。   .

   Kinoo biiru wo **san-bon** nomimashita.

   (I drank three bottles of beer yesterday.)

2. えんぴつが**二本**いります。

   Enpitsu ga **ni-hon** irimasu .

   (I need two pencils.)

~ Hai (Pai /Bai)

This is used to count cups, glasses and bowls of drinks or food.

1	ip-pai	8	hap-pai
2	ni-hai	9	kyuu-hai
3	san-bai	10	jup-pai
4	yon-hai	20	nijup-pai
5	go-hai	100	hyap-pai
6	rop-pai	1000	sen-bai
7	nana/shichi hai		

Interrogative: 何ばい nan-bai

1. 水を**二はい**持って来てください。

   Mizu wo **nihai** motte kite kudasai..

   (Please bring two glasses of water .)

2. 毎日コーヒーを**三ばい**ぐらい飲みます

   Mainichi koohii wo **san-bai** gurai nomimasu.

   (I drink about three cups of coffee every day.)

3. 酒は**何ばい**ぐらい飲めますか。

   Sake wa **nan-bai** gurai nomemasuka.

   (How many cups of sake can you drink?)

4. ご飯をもう**一ばい**ください。

   Gohan wo moo **ip-pai** kudasai.

   (Please give me another bowl of rice.)

~Nin

This is used to count human beings.

1	hitori	2	futari

3	san-nin	8	hachi-nin
4	yo-nin	9	kyuu-nin
5	go-nin	10	juu-nin
6	roku-nin	100	hyaku-nin
7	nana/shichi-nin	1000	sen-nin

Interrogative word: 何人 nan-nin

1. 友達が**三人**家に来ました。

   Tomodachi ga **san-nin** uchi ni kimashita.

   (Three of my friends came to my house.)

2. A: 兄弟は**何人**いますか。

   Kyoodai wa **nan-nin** imasuka?

   (How many brothers and sisters do you have?)

   B: 私は姉が**二人**います。

   Watashi wa ane ga **futari** imasu.

   (I have two big sisters.)

~Satsu

This is used to count bound books, magazines, etc.

1	is-satsu	8	has-satsu
2	ni-satsu	9	kyuu-satsu
3	san-satsu	10	jus-satsu
4	yon-satsu	20	nijus-satsu
5	go-satsu	100	hyaku-satsu
6	roku-satsu	1000	sen-satsu
7	nana-satsu		

Interrogative word: 何さつ nan-satsu

1. 先週本を**三さつ**読みました。

   Senshuu hon wo **san-satsu** yomimashita.

   (I read three books last week.)

2. 日本語の辞書が **一さつ**ほしいです。

   Nihon-go no jisho ga **is-satsu** hoshii desu.

   (I want one Japanese dictionary.)

~Hiki (Piki / Biki)

This is a general counter for animals but not for birds.

1	ip-piki	8	hap-piki
2	ni-hiki	9	kyuu-hiki
3	san-biki	10	jup-piki
4	yon-hiki	20	nijup-piki
5	go-hiki	100	hyap-piki
6	rop-piki	1000	sen-biki
7	nana-hiki		

Interrogative: 何びき nan-biki

1. 家にはねこが**二ひき**と犬が**一ぴき**います。

   Uchi ni wa neko ga **ni-hiki** to inu ga **ip-piki** imasu.

   (There are two cats and one dog in my house.)

2. 台所でネズミを**一ぴき**見ました。

   Daidokoro de nezumi wo **ip-piki** mimashita.

   (I saw one mouse in the kitchen.)

~Tsu

This counter is used for many objects that do not belong to any of the above categories.

1	hito-tsu	7	nana-tsu
2	futa-tsu	8	yat-tsu
3	mit-tsu	9	kokono-tsu
4	yot-tsu	10	too
5	itsu-tsu	11	juu-ichi
6	mut-tsu	12	juu-ni

Interrogative word: いくつ ikutsu

1. 質問が**一つ**あります。

   Shitsumon ga **hitotsu** arimasu.

   (I have a question.)

2. A: 今日漢字を**いくつ**勉強しましたか。

   Kyoo kanji wo **ikutsu** benkyoo shimashita ka.

   (How many kanji did you study today?)

B: **四つ**勉強しました。

    Yottsu benkyoo shimashita.

    (I studied four kanji).

3. (At a store)

    りんごを**五つ**ください。

    Ringo wo **itsutsu** kudasai.

    (I will take five apples. / Lit. Give me five apples.)

4. Fill each blank with the given number or word and the appropriate counter .

    Ex. 図書館で本を<u>5 さつ</u>借りました。   (5)

        Toshokan de hon wo <u>go-satsu</u> karimashita.

    1. ペンが_____あります。   (10)

       Pen ga _____ arimasu.

    2. この学校に日本語の先生が_____いますか。   (how many)

       Kono gakkoo ni nihon-go no sensei ga _____ imasu ka.

    3. 山田さんにかわいいねこを_____もらいました。   (2)

       Yamada-san ni kawaii neko wo _____ moraimashita.

    4. 切手を_____買いましたか。   (how many)

       Kitte wo _____ kaimashita ka.

    5. 毎日りんごを_____とバナナを_____食べます。   (2), (3)

       Mainichi ringo wo _____ to banana wo _____ tabemasu.

    6. パーティにビールを_____ぐらい持って来てください。   (20 bottles)

       Partii ni biiru wo _____ gurai motte kite kudasai.

    7. ケーキを_____買いましょうか。   (how many)

       Keeki wo _____ kaimashoo ka.

    8. 音楽の CD を_____友だちにあげました。   (4)

       Ongaku no CD wo _____ tomodachi ni agemashita.

    9. レストランでおいしいワインを_____飲みました。   (3 glasses)

       Resutoran de oishii wain wo _____ nomimashita.

   10. 私は兄が_____います。(1)

       Watashi wa ani ga _____ imasu.

Review

5. Give the Japanese equivalents to the given words.

    Ex. February 4th   <u>ni-gatsu yokka</u>

        28 (books)   <u>nijuu has-satsu</u>

        4:00   <u>yo-ji</u>

  1. 3:45 _____

  2. 9:10 _____

  3. June 30th _____

  4. January 1st _____

  5. November 3rd _____

  6. 610 (sheets of papers) _____

  7. 16 (cups/glasses) _____

  8. 10 (cats) _____

  9. 7 (apples) _____

10. 1,392 (people) _____

11. 90 (pencils) _____

6. Translate the following into Japanese.

1. A: What day is today?

   B: It is Monday, October 16.

2. A: What time is it now?

   B: It is four fifty.

3. I ate three cakes last night.

4. I will be in Japan from April 11 to September 30.

5. There are eight Japanese magazines in the library.

6. A: How many watches do you have?

   B: I have only two.

7. I drank six bottles of beer yesterday.

Chapter 6

Particles

WA

Topic

The particle "**wa**" marks a topic of a sentence. The topic could be anything, the subject, object, location, etc. A word or phrase preceding "**wa**" is something already mentioned before or obvious from the context or universally accepted facts. The focus of a sentence is placed on the part which follows "**wa.**"

1. 友子さん**は**学生です。

   Tomoko-san **wa** gakusei desu.

   (Tomoko is a student.)

2. あの映画**は**面白かったです。

   Ano eiga **wa** omoshirokatta desu.

   (That movie was interesting.)

3. ここ**は**寒くありません。

   Koko **wa** samuku arimasen.

   (This place is not cold.)

4. 朝ご飯**は**もう食べましたか。

   Asa gohan **wa** moo tabemashita ka?

   (Did you already eat breakfast?)

Contrast

The particle "**wa**" also shows the contrast of a word or phrase marked by "**wa**" with something else. "**Wa**" also indicates the contrastive element, when it is used in negative sentences.

1. 私は朝たいてい紅茶を飲みます。でも、けさ**は**コーヒーを飲みました。

    Watashi wa asa taitei koocha wo nomimasu. Demo, kesa **wa** koohii wo nomimashita.

    (Usually I drink tea in the morning. But I drank coffee this morning.)

2. 疲れたから、勉強**は**しないでビデオゲームをしてしまいました。

    Tsukareta kara, benkyoo **wa** shinai de bideogeemu wo shite shimaimashita.

    (Becasuse I became tired, I did not study and ended up playing video games.)

3. 去年日本へ行った時、東京へ**は**行きましたが、京都へ**は**行きませんでした。

    Kyonen Nihon e itta toki, Tokyo e **wa** ikimashita ga, Kyoto e **wa** ikimasen deshita.

    (When I went to Japan last year, I went to Tokyo, but I didn't go to Kyoto.)

GA

The subject of a sentence

The particle "**ga**" marks the subject of a sentence. A word or phrase preceding "**ga**" is the subject of a sentence which is introduced as a new information in the discourse. It puts a focus on the elements preceding "**ga**." In case the subject has a contrastive element, its subject-marker, "**ga**," is replaced by "**wa**." When a WH-word is the subject of a sentence, it is always followed by the particle "**ga**" and in the response to the question, the subject is also marked by "**ga**."

1. 今日、一時にケンさん**が**来ます。

    Kyoo, ichi-ji ni Ken-san **ga** kimasu.

    (Today, Ken will come at one o'clock.)

2. 誰**が**これを持って来たんですか。

    Dare **ga** kore o motte kita n' desu ka.

    (Who brought this?)

3. A: あのレストランは何**が**おいしいですか。

       Ano resutoran wa nani **ga** oishii desu ka.

       (What is good in that restaurant?)

    B: あそこはてんぷら**が**おいしいですよ。

       Asoko wa tempura **ga** oishii desu yo.

       (As for that place, tempura is good, you know.)

4. A: そのセーターはとてもいいですね。

       Sono seetaa wa totemo ii desu ne.

       (Your (Lit. the) sweater is very nice.)

CHAP. 6]   PARTICLES   51

B: そうですか。母が買ってくれたんです。

Soo desu ka. Haha ga katte kureta n' desu

(Really ? My mother bought it for me.)

5. A: どのビルがトランプ・タワーですか。

Dono biru **ga** Toranpu Tawaa (Trump Tower) desu ka.

(Which building is Trump Tower?)

B: あのビルがそうです。

Ano biru **ga** soo desu.

(That building is the one./Lit. That building is so.)

6. A: 日本は何月がいいですか。

Nihon wa nan-gatsu **ga** ii desu ka.

(Which month is nice in Japan?)

B: そうですねえ。四月がいいです.

Soo desu nee . . . Shigatsu **ga** ii desu .

(Let me see . . . in Japan it is nice in April.)

The subject in a subordinate clause

The subject in a subordinate clause is marked by "**ga**," when it is not the same as the subject of the main clause.

1. お姉さんが結婚した時、幸子さんは十才でした。

Oneesan **ga** kekkon shita toki, Sachiko-san wa jus-sai deshita.

(Sachiko was ten years old, when her sister got married.)

2. 敏夫さんが見たら、その子は泣き始めました。

Toshio-san **ga** mitara, sono ko wa nakihajimemashita.

(When Toshio looked at the child, she started to cry.)

3. 友達が来たから、仕事をしませんでした。

Tomodachi **ga** kita kara, shigoto wo shimasen deshita.

(Since my friend came, I did not work.)

Note: In a relative clause the subject may be followed by "**no**" as well as "**ga**."

田中さんが買った時計はとても高かったです。

Tanaka-san **ga** katta tokei wa totemo takakatta desu.

(The watch Ms. Tanaka bought was very expensive.)

田中さんの買った時計はとても高かったです。

Tanaka-san **no** katta tokei wa totemo takakatta desu.

(The watch Ms. Tanaka bought was very expensive.)

Direct object

The direct object of stative verbs and some auxiliary adjectives is usually marked by "**ga**." If the object has a contrastive element, "**ga**" is replaced by "**wa**."

1. ここから富士山**が**よく見えますよ。

   Koko kara Fuji-san **ga** yoku miemasu yo.

   (We can see Mt. Fuji well from here/Lit. Mt. Fuji is well visible from here, you know.)
2. 今度の休みには、十日ぐらいヨーロッパ旅行**が**したいです。

   Kondo no yasumi ni wa, tooka gurai no Yooroppa ryokoo **ga** shitai desu.

   (I want to take a ten-day European trip during the next vacation.)
3. 鈴木さんはジャズ**が**とても好きです。

   Suzuki-san wa jazu **ga** totemo suki desu.

   (Mr. Suzuki likes jazz very much.)

A list of special predicates that need "**ga**" for object-marking is as follows.
iru (need), **dekiru** *(can do)*, **hoshii** *(want)*, **mieru** *(can see)*, **kikoeru** (can hear), **wakaru** *(understand)*, **-tai** *(want to)*.

1. Choose the right particle from the two shown in parentheses.
   1. 兄（**は**、**が**）結婚した人は中国人です。

      Ani (**wa, ga**) kekkon shita hito wa chuugoku-jin desu.
   2. 私（**は**、**が**）今年大学を卒業します。

      Watashi (**wa, ga**) kotoshi daigaku wo sotsugyoo shimasu.
   3. ロシア（**は**、**が**）とても大きい国だ。

      Roshia (**wa, ga**) totemo ookii kuni da.
   4. 日本で何（**は**、**が**）一番面白かったですか。

      Nihon de nani (**wa, ga**) ichiban omoshirokatta desu ka..
   5. 田中さんは誕生日に車（**は**、**が**）ほしいそうです。

      Tanaka-san wa tanjoobi ni kuruma (**wa, ga**) hoshii soo desu.

2. Fill in the blanks in the following passage with either "**wa**" or "**ga**."
   私 ＿＿＿＿＿ 去年アメリカに来ました。

   Watashi ＿＿＿＿＿ kyonen Amerika ni kimashita.

私 _____ 行ったところ _____ボストンとワシントンとニューヨークです。

Watashi _____ itta tokoro _____ Bosuton to Washinton to Nyuuyooku desu.

その中で私 _____ ワシントン _____ 一番好きです。

Sono naka de watashi _____ Washinton _____ ichiban suki desu.

ワシントン _____ とてもきれいで、おもしろい所 _____ たくさんあります。

Washinton _____ totemo kirei de, omoshiroi tokoro _____ takusan arimasu.

来年 _____ サンフランシスコに行こうと思います。

Rainen _____ San Furanshisuko ni ikoo to omoimasu.

WO

The direct object

The particle "**wo**" marks the preceding word or phrase as a direct object in the sentence.

1. 先週おもしろい映画**を**見ました。

   Senshuu omoshiroi eiga **wo** mimashita.

   (Last week I saw an interesting movie.)

2. 去年父が古い切手**を**くれました。

   Kyonen chichi ga furui kitte **wo** kuremashita.

   (Last year my father gave me some old stamps.)

3. トムさんは毎日コーヒー**を**飲みます。

   Tom-san wa mainichi koohii **wo** nomimasu.

   (Tom drinks coffee every day.)

Place with a verb of motion

The particle "**wo**" marks a place word through which the motion takes place. It also indicates a place from which the movement starts.

1. この道**を**通って行きましょう。

   Kono michi **wo** tootte ikimashoo.

   (Let's go through this street.)

2. 次の角**を**曲がってください。

   Tsugi no kado **wo** magatte kudasai.

   (Please turn the next corner.)

3. 明日二時に家**を**出ます。

Ashita ni-ji ni uchi **wo** demasu.

(Tomorrow I will leave home at two o'clock.)

4. 地下鉄**を**おりたら、すぐ電話してください。

Chikatetsu **wo** oritara, sugu denwa shite kudasai.

(When you get off the subway, please call me right away.)

NI

Indirect object

The particle "**ni**" marks its preceding word or phrase as an indirect object in the sentence. (cf. A direct object is marked by "**wo.**")

1. 私**に**その辞書をください。

Watashi **ni** sono jisho wo kudasai.

(Please give me that dictionary.)

2. 猫**に**食べ物をやりました。

Neko **ni** tabemono wo yarimashita.

(I gave the cat some food.)

3. 父はニューヨークの会社**に**よく電話をかけます。

Chihi wa Nyuuyooku no kaisha **ni** yoku denwa wo kakemasu.

(My father often calls a company in New York.)

Location

The particle "**ni**" marks the location of objects.

1. あの店**に**とてもいいカメラがありますよ。

Ano mise **ni** totemo ii kamera ga arimasu yo.

(There are very good cameras in that store.)

2. デパートの前**に**たくさん人がいます。

Depaato no mae **ni** takusan hito ga imasu.

(There are many people in front of the department store.)

3. 子供のころ私のうち**に**は犬が三匹いました。

Kodomo no koro watashi no uchi **ni** wa inu ga san-biki imashita.

(When I was a child, there were three dogs in my house.)

Point in time

The particle "**ni**" marks a point in time and it corresponds to "at," "on," or "in" in English. It usually follows the time expressions which need "at," "on," or "in" in English, such as "at three o'clock," "on Monday," and "in May." "**Ni**" does not follow the time words which do not need any prepositions in English, such as "today," "last week," and "next year."

1. 毎朝七時に おきます。

   Maiasa shichi-ji **ni** okimasu.

   Every morning I get up at seven o'clock.)

2. 五月に 日本へ行きます。

   Go-gatsu **ni** Nihon e ikimasu.

   I am going to Japan in May.)

3. ジョージ・ワシントンは千七百三十二年に生まれました。

   Jooji Washinton wa sen-nanahyaku-sanjuu-ni-nen **ni** umaremashita.

   (George Washington was born in 1732.)

4. 去年大学をそつぎょうしました。

   Kyonen dagaku wo sotsugyoo shimashita.

   (I graduated from college last year.)

5. 父は朝一時間泳ぎます。

   Chichi wa asa ichi-jikan oyogimasu.

   (My father swims for one hour in the morning.)

Note: In case of "in the morning" and "at night" Japanese equivalents do not use "**ni**."

Destination

The particle "**ni**" marks the destination of a motion verb.

1. 今晩映画に行きませんか。

   Konban eiga **ni** ikimasen ka.

   (Would you like to go to a movie tonight?)

2. 弟は来年大学に入ります。

   Otooto wa rainen daigaku **ni** hairimasu.

   (My younger brother will enter college next year.)

3. 恵美さんは来年日本に帰るそうです。

   Emi-san wa rainen Nihon **ni** kaeru soo desu.

   (I have heard that Emi is going back to Japan next year.)

Purpose of motion verb

"V-stem + **ni**" with a motion verb indicates the purpose of the verb.

1. 子供とパンダを**見に**動物園へ行きました。

    Kodomo to panda wo **mi ni** doobutsu-en e ikimashita.

    (I went to the zoo with my child to see a panda.)

2. プレゼントを**買いに**ショッピング・センターへ行きました。

    Purezento wo **kai ni** shoppingu sentaa e ikimashita.

    (I went to a shopping mall to buy a present.)

3. ピエールさんは毎日昼ご飯を**食べに**家へ帰ります。

    Pieeru-san wa mainichi hiru-gohan wo **tabe ni** uchi e kaerimasu.

    (Pierre goes back home to eat lunch every day.)

Agent of passive, causative or causative passive verbs

The particle "**ni**" marks the agent of the action expressed by passive, causative or causative passive verbs.

1. 小さい時、母**に**よく叱られた。

    Chiisai toki, haha **ni** yoku shikarareta.

    (When I was a child, I was often scolded by my mother.)

2. 昨日妹は学校で先生**に**ほめられたそうです。

    Kinoo imooto wa gakkoo de sesnei **ni** homerareta soo desu.

    (I heard that my younger sister was praised by a teacher at school yesterday.)

3. 私は子供**に**毎日野菜を食べさせます。

    Watashi wa kodomo **ni** mainichi yasai wo tabesasemasu.

    (I make my children eat vegetables every day.)

4. 私**に**その話を聞かせてください。

    Watashi **ni** sono hanashi wo kikasete kudasai.

    (Please let me hear the story.)

5. 友子ちゃんはお母さん**に**ピアノの練習をさせられます。

    Tomoko-chan wa okaasan **ni** piano no renshuu wo saseraremasu.

    (Tomoko is made to practice the piano by her mother.)

6. 私は先生**に**一週間でひらがなを覚えさせられました。

    Watashi wa sensei **ni** Hiragana wo is-shuukan de oboesaseraremasnita.

    (I was made to memorize hiragana in a week by a teacher.)

E

The particle "**e**" indicates the direction of motion verbs. It corresponds to "toward" or "to" in English and is usually interchangeable with the particle "**ni**."

1. 今年の夏ロンドン**へ**行きます。

   Kotoshi no natsu Rondon **e** ikimasu.

   (This summer I am going to London.)

2. 今日何時ごろうち**へ**帰りますか。

   Kyoo nan-ji goro uchi **e** kaerimasu ka.

   (Around what time do you go home today?)

3. 明日八時に学校**へ**来てください。

   Ashita hachi-ji ni gakkoo **e** kite kudasai.

   (Please come to school at eight o'clock tomorrow.)

4. 外**へ**出たら、雨が降っていました。

   Soto **e** detara, ame ga futte imashita.

   (When I went outside, it was raining.)

DE

Place

The particle "**de**" marks the place where an action takes place or an event occurs. It is equivalent to "in" or "at" in English.

1. キムさんはアメリカ**で**日本語を勉強しました。

   Kimu-san wa Amerika **de** nihon-go wo benkyoo shimashita.

   (Ms. Kim studied Japanese in the United States.)

2. 道子さんは銀行**で**働いています。

   Michiko-san wa ginkoo **de** hataraite imasu.

   (Michiko is working at a bank.)

3. このネクタイは日本**で**買いました。

   Kono nekutai wa Nihon **de** kaimashita.

   (I bought this tie in Japan.)

4. 今晩八時半から友子さんのうち**で**パーティーがあります。

   Konban hachi-ji han kara Tomoko-san no uchi **de** paatii ga arimasu.

(There is a party tonight starting from eight thirty at Tomoko's house.)

5. 昨日学校でチェロのコンサートがありました。

Kinoo gakkoo **de** chero no konsaato ga arimashita.

(There was a cello concert at school yesterday.)

Means

The particle "**de**" indicates the means for doing something. It is equivalent to "by'" or "with" in English.

1. 黒いペンで名前を書いてください。

Kuroi pen **de** name wo kaite kudasai.

(Please write your name with black pen.)

2. 雨が降っているから、タクシーで来ました。

Ame ga futte iru kara, takushii **de** kimashita.

(I came by taxi, because it was raining.)

3. ジムさんは日本語で話しました。

Jimu-san wa nihon-go **de** hanashimashita.

(Jim spoke in Japanese.)

Cause

The particle "**de**" indicates the cause. It is equivalent to "because of" or "due to" in English.

1. 林さんはかぜで会社を休みました。

Hayashi-san wa kaze de kaisha wo yasumimashita.

(Mr. Hayashi was absent from work because of a cold.)

2. 仕事でシカゴへ行きます。

Shigoto **de** Shikago e ikimasu.

(I am going to Chicago on business.)

3. 雨でピクニックができませんでした。

Ame **de** pikunikku ga dekimasen deshita.

(We could not have a picnic because of rain.)

Required time or quantity

The particle "**de**" indicates the required time or quantity.

1. このレポートを二日**で**書かなければなりません。

   Kono repooto wo futsuka **de** kakanakereba narimasen.

   (I must write this report in two days.)

2. あの車は一万ドル**で**は買えないでしょう。

   Ano kuruma wa ichiman-doru **de** wa kaenai deshoo.

   (Probably one cannot buy that car with $10,000.)

3. 千恵さんはあと一年**で**大学を卒業します。

   Chie-san wa ato ichi-nen **de** daigaku wo sotsugyoo shimasu.

   (Chie is going to graduate from college in a year.)

3. Choose the right particle from the choises given in parentheses.

1. 明日二時（**を、に、へ、で**）講演があります。

   Ashita ni-ji (**wo, ni, e, de**) kooen ga arimasu.

2. 日本人はご飯をたいてい箸（**を、に、へ、で**）食べます。

   Nihon-jin wa gohan wo taitei hashi (**wo, ni, e, de**) tabemasu.

3. 私はきのう母（**を、に、へ、で**）くつ（**を、に、へ、で**）買ってもらいました。

   Watashi wa kinoo haha (**wo, ni, e, de**) kutsu (**wo, ni, e, de**) katte moraimashita.

4. 「キャッツ」はブロードウェー（**を、に、へ、で**）見ました。

   「Kyattsu」 wa Buroodowee (**wo, ni, e, de**) mimashita.

5. 来月友達とマイアミ（**を、に、へ、で**）行きます。

   Raigetsu tomodachi to Maiami (**wo, ni, e, de**) ikimasu.

6. 土曜日の四時からYMCA（**を、に、へ、で**）コンサートがあります。

   Doyoobi no yo-ji kara YMCA (**wo, ni, e, de**) konsaato ga arimasu.

7. あの店（**を、に、へ、で**）日本のビールがありますよ。

   no mise (**wo, ni, e, de**) Nihon no biiru ga aimasu yo.

8. 毎日同じ道（**を、に、へ、で**）散歩します。

   Mainichi onaji michi (**wo, ni, e, de**) sanpo shimasu.

9. ジョージさんは病気（**を、に、へ、で**）寝ています。

   Jooji-san wa byooki (**wo, ni, e, de**) nete imasu.

10. きのう本（**を、に、へ、で**）返し（**を、に、へ、で**）図書館（**を、に、へ、で**）行きました。

    Kinoo hon (**wo, ni, e, de**) kaeshi (**wo, ni, e, de**) toshokan (**wo, ni, e, de**) ikimashita.

11. 宿題（**を、に、へ、で**）忘れて、先生（**を、に、へ、で**）叱られてしまいました。

    Shukudai (**wo, ni, e, de**) wasurete, sensei (**wo, ni, e, de**) shikararete shimimashita.

12. あと三日（**を、に、へ、で**）ガールフレンドがコロラドから来ます。

    Ato mik-ka (**wo, ni, e, de**) gaarufurendo ga Kororado kara kimasu.

4. Fill in the blanks in the following passage with the particle "**wo**," "**ni**," "**e**," or "**de**."

金曜日の八時 ＿＿＿＿＿ 学校 ＿＿＿＿＿ 来てください。

Kinyoobi no hachi-ji ＿＿＿＿＿ gakkoo ＿＿＿＿＿ kite kudasai.

ケントホール ＿＿＿＿＿ しけん ＿＿＿＿＿ します。

Kento hooru ＿＿＿＿＿ shiken ＿＿＿＿＿ shimasu.

ケントホール ＿＿＿＿＿ は教室がたくさんありますが、32 A ＿＿＿＿＿ 来てください。

Kento hooru ＿＿＿＿＿ wa kyooshitsu ga takusan arimasu ga, 32 A ＿＿＿＿＿ kite

kudasai.

32 A ＿＿＿＿＿ 先生が三人います。先生 ＿＿＿＿＿ I.D. ＿＿＿＿＿ 見せてください。

32 A ＿＿＿＿＿ sensei ga san-nin imasu. Sensei ＿＿＿＿＿ I.D. ＿＿＿＿＿ misete kudasai.

しけんはペン ＿＿＿＿＿ 書いてはいけません。えんぴつ ＿＿＿＿＿ 持って来てください。

Shiken wa pen ＿＿＿＿＿ kaite wa ikemasen. Enpitsu ＿＿＿＿＿ motte kite kudasai.

えんぴつは三本 ＿＿＿＿＿ いいでしょう。

Enpitsu wa san-bon ＿＿＿＿＿ ii deshoo.

仕事 ＿＿＿＿＿ 来ることができない人は田中先生 ＿＿＿＿＿ 電話 ＿＿＿＿＿ かけてください。

Shigoto ＿＿＿＿＿ kuru koto ga dekinai hito wa Tanaka sensei ＿＿＿＿＿ denwa ＿＿＿＿＿

kakete kudasai.

KA

Interrogative

The sentence final particle "**ka**" indicates the preceding sentence to be an interrogative.

1. アンさんは学生です**か**。

    An san wa gakusei desu **ka**.

    (Is Ann a student?)

2. どんな音楽が好きです**か**。

    Donna ongaku ga suki desu **ka**.

    (What kind of music do you like?)

3. この白いチョコレートはおいしいです**か**。

    Kono shiroi chokoreeto wa oishii desu **ka**.

    (Does this white chocolate taste good?)

4. 令子さんのお子さんは女の子ですか、男の子ですか。

    Reiko-san no o-kosan wa onna no ko desu ka, otko no ko desu ka.

    (Is Reiko's child a girl or a boy?)

Note: When two interrogative sentences are combined, as in "X **ka**, Y **ka**," this corresponds to "X or Y?" in English.

Alternative

The particle "**ka**" marks an alternative. "X **ka** Y" corresponds to "(either) X or Y" in English.

1. 今晩は日本料理か韓国料理を食べに行きましょう。

    Konban wa nihon-ryoori **ka** kankoku-ryoori wo tabe ni ikimashoo.

    (Let's go to eat either Japanese or Korean food tonight.)

2. 利夫さんはアメリカかイギリスに住みたいそうです。

    Toshio-san wa Amerika **ka** Igirisu ni sumitai soo desu.

    (I heard that Toshio would like to live either in the United States or in England.)

3. 今年の夏は兄か姉と旅行をします。

    Kotoshi no natsu wa ani **ka** ane to ryokoo wo shimasu.

    (I will go on a trip this summer either with my older brother or with my sister.)

Embedded question

The expression "**ka doo ka**" indicates that the preceding sentence is an embedded yes-no question. It is equivalent to "whether (or not)" in English.

1. 良江さんがイタリア語を話すかどうか知っていますか。

    Yoshie-san ga itaria-go wo hansu **ka doo ka** shitte imasu ka.

    (Do you know whether Yoshie speaks Italian?)

2. キムさんが肉を食べるかどうか知りません。

    Kimu-san ga niku wo taberu **ka doo ka** shirimasen.

    (I do not know whether Mr. Kim eats meat.)

3. 明日までに仕事が終わるかどうか分かりません。

    Ashita made ni shigoto ga owaru **ka doo ka** wakarimasen.

    (I can not tell (Lit. understand) whether the work will be done by tomorrow.)

4. 日本へいつ行くか教えてください。

    Nihon e itsu iku **ka** oshiete kudasai.

    (Please let me know (Lit. teach me) when you are going to Japan.)

5. あの人にどこで会ったか覚えていません。

    Ano hito ni doko de atta **ka** oboete imasen.

    (I do not remember where I met her/him.)

Note: When an embedded sentence is a WH-question, just "**ka**" alone is used.

NE

The particle "**ne**" is a sentence final particle indicating that the speaker seeks for an agreement or confirmation from the listener about the statement. It is often regarded as a tag question in English.

1. このアパートは大きいです**ね**。

   Kono apaato wa ookii desu **ne**.

   (This apartment is large, isn't it?)

2. 水野先生の講演はよかったです**ね**。

   Mizuno sensei no kooen wa yokatta desu **ne**.

   (Professor Mizuno's lecture was good, wasn't it?)

3. しげるさんは歌が上手です**ね**。

   Shigeru-san wa uta ga joozu desu **ne**.

   (Shigeru sings well, doesn't he? /Lit. Shigeru is good at singing, isn't he?)

YO

The particle "**yo**" is a sentence final particle of emphasis showing the speaker's conviction.

1. あの店は高いです**よ**。

   Ano mise wa takai desu **yo**.

   (That store is expensive, you know.)

2. ここは日曜はとてもこみます**よ**。

   Koko wa nichiyoo wa totemo komimasu **yo**.

   (This place is very crowded on Sundays, I tell you.)

3. 電子辞書は便利です**よ**。

   Denshi-jisho wa benri desu **yo**.

   (An electronic dictionary is convenient, you know.)

5. Fill in the blanks in the following dialogue with the particle "**ka**," "**ne**," or "**yo**."

(In this dialogue between A and B, they are taking a walk in a park with which B is familiar.)

A: この公園は大きいです ＿＿＿＿＿。何と言う公園です ＿＿＿＿＿。

　　Kono kooen wa ookii desu ＿＿＿＿＿.　　Nan to iu kooen desu ＿＿＿＿＿.

B: 桜公園です ＿＿＿＿＿。

　　Sakura kooen desu ＿＿＿＿＿.

A: ああ、そうです ＿＿＿＿＿。本当にたくさん桜の木があります ＿＿＿＿＿。

　　Aa, soo desu ＿＿＿＿＿.　　Hontoo ni takusan sakira no ki ga arimasu ＿＿＿＿＿.

B: ええ。春になると、花が咲いて、とてもきれいです ＿＿＿＿＿。

　　Ee.　Haru ni naru to, hana ga saite, totemo kirei desu ＿＿＿＿＿.

A: そうでしょう ＿＿＿＿＿。そのころ、ここで桜祭りがある ＿＿＿＿＿ どうか知っていますか。

　　Soo deshoo ＿＿＿＿＿. Sono koro, koko de sakura-matsuri ga aru ＿＿＿＿＿ doo ka shitte

　　imasu ＿＿＿＿＿.

B: ああ、桜祭りです ＿＿＿＿＿。あります ＿＿＿＿＿。でもいつある ＿＿＿＿＿よく覚えてい

　　Aa, Sakura matsuri desu ＿＿＿＿＿.　　Arimasu ＿＿＿＿＿.　　Demo itsu aru ＿＿＿＿＿ yoku

　　ません。四月五日 ＿＿＿＿＿ 十日だと思います＿＿＿＿＿。

　　oboete imasen.　　Shi-gatsu itsuka ＿＿＿＿＿ tooka da to omoimasu ＿＿＿＿＿.

A: じゃあ、もうすぐです ＿＿＿＿＿。また、一緒に来ません＿＿＿＿＿。

　　Jaa, moo sugu desu ＿＿＿＿＿.　　Mata, issho ni kimasen ＿＿＿＿＿.

B: それはいいです＿＿＿＿＿。そうしましょう。

　　Sore wa ii desu ＿＿＿＿＿.　　Soo shimashoo.

NO

The particle "**no**" marks the modifier of the noun following it.

Possessive

The particle "**no**" indicates the possessive of its preceding noun.

1. ジム**の**お母さんはシカゴに住んでいます。

　　Jimu no okaasan wa Shikago ni sunde imasu.

　　(Jim's mother lives in Chicago.)

2. A: これは誰**の**めがねですか。

　　　Kore wa dare **no** megane desu ka.

　　　(Whose glasses are these?)

　B: あぁ、それですか。私**の**です。

　　　Aa, sore desu ka. Watashi **no** desu.

(Oh, those? They are mine.)

Note: The modified noun is omitted when it is understood from the context.

Equivalent

The particle "**no**" indicates that the preceding and the following nouns are equivalent.

1. 私の犬**の**チロはテリアです。

   Watashi no inu **no** Chiro wa teria desu.

   (My dog, Chiro, is a terrier.)

2. あの本は友達**の**弘子さんにあげました。

   Ano hon wa tomodachi **no** Hiroko-san ni agemashita.

   (I gave that book to my friend, Hiroko.)

3. 弟**の**正樹は今年二十になりました。

   Otooto **no** Masaki wa kotoshi hatachi ni narimashita.

   (My younger brother, Masaki, turned (Lit. became) twenty years old this year.)

Location

The particle "**no**" marks the location of the noun following it. "X **no** Y" means "Y in/at X" in English.

1. 東京**の**会社につとめたいです。

   Tookyoo **no** kaisha ni tsutome-tai desu.

   (I want to work at a company in Tokyo.)

2. この町**の**公園はきれいですね。

   Kono machi **no** kooen wa kirei desu ne.

   (The park in this town is beautiful, isn't it?)

3. 静子さんの部屋**の**テレビはとても小さい。

   Shizuko-san no heya **no** terebi wa totemo chiisai.

   (The TV in Shizuko's room is very small.)

Subject

The particle "**no**" marks the subject of a sentence modifier. This "**no**" may be interchangeable with the particle "**ga**" (cf. Chapter 11, Modification of a Noun, pp.151-152: Sentence Modifier)

1. これは私**の/が**作ったケーキです。

    Kore wa watashi **no/ga** tsukutta keeki desu.

    (This is the cake I made.)

2. ブライアンさん**の/が**言ったことは分かりませんでした。

    Buraian-san **no/ga** itta koto wa wakarimasen deshita.

    (I did not understand what Brian said.)

3. 妻**の/が**乗る飛行機は JAL の 747 です。

    Tsuma **no/ga** noru hikooki wa JAL no 747 desu.

    (The plane which my wife will fly is JAL 747.)

MO

Similarity

The particle "**mo**" indicates similarity. It is equivalent to "also" in an affirmative sentence and "either" in a negative sentence.

1. A: わたしの誕生日は六月六日です。

    Watashi no tanjoobi wa roku-gatsu muika desu.

    (My birthday is the 6th of June.)

    B: えっ、僕の**も**です。

    E! boku no **mo** desu .

    (Really! So is mine.)

2. リーさんは肉は食べません。魚**も**食べません。

    Ree-san wa niku wa tabemasen. Sakana **mo** tabemasen.

    (Mr. Lee does not eat meat. He does not eat fish, either)

3. 去年京都へ行きました。大阪へ**も**行きました。

    Kyonen Kyooto e ikimashita. Oosaka e **mo** ikimashita.

    (I went to Kyoto last year. I also went to Osaka.)

Note: Particles "**wa**," "**ga**," and "**wo**" are replaced by "**mo**," but other particles coexist with "**mo**" by preceding it.

Emphasis

The particle "**mo**" which follows a quantitative word with a numeral emphasizes how much or how little the amount is.

1. 田中先生の講演を聞きに**三百人も**人が来ました。

   Tanaka sensei no kooen wo kiki ni **sanbyaku-nin mo** hito ga kimashita.

   (As many as three hundred people came to listen to Professor Tanaka's talk.)

2. 昨日は**二時間も**寝ませんでした。

   Kinoo wa **ni-jikan mo** nemasen deshita.

   (Yesterday I did not sleep for not even two hours.)

3. ゆうべ友達の家でビールを**五本も**飲んでしまいました。

   Yuube tomodachi no uchi de biiru wo **go-hon mo** nonde shimaimashita.

   (I ended up drinking as many as five bottles of beer at my friend's last night.)

~ MO ~ MO

The repetition of the particle "**mo**" in an affirmative sentence is equivalent to "both ~ and ~" and in a negative sentence "neither ~ nor ~" in English.

1. 始さんのお父さん**も**お母さん**も**先生です。

   Hajime-san no otoosan **mo** okaasan **mo** sensei desu.

   (Hajime's father and mother both are teachers.)

2. 東京で敏子さんに**も**郁子さんに**も**会いました。

   Tokyo de Toshiko-san ni **mo** Ikuko-san ni **mo** aimashita.

   (I saw both Toshiko and Ikuko in Tokyo.)

3. 花子さんは肉**も**魚**も**食べません。

   Hanako-san wa niku **mo** sakana **mo** tabemasen.

   (Hanako eats neither meat nor fish.)

4. アメリカでは映画館で**も**レストランで**も**タバコをすってはいけません。

   Amerika de wa eigakan de **mo** restoran de **mo** tabako wo sutte wa ikemasen.

   (One must not smoke in a movie theater or in a restaurant in the United States.)

Note: Particles "**wa**," "**ga**," and "**wo**" are replaced by "**mo**," but other particles coexist with "**mo**" by preceding it.

TO

Complete listing

The particle "**to**" joins nouns. It is equivalent to "and" in English.

1. 夏にカナダとアラスカへ行きました。

   Natsu ni Kanada **to** Arasuka e ikimashita.

   (I went to Canada and Alaska during the summer.)

2. 来週家に山田さんと田中さんとミラーさんが来ます。

   Raishuu uchi ni Yamada san **to** Tanaka-san **to** Miraa-san ga kimasu.

   (Mr. Yamada, Ms. Tanaka, and Mr. Miller will come to my house next week.)

3. ケーキを作るから、卵とバターと砂糖を買って来てください。

   Keeki wo tsukuru kara, tamago **to** bataa **to** satoo wo katte kite kudasai.

   (Please go and buy eggs, butter, and sugar, because I am going to make a cake.)

Reciprocal relationship

The particle "**to**" marks the person(s) with whom one does things. It is equivalent to "with" in English.

1. 私は友達とアパートに住んでいます。

   Watashi wa tomodachi **to** apaato ni sunde imasu.

   (I live in an apartment with a friend.)

2. 先月兄はナオミさんとカナダへ行きました。

   Sengetsu ani wa Naomi-san **to** Kanada e ikimashita.

   (My older brother went to Canada with Naomi last month.)

3. 毎朝父は母と散歩します。

   Maiasa chichi wa haha **to** sanpo shimasu.

   (My father takes a walk with my mother every morning.)

4. きのう友達と三時間も話しました。

   Kinoo tomodachi **to** san-jikan mo hanashimashita.

   (I talked with my friend for three long hours yesterday.)

Quotation

The particle "**to**" indicates the preceding sentence or word to be a quotation, one's thought, onomatopoeia, etc.

1. 上田さんが電話で明日来ると言いました。

   Ueda-san ga denwa de ashita kuru **to** iimashta.

   (Mr. Ueda said by phone that he would come tomorrow.)

2. 今度ボストンへ車で行こうと思います。

   Kondo Bosuton e kuruma de ikoo **to** omoimasu.

   (I think that next time I will go to Boston by car.)

3. 犬がワンワンとなきました。

   Inu ga wanwan **to** nakimashita

   (A dog barked, "Ruff, ruff.")

4. 山下多恵子さんという人を知っていますか。

   Yamashita Taeko-san **to** iu hito wo shitte imasu ka.

   (Do you know a person called Taeko Yamashita?)

Similarity and difference

The particle "**to**" indicates that the preceding noun is "same as ~" or "different from ~."

1. 友子さんのスーツは私のと同じだ。

   Tomoko-san no suutsu wa watashi no **to onaji** da.

   (Tomoko's suits are the same as mine.)

2. これと同じものがもう一つありますか。

   Kore **to onaji** mono ga moo hitotsu arimasu ka?

   (Do you have another one just like this?)

3. 一郎さんはお兄さんとぜんぜん違いますね。

   Ichiroo-san wa oniisan **to** zenzen **chigaimasu** ne.

   (Ichiroo is completely different from his older brother, isn't he?)

4. アメリカのなすは日本のとちょっと違います。

   Ameika no nasu wa Nihon no **to** chotto **chigaimasu**.

   (An American eggplant is a little different from a Japanese one.)

YA

The particle "**ya**" connects nouns and implies that there would be more things besides those on the list. It is equivalent to "~ and others," and "~ and so forth" in English.

1. 令子さん**や**武さんもパーティーに来ました。

   Reiko-san **ya** Takeshi-san mo paatii ni kimashita.

   (Reiko, Takeshi, and others also came to the party.)

2. 休みには山**や**海に行きたいですね。

   Yasumi ni wa yama **ya** umi ni ikitai desu ne.

   (I want to go to the mountain, the sea, and so forth during holidays.)

3. 野菜**や**果物などは体にいい。

   Yasai **ya** kudamono nado wa karada ni ii.

   (Vegetables, fruits, and the like are good for the health (Lit./ body).)

Note: The particle "**nado**" is optional.

6. Choose the right particle from the choices given in parentheses.

1. 弟（**の、も、と、や**）友達は一人でU．S．オープンに行きました。

   Otooto (**no, mo, to, ya**) tomodachi wa hitori de U.S. oopun (Open) ni ikimashita.

2. 敏子さんは犬が大好きです。私（**の、も、と、や**）そうです。

   Toshiko-san wa inu ga daisuki desu. Watashi (**no, mo, to, ya**) soo desu.

3. 美佐子さん（**の、も、と、や**）安子さんはニューヨーク大学の学生です。

   Misako-san (**no, mo, to, ya**) Yasuko-san wa Nyuuyooku daigaku no gakusei desu.

4. 日本語のクラスにはアメリカ人（**の、も、と、や**）中国人（**の、も、と、や**）韓国人

   Nihongo no kurasu ni wa amerika-jin (**no, mo, to, ya**) chuugoku-jin (**no, mo, to, ya**)
   などいろいろな人がいます。

   kankoku-jin nado irorio na hito ga imasu.

5. 子供のテレビ番組(program)（**の、も、と、や**）「セサミストリート」は有名です。

   Kodomo no terebi bangumi(program) (**no, mo, to, ya**) 「Sesami Sutoriito」 wa yuumei desu.

6. ショルツさんのうちにはピカソの絵が十枚（**の、も、と、や**）あるそうです。

   Shorutsu-san no uchi ni wa Pikaso no e ga juu-mai (**no, mo, to, ya**) aru soo desu.

7. いつか本を書きたい（**の、も、と、や**）思っています。

   Itsu ka hon wo kakitai (**no, mo, to, ya**) omotte imasu.

8. 父（**の、も、と、や**）一緒によくテニスをします。

   Chichi (**no, mo, to, ya**) issho ni yoku tenisu wo shimasu.

9. 東京（**の、も、と、や**）地下鉄はいつもこんでいる。

   Tookyoo (**no, mo, to, ya**) chikatetsu wa itsumo konde iru.

10. これは二十年前に先生（**の、も、と、や**）お書きになった本です。

    Kore wa nijuu-nen mae ni sensei (**no, mo, to, ya**) o-kaki ni natta hon desu.

11. みどりさんは若い時（**の、も、と、や**）ぜんぜん違う。

   Midori-san wa wakai toki (**no, mo, to, ya**) zenzen chigau.

12. 父はテニス（**の、も、と、や**）ゴルフ（**の、も、と、や**）しません。

   Chichi wa tenisu (**no, mo, to, ya**) gorufu (**no, mo, to, ya**) shimasen.

13.「はる」（**の、も、と、や**）いうレストランに行ったことがありますか。

   "Haru" (**no, mo, to, ya**) iu resutoran ni itta koto ga arimasu ka.

7. Fill in the blanks in the following passage with the particle "**no**," "**mo**," "**to**," or "**ya**."

   私は先月友達 ＿＿＿ ケイト＿＿＿ アジアを旅行しました。

   Watashi wa sengetsu tomodachi ＿＿＿ Keito ＿＿＿ Ajia wo ryokoo shimashita.

   中国 ＿＿＿ 日本 ＿＿＿ 韓国などへ行きました。タイに ＿＿＿ 行きました。

   Chuugoku ＿＿＿ Nihon ＿＿＿ Kankoku nado e ikimashita. Tai ni ＿＿＿ ikimashita.

   日本では東京 ＿＿＿ 京都に行って、いろいろな料理を食べました。

   Nihon de wa Tookyoo ＿＿＿ Kyooto ni itte, iroiro na ryoori wo tabemashita.

   東京 ＿＿＿ パン屋で私 ＿＿＿ 買ったケーキはとてもおいしかったので、二人で

   Tookyoo ＿＿＿ pan-ya de watashi ＿＿＿ katta keeki wa totemo oishikatta node, futari de

   六つ ＿＿＿ 食べてしまいました。

   Mutts ＿＿＿ tabete shimaimashita.

   私 ＿＿＿ 母はそれ ＿＿＿ 同じケーキが食べてみたい ＿＿＿ 言っています。

   Watashi ＿＿＿ haha wa sore ＿＿＿ onaji keeki ga tabete mitai ＿＿＿ itte imasu.

   来年は母 ＿＿＿ 一緒に日本へ行きます。

   Rainen wa haha ＿＿＿ ishho ni Nihon e ikimasu.

KARA

The particle "**kara**" indicates a starting point. It is equivalent to "from" in English.

1. 昨日ボストン**から**車で来ました。

   Kinoo Bosuton **kara** kuruma de kimashita.

   (I came from Boston by car yesterday.)

2. 講演は一時**から**です。

   Kooen wa ichi-ji **kara** desu.

   (The lecture starts at (Lit. is from) one o'clock.)

3. これは姉**から**もらいました。

   Kore wa ane **kara** moraimashita.

(I received this from my older sister.)

MADE

The particle "**made**" corresponds to "up to," "until," or "as far as" in English.

1. 家から会社**まで**歩いて行きます。

    Uchi kara kaisha **made** aruite ikimasu.

    (I walk to my office from home.)

2. 来週は月曜から水曜**まで**ひまです。

    Raishuu wa getsuyoo kara suiyoo **made** hima desu.

    (Next week I am not busy /Lit. free from Monday to Wednesday.)

3. この頃毎日九時頃**まで**仕事をしています。

    Kono goro mainichi ku-ji goro **made** shigoto wo shite imasu.

    (Recently I have been working until around nine o'clock every day.)

4. 岡田さんが来る**まで**ここにいましょう。

    Okada-san ga kuru **made** koko ni imashoo.

    (Let's stay here until Mr. Okada comes.)

MADE NI

The particle "**made ni**" marks the time limit. It corresponds to "by/by the time" in English.

1. 三月**までに**結果をお知らせします。

    San-gatsu **made ni** kekka wo oshirase shimasu.

    (I will notify you of the result by March.)

2. 今晩七時**までに**家に来てください。

    Konban shichi-ji **made ni** uchi ni kite kudasai.

    (Please come to my house by seven o'clock tonight.)

3. 来年日本に行く**までに**漢字を三百覚えるつもりだ。

    Rainen Nihon ni iku **made ni** kanji wo sanbyaku oboeru tsumori da.

    (I intend to memorize three hundred kanji by the time I go to Japan next year.)

8. Choose the appropriate particle from the ones shown in parentheses.

1. 来週 （**から、まで、までに**） この仕事は終わりますか。

   Raishuu   (**kara, made, made ni**)   kono shigoto wa owarimasu ka.

2. 月曜日 （**から、まで、までに**） 新しい仕事を始めます。

   Getsuyoo-bi (**kara, made, made ni**) atarashii shigoto wo hajimemasu.

3. 今日は家 （**から、まで、までに**） 学校にタクシーで来ました。

   Kyoo wa uchi (**kara, made, made ni**) gakkoo ni takushii de kimashita.

4. 北海道 （**から、まで、までに**） 九州 （**から、まで、までに**） 飛行機で何時間ぐらい

   Hokkaidoo (**kara, made, made ni**) Kyuushuu (**kara, made, made ni**) hikooki de
   かかりますか。

   nan-jikan gurai kakarimasu ka.

9. Fill in the blanks in the following passage with the particle "**kara**," " **made**," or "**made ni**."

今日のコンサートは八時 ＿＿＿＿ですから、七時半 ＿＿＿＿ コンサートホールの前 ＿＿＿＿

Kyoo no konsaato wa hachi-ji ＿＿＿＿ desu kara, shichi-ji han ＿＿＿＿ konsaato hooru no
来てください。

mae ＿＿＿＿ kite kudasai.

会社 ＿＿＿＿ コンサートホール ＿＿＿＿ はバスで三十分ぐらいでしょう。

Kaisha ＿＿＿＿ konsaato hooru ＿＿＿＿ wa basu de sanjup-pun gurai deshoo.
ですから、仕事は六時 ＿＿＿＿ してしまってください。

Desu kara, shigoto wa roku-ji ＿＿＿＿ shite shimatte kudasai.

八時五分前 ＿＿＿＿ 待っていますが、それ ＿＿＿＿ 来ない時は、一人でホールに入ります。

Hachi-ji go-fun mae ＿＿＿＿ matte imasu ga, sore ＿＿＿＿ konai toki wa, hitori de hooru
ni hairimasu.

YORI

The particle "~ **yori**" indicates that the preceding noun or verb shows the measure for comparison. It is equivalent to "than ~" in English.

1. 林さんは**私より**背が高い。

   Hayashi-san wa **watshi yori** se ga takai.

   (Ms. Hayashi is taller than I.)

2. 中山さんは**藤田さんより**年上でしょう。

   Nakayama-san wa **Fujita-san yori** toshiue deshoo.

(Mr. Nakayama is probably older than Ms. Fujita.)

3. 地下鉄で行く方がバスで**行くより**早いです。

Chikatetsu de iku hoo ga, basu de **iku yori** hayai desu.

(Going by subway is faster than going by bus.)

HODO

The particle "~ **hodo** + negative expression" indicates that the preceding noun or verb shows the "standard" of negative comparison. It is equivalent to "not as ....as ~" in English.

1. 奈良は**京都ほど有名じゃありません**。

Nara wa **Kyooto hodo yuumei ja arimasen**.

(Nara is not as famous as Kyoto.)

2. 今年の冬は**去年ほど寒くありません**。

Kotoshi no fuyu wa **kyonen hodo samuku arimasen**.

(This winter is not as cold as the last one.)

3. 泳ぐのは**考えていたほどやさしくない**。

Oyogu no wa **kangaete ita hodo yasashiku nai**.

(Swimming is not as easy as I thought.)

DAKE

The particle "**dake**" indicates that the preceding noun or sentence shows restriction or limitation. It is equivalent to "just" or "only" in English.

1. やさしい漢字**だけ**覚えました。

Yasashii kanji **dake** oboemashita.

(I memorized just easy kanji.)

2. インドへ一度**だけ**行ったことがあります。

Indo e ichi-do **dake** itta koto ga arimasu.

(I have been to India just once.)

3. きのうはテレビを見た**だけ**です。

Kinoo wa terebi wo mita **dake** desu.

(I only watched TV yesterday.)

4. あの人は有名な**だけ**です。

   Ano hito wa yuumei na **dake** desu.

   (That person is just famous, that's all.)

SHIKA

The particle "**shika** + negative expression" is equivalent to "only" or "nothing but" in English.

1. 田中さんと吉田さん**しか来ませんでした**。

   Tanaka-san to Yoshida san **shika kimasen deshita**.

   (Only Mr. Tanaka and Ms. Yoshida came.)

2. ティムさんは野菜**しか食べません**。

   Timu-san wa yasai **shika tabemasen**.

   (Tim eats nothing but vegetables.)

3. あそこへはタクシーで**しか行けません**。

   Asoko e wa takushii de **shika ikemasen**.

   (You can go there only by taxi.)

10. Choose the appropriate particle from the ones shown in parentheses.

1. 日本は中国（**より、ほど、だけ、しか**）古い国ではありません。

   Nihon wa chuugoku (**yori, hodo, dake, shika**) furui kuni de wa arimasen.

2. 健三さんは日本語（**より、ほど、だけ、しか**）話せません。

   Kenzoo-san wa nihon-go (**yori, hodo, dake, shika**) hanasemasen.

3. 今私はニドル（**より、ほど、だけ、しか**）持っていません。

   Ima watashi wa ni-doru (**yori, hodo, dake, shika**) motte imasen.

4. 林さんはお父さん（**より、ほど、だけ、しか**）背が高くない。

   Hayashi-san wa otoosan (**yori, hodo, dake, shika**) se ga takaku nai.

5. 私はケーキ（**より、ほど、だけ、しか**）果物の方が好きです。

   Watashi wa keeki (**yori, hodo, dake, shika**) kudamono no hoo ga suki desu.

11. Fill in the blanks in the following passage with the particle "**yori**," "**hodo**," "**dake**," or "**shika**."

私は京都には一度 ＿＿＿ 行ったことがありませんが、京都が大好きです。

Watashi wa Kyoto ni wa ichido ＿＿＿ itta koto ga arimasen ga, Kyooto ga daisuki desu.

東京は京都 ＿＿＿ 新しいですが、京都 ＿＿＿ きれいじゃありません。

Tookyoo wa Kyooto ＿＿＿ atarashii desu ga, Kyooto ＿＿＿ kirei ja arimasen.

東京から京都まで飛行機で行ったので、一時間 _____ かかりませんでした。

Tookyoo kara Kyooto made hikooki de itta node, ichi-jikan _____ kakarimasen deshita.

その時はとても忙しかったから、京都には三日 _____ いて、すぐ東京に帰ってきました。

Sono toki wa totemo isogashikatta kara, Kyooto ni wa mik-ka _____ ite, sugu Tookyoo ni kaette kimashita.

今はその時 _____ 忙しくないので、又京都に行って、前 _____ 長い間京都にいたいです。

Ima wa sono toki _____ isogashiku nai node, mata Kyooto ni itte, mae _____ nagai aida Kyooto ni itai desu.

Review

12. Choose the appropriate particle from the two in parentheses.

1. 銀行の前（**で、に**）人（**は、が**）たくさんいる。

   Ginkoo no mae (**de, ni**) hito (**wa, ga**) takusan iru.

2. 父は公園（**を、に**）よく散歩します。

   Chichi wa kooen (**wo, ni**) yoku sanpo shimau.

3. きのうすし（**を、は**）食べ（**を、に**）日本のレストラン（**へ、で**）行った。

   Kinoo sushi (**wo, wa**) tabe (**wo, ni**) nihon no resutoran (**e, de**) itta.

4. このかばんはだれ（**の、を**）です（**ね、か**）。

   Kono kaban wa dare (**no, wo**) desu (**ne, ka**).

5. スミスさんはスペイン語（**が、を**）分かります。

   Sumisu-san wa supein-go (**ga, wo**) wakarimasu.

6. デパート（**に、で**）スイス（**は、の**）時計（**が、を**）買いました。

   Depaato (**ni, de**) Suisu (**wa, no**) tokei (**ga, wo**) kaimashita.

7. 今晩ケント・ホール（**で、に**）コンサート（**が、は**）ある。

   Konban Kento Hooru (**de, ni**) konsaato (**ga, wa**) aru.

8. このケーキはスプーン（**で、に**）食べてください。

   Kono keeki wa supuun (**de, ni**) tabete kudasai.

9. 友達が辞書（**は、を**）くれる（**を、と**）言いました。

   Tomodachi ga jisho (**wa, wo**) kureru (**wo, to**) iimashita.

10. 今日は二ドル（**だけ、しか**）持っていません。

    Kyoo wa ni-doru (**dake, shika**) motte imasen.

11. 純子さん（**と、も**）美子さん（**と、も**）大学生です。

    Sumiko-san (**to, mo**) Yoshiko-san (**to, mo**) daigaku-sei desu.

12. 日本は中国（**ほど、より**）大きくない。

Nihon wa Chuugoku (**hodo, yori**) ookiku nai.

13. 今日は七時（**までに、まで**）仕事をするつもりです。

Kyoo wa shichi-ji (**made ni, made**) shigoto wo suru tsumori desu.

14. 明日は会社（**に、で**）八時（**までに、まで**）来てください

Ahita wa kaisha (**ni, de**) hachi-ji (**made ni, made**) kite kudasai.

13. Fill in the blanks with an appropriate particle.

去年私 ＿＿＿ フランス ＿＿＿ 行きました。　パリ ＿＿＿ 一週間いました。

Kyonen watashi ＿＿＿ Furansu ＿＿＿ ikimashita.　Pari ＿＿＿ is-shuukan imashita.

毎朝カフェ ＿＿＿ 行って、コーヒー ＿＿＿ 飲みました。コーヒー ＿＿＿ 飲みながら

Mai-asa kafe (Café) ＿＿＿ itte, koohii (coffee) ＿＿＿ nomimashita.　Koohii ＿＿＿ nomi

道 ＿＿＿ 歩いている人々 ＿＿＿ 見るの ＿＿＿ とてもおもしろかったです。

nagara michi ＿＿＿ aruite iru hito-bito ＿＿＿ miru no ＿＿＿ totemo omoshirokatta desu.

旅行している人 ＿＿＿ 学生 ＿＿＿ 会社員 ＿＿＿ 子供など、いろいろな人 ＿＿＿ いまし

Ryokoo shite iru hito ＿＿＿ gakusei ＿＿＿ kaisha-in ＿＿＿ kodomo nado, iroiro na hito ＿＿＿

た。私はフランス語 ＿＿＿ 五年 ＿＿＿ 習っているのに、フランス人 ＿＿＿ 話している

imashita.　Watashi wa furansu-go ＿＿＿ go-nen ＿＿＿ naratte iru noni, furansu-jin ＿＿＿

こと ＿＿＿ 少し ＿＿＿ 分かりませんでした。フランス語 ＿＿＿ 英語 ＿＿＿ もっと難しい

hanashite iru koto ＿＿＿ sukoshi ＿＿＿ wakarimasen deshita.　Furansu-go ＿＿＿

＿＿＿ 思いました。

ei-go ＿＿＿ motto muzukashii ＿＿＿ omoimashita.

パリ ＿＿＿ 地下鉄は便利なので、地下鉄 ＿＿＿ いろいろな所 ＿＿＿ 見 ＿＿＿ 行きま

Pari ＿＿＿ chikatetsu wa benri na node, chikatetsu ＿＿＿ iroiro na tokoro ＿＿＿ mi ＿＿＿

した。ルーブル＿＿＿絵＿＿＿見たり、エッフェル塔＿＿＿登ったり、シャンゼリゼ ＿＿＿

ikimashita.　Ruuburu (the Louvre) ＿＿＿ e ＿＿＿ mita-ri, Efferu-too (the Eiffel Tower) ＿＿＿

歩いたりしました。

nobotta-ri, Shanzerize (Champs-Elysees) ＿＿＿ aruita-ri shimashita.

二年前 ＿＿＿ 日本語 ＿＿＿ 習っているから、来年は日本 ＿＿＿ 行こう ＿＿＿ 思って

Ni-nen mae ＿＿＿ nihon-go ＿＿＿ naratte iru kara, rainen wa Nihon ＿＿＿ ikoo ＿＿＿

います。

omotte imasu.

Chapter 7

Conjunctions

COORDINATING CONJUNCTION

Ga

"**Ga**" is a conjunctive word that corresponds to "but" in English and connects two contrastive sentences.

1. ひまはあります**が**、お金はありません。

   Hima wa arimasu **ga**, okane wa arimasen.

   (I have free time, but I don't have money.)

2. 今日は天気は悪いです**が**、あまり寒くありません。

   Kyoo wa tenki wa warui desu **ga** amari samuku arimasen.

   (The weather is bad, but it's not so cold today.)

3. 薬を飲みました**が**、まだよくなりません。

   Kusuri wo nomimashita **ga**, mada yoku narimasen.

   (I took medicine, but I haven't gotten better yet.)

4. 料理はおいしかったです**が**、あまり食べられませんでした。

   Ryoori wa oishikatta desu **ga**, amari taberaremasen deshita.

   (The food was delicious, but I could not eat much.)

SUBORDINATING CONJUNCTIONS

Toki

The clause of "**toki**" indicates "the time when ~" in English. Since this is a subordinate clause, the subject in a "**toki**" clause is marked by "**ga.**"   The particle "**ni,**" "**wa,**" or "**ni wa**" may be added to "**toki**" depending on the context.

I. Noun + no toki (ni) (wa)

1. 休みの時父はたいていゴルフに行きます。

    Yasumi no toki chichi wa taitei gorufu ni ikimasu.

    (*My father usually goes golfing when he is not at work.*)

2. 子供の時はよく兄と公園で遊びました。

    Kodomo no toki wa yoku ani to kooen de asobimashita.

    (*When I was a child, I often played with my brother in the park.*)

3. 学生の時にフランス語を勉強しました。.

    Gakusei no toki furansu go wo benkyoo shimashita.

    (*I studied French when I was a student.*)

II. I-adjective + toki

1. 頭が痛い時はこの薬を飲んでください.

    Atama ga itai toki wa kono kusuri wo nonde kudasai.

    (*Please take this medicine when you have a headache.*)

2. 暑い時はよく眠れませんね。

    Atsui toki wa yoku nemuremasen ne.

    (*We can't sleep well when it is hot, can we?*)

3. 弟は小さい時よく病気になりました。

    Otooto wa **chiisai toki** yoku byooki ni narimashita.

    (*My little brother often got sick when he was young.*)

III. Na-adjective + toki

1. ひまな時は何をしますか。

    Hima na toki wa nani wo shimasu ka.

    (*What do you do when you are free?*)

2. 祖母が元気な時よく本を読んでもらいました。

   Sobo ga genki na toki yoku hon wo yonde moraimashita.

   (*When my grandmother was well, I used to have her read a book to me.*)

IV. <u>Verb + toki</u>

The event in the subordinate "**toki**" clause is stated in the past plain form when it takes place before the event in the main clause.   On the other hand, the event in the "**toki**" clause is always stated in the non-past plain form when it takes places after the event of the main clause, regardless of the tense.

1. 昨日バスに乗る時吉田さんに会いました。

   Kinoo basu ni noru toki yoshida-san ni aimashita.

   (*Yesterday I met Mr. Yoshida when I rode a bus.*)

2. 家に帰った時いつもイーメールを見ます。

   Uchi ni kaetta toki itsumo e-mail wo mimasu.

   (*I always see e-mails when I get home.*)

3. 日本人は食べる時「いただきます」と言います。

   Nihon-jin wa **taberu toki** "itadakimasu" to iimasu.

   (*Japanese say "itadakimasu" when they eat.*)

4. レストランで食事をした時はチップをあげます。

   Resutoran de **shokuji wo shita toki wa** chippu wo agemasu.

   (*We give tips when we eat at a restaurant.*)

A negative sentence in a "**toki**" clause is commonly described in the non-past negative plain form whether the statement refers to the non-past event or the past event.

1. 金がない時は本も酒も買えなかった。

   Kane ga nai toki wa hon mo sake mo kaenakatta.

   (*When I had no money, I could buy neither a book nor sake.*)

2. 宿題ができない時よく父が手伝ってくれた。

   Shukudai ga dekinai toki yoku chichi ga tetsudatte kureta.

   (*When I couldn't do my homework, my father often helped me .*)

3. 眠れない時はハーブ茶を飲みます。

   Nemurenai toki wa haabu-cha wo nomimasu.

   (*I drink herb tea when I can not sleep.*)

1. Connect the given two sentences using "**toki**".

Ex. 子供だった / よく兄と遊んだ → <u>子供の時よく兄と遊びました。</u>

Kodomo datta / Yoku ani to asonda. → <u>Kodomo no toki yoku ani to asobimshita.</u>

1. 本を借りた / ID を見せた。

Hon wo karita / ID wo miseta.   _____

2. 車に乗る / 酒を飲まない

Kuruma ni noru / Sake wo namanai   _____

3. 先生に会う / 質問する

Sensei ni au / Shitsumon suru   _____

4. 日本へ行く / かぶきが見たい

Nihon e iku / Kabuki ga mitai   _____

2. Translate the following English into Japanese.

1. I will borrow a book when I go to the library.

2. I can not come home early when I am busy.

3. I will call you when I leave home.

4. I used my credit card when I bought a bag and shoes.

Mae

"**Mae**" is an independent noun which means "the front" in English. The clause or noun phrase of "**mae**" indicates "the time before ~" in English. The subject in the clause of "**mae**" is marked by "**ga**" because it is a subordinate clause. The particle "**ni**," "**wa**," or "**ni wa**" may follow "**mae**" depending on the context.

I. <u>Noun +no mae ni</u>

1. **試験**の**前に**何度も漢字を練習した。

Shiken no mae ni nando mo kanji wo renshuu shita.

(I practiced kanji many times before the examination.)

2. 仕事の前にいつも新聞を読みます。.

Shigoto no mae ni itsumo shinbun wo yomimasu.)

(I always read a newspaper before work.)

3. 食事の前に手が洗いたいです。

Shokuji no mae ni te ga araitai desu.

(I want to wash my hands before the meal.)

II. <u>Verb + mae ni</u>

The verb in the "**mae**" clause is always in the non-past plain form regardless of the tense.

1. クラスが**始まる前に**宿題をしてしまった。

   Kurasu ga hajimaru mae ni shukudai wo shite shimatta.

   (I finished the homework before the class began.)

2. 友達が**来る前に**部屋をそうじしておきます。

   Tomodachi ga kuru mae ni heya wo sooji shite okimasu.

   (I will clean up the room before my friend comes.)

3. ゆうべ**寝る前に**本を読みました。

   Yuube **neru mae ni** hon wo yomimashita.

   (I read a book before I went to bed last night.)

<u>Ato</u>

A phrase or a sentence followed by "**ato**" indicates "the time after doing so and so ~" in English. When the subject in the subordinate clause is different from the one in the main clause, it is marked by the particle "**ga**." The particle "**de**" or "**wa**" may be added to "**ato**" depending on the context.

I. <u>Noun + no ato (de)</u>

1. クラスの**後で**図書館に行くつもりです。

   Kurasu no ato de toshokan ni iku tsumori desu.

   (I intend to go to a library after the class.)

2. 食事の**後で**さんぽしました。

   Shokuji no ato de sanpo shimashita.

   (I took a walk after the meal.)

II. <u>Verb (past-plain)+ ato (de)</u>

The verb in the subordinate clause of "**ato**" is always in the plain past form whether the statement is about the present or the future event.

1. 本屋に**寄った後**すぐ家へ帰ります。

   Hon-ya ni yotta ato sugu uchi e kaerimasu.

   (I will go home right after I stop by the bookstore.)

2. 魚を食べた後でお腹が痛くなりました。

   Sakana wo tabeta ato de onaka ga itaku narimashita.

   (*I got a stomachache after I ate a fish.*)

3. 雨が降った後少し寒くなりました。

   Ame ga futta ato sukoshi samuku narimashita ne.

   (*It has become a little cold after it rained.*)

3. Connect the following two sentences using either "**mae**" or "**ato**."

   Ex. 雨が降る ／ 家へ帰る

   Ame ga furu / Uchi e kaeru   <u>Ame ga furu mae ni uchi e kaerimasu.</u>

   1. 手紙を書く／ 郵便局へ行く

   Tegami wo kaku / yuubinkyoku e iku   _____

   2. 日本へ行く ／ 東京のホテルに予約しておく

   Nihon e iku / Tookyoo no hoteru ni yoyaku shite oku   _____

   3. ジョギングをする ／ シャワーをあびる

   Jogingu wo suru / Shåwaa(shower) wo abiru   _____

   4. 食事をする ／ デザートを食べる

   Shokuji wo suru / Dezaato (dessert) wo taberu   _____

4. Translate the following English sentences into Japanese.

   1. I practiced kanji before the examination.

   2. I will go out after I do my homework.

   3. I called my friend before I went to China.

   4. I am going to bed after I take a bath.

Aida / Aida (ni)

"**Aida**" is an independent noun which means " between" in English.   When "**aida**" follows a phrase or a sentence, it indicates "during the time when ~" or "while ~."   When the subject in the clause of "**aida**" is different from the one in the main clause, it is marked by "**ga**"

The event or action of the main clause takes place throughout the span of time described in the "**aida**" phrase or clause. On the other hand, the event or action stated in the main clause takes place at a certain point during the time described in the "**aida ni**" phrase or clause.

I. <u>Noun + no aida /aida ni</u>

  1. 病気の間何も食べられませんでした。

    Byooki no aida nani mo taberaremasen deshita.

    (I couldn't eat anything while I was sick.)

  2. 休みの間にボストンへ行って来ます。

    Yasumi no aida ni Bosuton e itte kimasu.

    (I will go to Boston during vacation.)

  3. 学生の間にたくさん旅行をするつもりだ。

    Gakusei no aida ni takusan ryokoo wo suru tsumori da.

    (I will travel a lot while I am a student.)

II. <u>I-adjective + aida /aida ni</u>

  1. 魚が新しい間にすしを作りましょう。

    Sakana ga **atarashii aida ni** sushi wo tsukurimashoo.

    (Let's make sushi while the fish is fresh.)

  2. 仕事で忙しい間は何もできない.

    Shigoto de **isogashii aida wa** nani mo dekinai.

    (I can't do anything while I am busy with work.)

  3. 父は若い間は東京に住んでいた。

    Chichi wa **wakai aida wa** Tookyoo ni sunde ita.

    (My father lived in Tokyo when he was young.)

III. <u>Na-adjective + aida /aida ni</u>

  1. 仕事が大変な間はテレビは見られません。

    Shigoto ga taihen na aida wa, terebi wa miraremasen.

    (I cannot watch TV while I am busy with work.)

  2. ひまな間に先生に手紙を書きます。

    Himana aida ni sensei ni tegami wo kakimasu.

    (I will write a letter to my teacher while I am free.)

IV. <u>Verb + aida /aida ni</u>

    When the verb in the "**aida (ni)**" clause indicates an action, it is always stated in the form of "**~te iru**" whether it refers to the past or non-past event.

1. 雨が**降っている間は**ずっと家にいた。

   Ame ga **futte iru aida wa** zutto uchi ni ita.

   (I was home while it was raining.)

2. 子供が**寝ている間は**へやが静かです。

   Kodomo ga **nete iru aida wa** heya ga shizuka desu.

   (The room is quiet while my child is sleeping.)

3. バスを**待っている間に**新聞を買いました。

   Basu wo **matte iru aida ni** shinbun wo kaimashita.

   (I bought a newspaper while I was waiting for the bus.)

4. いつもルームメートが**いない間に**晩ごはんを作る。

   Itsumo roomumeete ga **inai aida ni** ban gohan wo tsukuru.

   (I always make supper when my roommate is not around.)

5. Connect each pair of sentences with either "**aida**" or "**aida ni**."

   Ex. ジョギングをしていた / いい天気だった   ジョギングをしている間いい天気でした。

   Joging (jogging) o shite ita / Ii tenki datta.   Joging o shite iru aida ii tenki deshita.

   1. 飛行機に乗っていた / 映画を二つ見た

      Hikooki ni notte ita / Eiga wo futatsu mita.   _____

   2. セールがある / 店がこんでいる

      Seeru ga aru / Mise ga konde iru   _____

   3. 日本にいる / ふじ山が見たい

      Nihon ni iru / Fuji-san (Mt. Fuji) ga mitai.   _____

   4. 学校が休みだ / ジムは閉まっている

      Gakkoo ga yasumi da / Jimu (gym) wa shimatte iru   _____

6. Translate the following English sentences into Japanese.

   1. I want to buy a coat while there is a sale.

   2. The beach is quiet during winter.

   3. My father left home while I was still sleeping.

Kara

   The "**kara**" clause indicates the "reason" for the main clause, and it corresponds to "because" in English. Since the "**kara**" clause is a subordinate one, the predicate in the clause is usually described in the plain form, and the subject in the clause is marked by "**ga**" when it is different from the one in the main clause.

I. <u>Copula + kara</u>

1. 弟が**病気だから**、母は家にいます。

   Otooto ga **byooki da kara,** haha wa uchi ni imasu.

   (My mother is home because my younger brother is sick.)

2. 昨日は**ひまだったから**、映画を見に行きました。

   Kinoo wa **hima datta kara,** eiga wo mi ni ikimashita.

   (I went to see a movie because I was free yesterday.)

3. 妹は音楽が**好きだから**、よくＣＤを聞きます。

   Imooto wa ongaku ga **suki da kara,** yoku CD wo kikimasu.

   (My little sister often listens to CDs because she likes music.)

4. 週末は**いい天気だったから**、出かけました。

   Syuumatsu wa **ii tenki datta kara,** dekakemashita.

   (I went out on the weekend, because the weather was nice.)

II. <u>I-adjective +kara</u>

1. **暑いから**、エアコンをつけましょう。

   Aatsui kara, eakon wo tsukemashoo.

   (Let's turn on the air conditioner because it is hot.)

2. **忙しかったから**、友達と話せませんでした。

   Isogashikatta kara, tomodachi to hanasemasen deshita.

   (I could not talk with my friend because I was busy.)

3. このレストランは料理が**おいしいから**、人気があります。

   Kono resutoran wa ryoori ga **oishii kara,** ninki ga arimasu.

   (This restaurant is popular because it serves delicious food.)

III. <u>Verb + kara</u>

1. 明日試験が**あるから**、家で勉強します。

   Ashita shiken ga **aru kara,** uchi de benkyoo shimasu.

   (I will study at home because there is a test tomorrow.)

2. お金が**ないから**、コンピューターは買えません。

   Okane ga **nai kara,** konpyuutaa wa kaemasen.

   (I cannot buy a computer because I have no money.)

3. バスが**来なかったから**、歩いて帰りました。

   Basu ga **konakatta kara,** aruite kaerimashita.

   (I walked home because the bus didn't come.)

4. 雨が**降っているから**、さんぽはしません。

   Ame ga **futte iru kara,** sanpo wa shimasen.

   (I will not take a walk because it's raining.)

7. Connect the pairs of two sentences using "**kara.**"

   Ex. 知らない言葉がありました　／辞書で調べました

   Shiranai kotoba ga arimashita / Jisho de shirabemashita.

   <u>知らない言葉があったから辞書で調べました。</u>

   Shiranai kotoba ga atta kara jisho de shirabemashita.

1. 部屋がきたないです　／　そうじをしてください。

   Heya ga kitanai desu / sooji wo shitekudasai

   _____

2. 時間がありません　／　急いでください

   Jikan ga arimasen / Isoide kudasai

   _____

3. みんなが**勉強しています**　／　静かに話しましょう

   Minna ga benkyoo shite imasu / Shizuka ni hanashimashoo

   _____

4. 試験が終わりました　／　遊びに行きたいです

   Shiken ga owarimashita / Asobi ni ikitai desu.

   _____

8. Translate the following English sentences into Japanese..

   1. I cannot go out because my parents are coming over.

   2. Let's have a party because it's your birthday.

   3. I always take a subway because it's cheap and fast.

   4. I have no money because I bought a new computer.

Node

   The "**node**" clause refers to a "cause" or a "reason" for the statement of the main clause. Since "**node**" is used in an objective statement, the subjective expression, such as "~ **mashoo** (= let's~)," "~ te kudasai (= please do ~)," and so on, does not take place in the main clause, while "**kara**" allows those subjective expressions in the main clause.

I. Noun / Na-adjective +node

The plain non-past copula "**da**" is replaced by "**na**" when the statement in the "**node**" clause is in the present tense.

1. いい**天気なので**、公園は人が多いです。

   Ii **tenki na node,** kooen wa hito ga ooi desu.

   (The park is full of people because of the nice weather.)

2. 歌が**好きなので**、よくカラオケバーに行きます。

   Uta ga **suki na node,** yoku karaoke baa ni ikimasu.

   (I like singing, so I often go to a karaoke bar.)

3. 花が**きれいだったので**、少し買いました。

   Hana ga **kirei datta node,** sukoshi kaimashita.

   (I bought some flowers because they were pretty.)

4. バスはあまり**便利じゃないので**、乗りません。

   Basu wa amari **benri ja nai node,** norimasen.

   (I do not ride a bus because it's not so convenient.)

II. I-adjective + node

1. 部屋が**せまいので**、**大きい**ベッドは買えません。

   Heya ga **semai node,** ookii beddo wa kaemasen.

   (I cannot buy a big bed because my room is small.)

2. 家はここから**遠くないので**、歩いて帰ります。

   Uchi wa koko kara **tooku nai node,** aruite kaerimasu.

   (My house is not far from here, so I will walk home.)

3. お金が**ほしいので**、アルバイトを探している。

   Okane ga **hoshii node,** arubaito wo sagashite iru.

   (I'm looking for a part-time job because I want money.)

III. Verb + node

1. 来年中国へ**行くので**、中国語の勉強を始めた。

   Rainen Chuugoku e **iku node,** chuugoku-go no benkyoo wo hajimeta.

   (I began to study Chinese because I will go to China next year.)

2. 母がお金を**くれたので、**スーツを買いました。

   Haha ga okane wo **kureta node,** suutsu wo kaimashita.

   (My mother gave me money so I bought suits.)

3. 図書館が**閉まっているので、**本が借りられません.

   Toshokan ga **shimatte iru node,** hon ga kariraremasen.

   (I cannot borrow a book because the library is closed.)

4. 勉強**しなかったので、**テストができなかった。

   Benkyoo **shinakatta node,** tesuto ga dekinakatta

   (I could not do well on the test because I did not study.)

Noni

   "**Noni**" corresponds to the English "in spite of the fact ~ or although ~" and follows a phrase or a sentence.   The main clause after "**noni**" usually states something which turns out to be contrary to the speaker's expectation.   Consequently, the statement with "**noni**" reflects the speaker's surprise, disappointment, and so on.   It also carries the speaker's reproachful tone depending on the context.

I. <u>Noun / Na-adjective + noni</u>

   Plain non-past form of copula "**da**" is replaced by "**na**" when the statement in the "**noni**" clause is in the present tense.

1. 父は**病気なのに、**仕事に行きました。

   Chichi wa **byooki na noni,** shigoto ni ikimashita.

   (My father went to work although he is sick.)

2. **日曜日なのに、**銀行が開いていますよ。   .

   Nichiyoo-bi na noni, ginkoo ga aite imasu yo.

   (The bank is open although it's Sunday.)

3. 兄は**ひまだったのに、**手伝ってくれませんでした。

   Ani wa **hima datta noni,** tetsudatte kuremasen deshita.

   (My older brother didn't help me although he was free.)

4. 子供が**好きじゃないのに、**ベビーシッターになった。

   Kodomo ga **suki ja nai noni,** bebii sittaa ni natta.

   (She became a baby sitter although she does not like children.)

II. <u>I-adjective + noni</u>

1. あの店は料理が**おいしくないのに、**高いです。

   Ano mise wa ryoori ga **oishiku nai noni,** takai desu.

   (That restaurant is expensive although the food is not tasty.)

2. この車はまだ**新しいのに、**よく故障します。

   Kono kuruma wa mada **atarashii noni,** yoku koshoo shimasu.

   (This car often breaks down although it is still new.)

3. 田中さんは**忙しかったのに、** 会いに来てくれました。

   Tanak-san wa **isogashikatta noni,** ai ni kite kuremashita.

   (Mr. Tanaka came to see me although he was busy.)

IV. <u>Verb + noni</u>

1. 雨が**降っているのに、**弟は外で遊んでいます。

   Ame ga **futte iru noni,** otooto wa soto de asonde imasu.

   (My little brother is playing outside although it is raining.)

2. 妹はお金が**ないのに、**高いドレスを買いました。

   Imooto wa okane ga **nai noni,** takai doresu wo kaimashita.

   (My little sister bought an expensive dress although she has no money.)

3. 和夫さんはそれを**知っていたのに、** 教えてくれませんでした.

   Kazuo-san wa sore wo **shitte ita noni**, oshiete kuremasen deshita.

   (In spite of the fact that Kazuo knew it, he did not tell me.)

9. Connect the pairs of sentences using either "**node**" or "**noni.**"

いい天気だった　/　一日中家にいた　　　いい天気だったのに、一日中家にいました。

Ex.　Ii tenki datta / Ichinichi juu uchi ni ita　　<u>Ii tenki datta noni, ichinichijuu uchi ni</u>

<u>imashita</u>.

1.宿題を忘れた　/　先生にしかられた

   Shukudai o wasureta / sensei ni shikarareta　　　_____

2. 歌が嫌いだ　/　カラオケで歌わされた

   Uta ga kirai da / karaoke de utawasareta　　　_____

3. この寺は有名だ　/　だれでも知っている

   Kono tera wa yuumei da / dare demo shitte iru　　_____

4. 古いアパートだ　/　家ちんが高い

   Furui apaato da / yachin ga takai　　　_____

5. 勉強しなかった　/　試験はやさしかった

Benkyoo shinakatta / shiken wa yasashikatta　＿＿＿＿＿＿＿＿＿＿＿＿＿＿

Nagara

　　"Verb (V-stem) + **nagara**" forms an adverbial phrase, and it refers to the secondary action which takes place simultaneously with the action in the main clause, and it is interpreted as "do something while ~ ing".　In this structure the agent of the action of　"V- **nagara**" and the agent of the action in the main clause should be the same person.

1. 父はビールを**飲みながら**、テレビを見ている。

　　Chichi wa biiru wo **nomi nagara,** terebi wo mite iru.

　　(My father is drinking beer while watching TV.)

2. 山田さんは**働きながら**、英語学校に通いました。

　　Yamada-san wa **hataraki nagara**, ei-go gakkoo ni kayoimashita.

　　(Mr. Yamada worked while going to an English school.)

3. よく友達と学校の話を**しながら**、食事をする。

　　Yoku tomodachi to gakkoo no hanashi wo **shinagara,** shokuji wo suru.

　　(My friend and I often talk about school when we are eating.)

10. Fill in the blanks with a "**nagara**" phrase that is appropriate with the given verb.

　　　　ラジオを聞きながらいろいろなことをする。（聞く）

　　Ex.　Rajio o <u>kiki-nagara</u> iroirona koto o suru.　(kiku)

1. たばこを　＿＿＿＿＿＿　バスを待っています。　（吸う）

　　Tabako wo ＿＿＿＿＿＿ basu wo matte imasu.　(suu)

2. コーヒーを　＿＿＿＿＿＿ざっしを読みました。　（飲む）

　　Koohii wo ＿＿＿＿＿＿ zasshi wo yomimashita.　(nomu)

3. 友達はいつも歌を　＿＿＿＿＿シャワーをします。　（歌う）

　　Tomodachi wa itsumo uta wo ＿＿＿＿＿＿ shawaa wo shimasu.　(utau)

4. ポップコーンを　＿＿＿＿＿＿映画を見るのは楽しいですね。　（食べる）

　　Poppu koon wo ＿＿＿＿＿＿ eiga wo miru no wa tanoshii desu ne.　(taberu)

11.　Translate the following English sentences into Japanese.

　　1. I wrote a letter while eating lunch.

　　2. I listened to the radio while making supper.

　　3. The teacher always walks while teaching the class.

Made

A noun phrase or a sentence followed by "**made**" is equivalent to "until ~", and a phrase or a sentence followed by "**made ni**" is equivalent to "by the time when ~" in English. The verb in the subordinate clause of "**made or made ni**" is always in the plain non-past form whether the statement refers to a past or non-past event.

I. Noun + made/made ni

1. 今週の土曜日までにレポートを書いてしまうつもりだ。

   Konshuu no doyoobi made ni repooto wo kaite shimau tsumori da.

   (I am going to finish writing the report by this Saturday.)
2. 二時までに来てください。

   Niji made ni kite kudasai.

   (Please come by two o'clock.)
3. 今日から来週の月曜日まで雨が降るそうだ。

   Kyoo kara **raishuu no getsuyoobi made** ame ga furu soo da.

   (I heard that it will rain starting today through next Monday.)
4. 今日は六時まで会社で仕事をしています。

   Kyoo wa **roku-ji made** kaisha de shigoto wo shite imasu.

   (I will be working in the office until six o'clock today.)

II. Verb + made/made ni

The subject in the subordinate clause of "**made (ni)**" is marked by "**ga**" when it is different from the subject in the main clause.

1. 客が来るまでにそうじを全部しておきたいです。

   Kyaku **ga kuru made ni** sooji wo zenbu shite okitai desu.

   (I want to finish cleaning by the time the guest comes.)
2. 学期が始まるまでにいいアパートを見つけなくてはいけない。

   Gakki **ga hajimaru made ni** ii apaato wo mitsukenakute wa ikenai.

   (I have to find a good apartment by the time the semester starts.)
3. 鈴木さんはアメリカに来るまで日本で働いていました。

   Suzuki-san wa Amerika ni **kuru made** Nihon de hataraite imashita.

   (Mr. Suzuki was working in Japan until he came to the United States.)
4. 上手になるまで日本語の勉強を続けるつもりです。

   Joozu ni naru made nihon-go no benkyoo wo tsuzukeru tsumori desu.

(I am going to continue the study of Japanese until I become good at it.)

12. Fill in the blanks with either "~ **made**" or "~ **made ni.**"   Refer to the given English phrases.

   Ex.   <u>雨がやむまで</u>家にいました。(the rain stopped)

   <u>Ame ga yamu made</u> uchi ni imashita.

   <u>八時までに</u>起きます。(eight o'clock)

   <u>Hachi ji made ni</u> okimasu.

   1.   _____ 家に帰ります。(seven thirty)

        _____ uchi ni kaerimasu.

   2.   _____ 外で遊びました。(it became dark)

        _____ soto de asobimashita.

   3.   _____ 何も知りませんでした。(I heard the news)

        _____ nani mo shirimasen deshita.

   4.   _____ この本を全部読んでしまいます。(the vacation ends)

        _____ kono hon wo zenbu yonde shimaimasu.

   5.   _____ 結婚したいです。(thirty years old)

        _____ kekkon shitai desu.

   6.   _____ 電話をください。(I leave home)

        _____ denwa wo kudasai.

Review

13. Fill in the blanks with the appropriate Japanese phrase. Refer to the given English phrases.

   1.   (watching a television)

        _____ 食事をしました。

        _____ shokuji wo shimashita.

   2.   (before I go to your house)

        _____電話をかけます。

        _____denwa wo kakemasu.

3. (while I was riding a train)

_____スナックを少し食べました。

_____snakku(snack)wo sukoshi tabemashita.

4. (while I was sick)

_____何もできませんでした。

_____nani mo dekimasen deshita.

5. (when I was writing a letter)

_____ルームメートが帰ってきました。

_____ruumu meeto(room mate)ga kaette kimashita.

6. (after we play tennis)

_____ビールを飲みましょう。

_____biiru wo nomimashoo.

7. (until I became well)

_____毎日病院に行きました。

_____ mainichi byooin ni ikimashita.

8. (even though he is a Japanese)

山田さんは_____日本の映画は見ないそうだ。

Yamada-san wa _____ Nihon no eiga wa minai soo da.

9. (because tomorrow is my mother's birthday),

_____、今日プレゼントを買うつもりです。

_____, kyoo purezento wo kau tsumori desu.

10.　(because we have no money),

_____、安いレストランで食べましょう。

_____, yasui resutoran de tabemasyoo.

14. Below is a record of how Mr. Takada spent his day.　After you read this list fill in the blanks.

   7:00   got up

   7:30   ate breakfast while listening to music

   8:00   read newspaper

   8:30   cleaned up the room

   9:00   left home

   9:30   got on a subway and read a book

 10:00   arrived at the office

10:30　had a meeting with Mr. Sasaki in the office

12:00　ate a sandwich with Mr. Sasaki in the office

　1:00　resumed the meeting with Mr. Sasaki

　2:00　wrote report about the meeting

　3:00　went to a coffee shop for a break and met Ms. Hayashi

　6:00　finished work and left the office

　6:30　bought some books at a bookstore

　7:00　ate supper at a restaurant

　8:30　returned home

高田さんは

Takada-san wa

1. ＿＿＿＿＿＿＿＿＿　ながら朝ご飯を食べました。

　 ＿＿＿＿＿＿＿＿＿ nagara asa-gohan wo tabemashita.

2. ＿＿＿＿＿＿＿＿＿　前に新聞を読みました。

　 ＿＿＿＿＿＿＿＿＿ mae ni shinbun wo yomimashita.

3. ＿＿＿＿＿＿＿＿＿　後で家を出ました。

　 ＿＿＿＿＿＿＿＿＿ ato de uchi wo demashita.

4. ＿＿＿＿＿＿＿＿＿　間本を読んでいました。

　 ＿＿＿＿＿＿＿＿＿ aida hon wo yonde imashita.

5. ＿＿＿＿＿＿＿＿＿　間にサンドイッチを食べました。

　 ＿＿＿＿＿＿＿＿＿ aida ni sando-icchi (sandwich) wo tabemashita.

6. ＿＿＿＿＿＿＿＿＿　時林さんに会いました。

　 ＿＿＿＿＿＿＿＿＿ toki Hayashi-san ni aimashita.

7. ＿＿＿＿＿＿＿＿＿　後で本を買いました。

　 ＿＿＿＿＿＿＿＿＿ ato de hon wo kaimashita.

8. ＿＿＿＿＿＿＿＿＿　前に晩ご飯を食べました。

　 ＿＿＿＿＿＿＿＿＿ mae ni ban-gohan wo tabemashita.

Chapter 8

Verbs

Japanese has mainly two speech styles, formal and informal. The "**masu**"- ending verb, which comes at the end of a sentence as a main verb, is considered to be formal and polite, whereas the plain form is used as an informal speech style between close friends, family members, and so forth.

STYLES

Formal speech styles

1. 私は日本語は話しますが、英語は話しません。

   Watashi wa nihon-go wa hanashimasu ga, ei-go wa hanashimasen.

   (I speak Japanese, but I do not speak English.)
2. 昨日すしを食べました。でも、てんぷらは食べませんでした。

   Kinoo sushi wo tabemashita. Demo, tempura wa tabemasen deshita.

   (I ate sushi yesterday, but I did not eat tempura.)

Informal speech styles

1. (Conversation between two friends)

   A: ご飯食べた？

   Gohan tabeta ?

   (Did you eat?)

B: うん、食べた。

Un, tabeta.

(Yes, I did.)

FORMS AND GROUPS

Ex.

	non-past	neg. non-past	past	neg. past
Plain	iku *(go)*	ikanai	it-ta	ika-nakatta
	taberu *(eat)*	tabe-nai	tabe-ta	tabe-nakatta
Polite	iki-masu	iki-masen	iki-mashita	iki-masen deshita
	tabe-masu	tabe-massen	tabe-mashita	tabe-masen deshita

The plain non-past form is identical with its dictionary form.   Japanese verbs are classified into three main groups; "**u**-verb," "**ru**-verb," and "irregular verb."

1. A verb which ends with "-**u**" in its dictionary form is called "**u**-verb."

2. A verb which ends with "-**ru**" in its dictionary form is called "**ru**-verb."

3. The irregular verbs refer to only two verbs, which are "**suru**" (to do) and "**kuru**" (to come).

U-verbs and **ru**-verbs are conjugated systematically to make other forms, whereas the irregular verbs are not.

Here are some examples of **u**-verbs and **ru**-verbs.

U-verbs		**Ru-verbs**		**Irregular verbs**	
Plain	-masu	Plain	-masu	Plain	-masu
yom-u	yom-imasu	oki-ru	oki-masu	kuru	kimasu
kak-u	kak-imasu	mi-ru	mi-masu	suru	shimasu
kaer-u	kaer-imasu	i-ru	i-masu		
ka-u	ka-imasu	ne-ru	ne-masu		
oyog-u	oyog-imasu	age-ru	age-masu		
mats-u	mach-imasu	mie-ru	mie-masu		
hanas-u	hanash-imasu	ake-ru	ake-masu		

Formation of the plain neg. non-past form

I. U-verb

The final vowel "-**u**" of the dictionary form is replaced by "-**anai**."

Ex. kik-**u** → kik-**anai**,   mats-**u** → mat-**anai**,

wara-**u** → wara-**wanai**

Note: The final "**u**" of two vowels "**au**," "**iu**," "**uu**," and "**ou**" of the u-verbs like "**kau** (*buy*),"

"**au** (*meet*)," "**iu** (*say*)," "**you** (*get drunk*),""**suu** (*smoke*)" are replaced by "-**wanai**."

II. Ru-verb

The final syllable "-**ru**" of the dictionary form is replaced by "-**nai**."

Ex. tabe-**ru** → tabe-**nai**,   ne-**ru** → ne-**nai**

III. Irregular verbs

suru → **shinai**,   **kuru** → **konai**

Formation of the plain neg. past form

Replace the final "-**nai**" of the plain neg. non-past form by "-**nakatt**a."

Ex: kak-**anai** → kak-**anakatta**, tabe-**nai** → tabe-**nakatta**

shinai → **shi-nakatta**

Formation of the plain past form

I. U-verb

Verbs which end with "-ku"

ka-**ku** → ka-**ita**,   ki-**ku** → ki-**ita**,   i-**ku** → i-**tta****

Verbs which end with "-**gu**"

oyo-**gu** → oyo-**ida**

Verbs which end with "-**mu**," "-**bu**," and "-**nu**"

yo-**mu** → yo-**nda**,   to-**bu** → to-**nda**,   shi-**nu** → shi-**nda**

Verbs which end with "-**u**," "-**tsu**," and "-**ru**"

ma-**tsu** → ma-**tta**,   kae-**ru** → kae-**tta**,   ka-**u** → ka-**tta**

Verbs which end with "-**su**"

hana-**su** → hana-**shita**

"**Iku** (to go)" is an exception. Its final syllable, "-**ku**," is replaced by "-**tta**."

II. Ru-verb

The final syllable "**ru**" of the dictionary form is replaced by "**ta**."

mi-**ru** → mi-**ta**,   tabe-**ru** → tabe-**ta**

III. Irregular verb

suru → **shita**,   **kuru** → **kita**

1. Change the following verbs from **masu-form** to the given plain forms.

	non-past	past	neg. non-past	neg. past
Ex. ka-imasu →	kau	katta	kawanai	kawanakatta
1. aruk-imasu	_____	_____	_____	_____
2. shin-imasu	_____	_____	_____	_____
3. nom-imasu	_____	_____	_____	_____
4. kake-masu	_____	_____	_____	_____
5. kaer-imasu	_____	_____	_____	_____
6. asob-imasu	_____	_____	_____	_____
7. tach-imasu	_____	_____	_____	_____
8. hajime-masu	_____	_____	_____	_____
9. shi-masu	_____	_____	_____	_____
10. su-imasu	_____	_____	_____	_____

2. Change the following verbs from plain form to **masu**-form.

Ex. ka-u   → kaimasu

1. mora-u   _____
2. kik-u   _____
3. mats-u   _____
4. hanas-u   _____
5. tsukur-u _____
6. de-ru   _____
7. age-ru   _____

BASIC TYPES OF JAPANESE VERB SENTENCE

"V-mashoo"

The expression of "~**mashoo**" means "Let's do such and such", and "~**mashoo ka**" corresponds to "Shall we or I do such and such?" in English.

1. 少し**休みましょう**。
   Sukoshi **yasumimashoo**.
   (Let's take a little break.)

2. あの喫茶店へ行って何か**飲みましょう**。

   Ano kissa-ten e itte nani ka **nomimashoo**.

   (Let's go to the coffee shop over there and drink something.)

3. 明日の朝電話**しましょう**か。

   Ashita no asa denwa **shimashoo** ka.

   (Shall I call you tomorrow morning?)

4. 今晩どこで**食べましょう**か。

   Konban doko de **tabemashoo** ka.

   (Where shall we eat tonight?)

Intransitive Verbs

Intransitive verbs require no object. The subject and the verb are the main elements in this structure.

1. 昨日**雨が降りました**。

   Kinoo **ame ga furimashita**.

   (It rained yesterday.)

2. **クラスは**すぐ**終わります**。

   Kurasu wa sugu **owarimasu**.

   (The class will end soon.)

3. **弟は**よく**泣きます**。

   Otooto wa yoku **nakimasu**.

   (My little brother often cries.)

4. けさ七時に**起きました**。

   Kesa shichi-ji ni **okimashita**.

   (I got up at 7:00 this morning.)

5. ゆうべはあまり**寝ませんでした**。

   Yuube wa amari **nemasen deshita**.

   (I did not sleep well last night.)

Transitive Verbs

I. <u>S + O + Transitive Action Verb</u> (S=Subject, O=Object)

In this structure, the subject is marked by the particle "**wa/ga**" and the direct object by the particle "**wo**."

1. 私は映画を見ました。

   Watashi **wa** eiga **wo mimashita**.

   (I saw a movie.)

2. よくＣＤを聞きますか。

   Yoku CD **wo kikimasu** ka.

   (Do you listen to CDs frequently?)

3. ゆうべ宿題をしましたか。

   Yuube shukudai **wo shimashita** ka.

   (Did you do your homework last night?)

4. この漢字は知りません。

   Kono kanji **wa shirimasen**.

   (I do not know this kanji.)

Note: In a negative sentence like one in item 4, the direct object marker "**wo**" is often replaced by the contrastive particle "**wa**."   As mentioned before, the subject is frequently omitted as long as it is understood in the context.

II. <u>S + I.O.+ D.O.+ Transitive Verb</u> (S=Subject, I.O.=Indirect Object, D.O.=Direct Object)

The indirect object is marked by the particle "**ni**" and the direct object is marked by "**wo**."   The indirect object usually precedes the direct object, though the reverse is acceptable.

1. 友達に電話番号を聞きます。

   Tomodachi **ni** denwa-bangoo **wo kikimasu**.

   (I will ask my friend for the phone number.)

2. 先生に宿題を見せませんでした。

   Sensei **ni** shukudai **wo misemasen deshita**.

   (I did not show my homework to the teacher.)

3. 母にセーターをあげました。

   Haha **ni** seetaa **wo agemashita**.

   (I gave my mother a sweater.)

4. 山田さんにトムさんを紹介しました。

   Yamada-san **ni** Tomu-san **wo shookai shimashita**.

   (I introduced Tom to Mr. Yamada.)

Motion Verbs

S + Direction + Motion Verb (S=Subject)

The direction or destination of a motion verb such as "go, come, return" is always marked by the particle "**ni/ e**."

1. 今年はヨーロッパ**へ行きます**。

   Kotoshi wa Yooroppa **e ikimasu**.

   (I am going to go to Europe this year.)

2. 昨日父は遅く家**に帰りました**。`

   Kinoo chichi wa osoku uchi **ni kaerimashita**.

   (My father came home late last night.)

3. 友達はここ**に来ませんでした**。

   Tomodachi wa koko **ni kimasen deshita**.

   (My friend did not come here.)

4. 友達ときっさ店**に入りました**。

   Tomodachi to kissaten **ni hairimashita**.

   (I went to a coffee shop with my friend.)

Existential Verbs

I. Place + S + Existential Verb (S=Subject)

This sentence structure indicates that something or someone exists in a certain place. The place precedes the subject of the sentence, and it is marked by the particle "**ni**." The subject is usually marked by "**ga**."   There are two existential verbs, that is, "**iru**" and "**aru**." "**Iru**" refers to the existence of human and animals, and "**aru**" refers to the existence of things.

1. この図書館に日本の新聞**がありますか**。

   Kono toshokan **ni** Nihon no shinbun **ga arimasu** ka.

   (Is there a Japanese newspaper in this library?)

2. 公園にかわいい子供**がいました**よ。

   Kooen **ni** kawaii kodomo **ga imashita** yo.

   (There was a cute child in the park.)

3. 私の家にねこ**はいます**が、犬**はいません**。

   Watashi no uchi **ni** neko **wa imasu** ga, inu **wa imasen**.

   (There is a cat but no dog in my house.)

4. ニューヨーク**には**外国のレストラン**が**たくさん**あります**。

   Nyuuyooku **ni** wa gaikoku no resutoran **ga** takusan **arimasu.**

(There are many foreign restaurants in New York.)

II. S + Place + Existential Verb (S=Subject))

This sentence structure refers to the location of something or someone, that is, "where the thing or the person in question is located." In this structure the subject, in other words the topic of the sentence, is always marked by the particle "**wa**," and the place is marked by "**ni**."

1. A: 山田さん**は**今どこ**にいます**か。

     Yamada-san **wa** ima doko **ni imasu** ka.

     (Where is Mr. Yamada now?)

  B: 図書館**にいます**よ。

     Toshokan **ni imasu** yo.

     (He is in the library.)

2. 私**は**きのう家**にいませんでした**。

   Watashi **wa** kinoo uchi **ni imasen deshita**.

   (I was not at home yesterday.)

3. A: ちょっとすみませんが、東京銀行**は**どこ**にあります**か。

     Chotto sumimasen ga, Tookyoo ginkoo **wa** doko **ni arimasu** ka.

     (Excuse me, sir/madam. *Where is the Bank of Tokyo?)*

  B: (東京銀行**は**) 駅のそば**に** あ**ります**よ。

     (Tookyoo ginkoo **wa**) eki no soba **ni arimasu** yo.

     (It is by the station.)

3. Fill in the blanks with an appropriate particle and either "**arimasu**" or "**imasu**."

    Ex. あそこ<u>に</u>　田中さん　<u>が</u>　<u>います</u>よ。

    Asoko <u>ni</u> Tanaka-san <u>ga</u> <u>imasu</u> yo.

   1. A: あの店＿＿日本の食べ物 ＿＿ ＿＿＿＿＿＿＿か。

       Ano mise ＿＿ Nihon no tabemono ＿＿ ＿＿＿＿＿ ka.

    B: いいえ、＿＿＿＿＿＿。

       Iie, ＿＿＿＿＿＿.

   2. 東京＿＿＿は外国人＿＿＿たくさん＿＿＿＿＿＿。

     Tookyoo ＿＿＿ wa gaikoku-jin ＿＿＿ takusan ＿＿＿＿＿＿.

   3. 日本語の辞書＿＿＿どこ＿＿＿ ＿＿＿＿＿＿か・

     Nihon-go no jisho ＿＿＿ doko ＿＿＿ ＿＿＿＿＿＿ ka.

4. あの動物園＿＿はおもしろい魚＿＿ ＿＿＿＿＿＿＿。

Ano doobutsuen ___ wa omoshiroi sakana ___ _____.

5. 私の父＿＿去年京都 ＿＿ ＿＿＿＿＿＿。

Watashi no chichi ___ kyonen Kyooto ___ _____.

Spontaneous Verbs

S + O + Spontaneous Verb   (S = Subject, O = Object)

Spontaneous verbs are verbs such as "**wakaru**" (comprehensible), "**mieru**" (visible), and "**kikoeru**" (audible).   The object of the verb is marked by "**ga**," not "**wo**," in this expression.

1. 私は日本語**が分ります**。

Watashi wa nihon-go **ga wakarimasu**.

(*I understand Japanese.*)

2. ここから富士山**が**よく**見えます**ね。

Koko kara Fuji-san **ga** yoku **miemasu** ne.

(*We can see Mt. Fuji well from here.*)

3. 声**が**よく**聞こえません**。

Koe **ga** yoku **kikoemasen**.

(*I cannot hear you well.*)

4. 中国語**は分かります**が、スペイン語**は分かりません**。

Chuugoku-go **wa wakarimasu** ga, supein-go **wa wakarimasen**.

(*I understand Chinese, but I do not understand Spanish.*)

4. Complete the sentences below using the appropriate word given here.

起きる (okiru) 読む (yomu) 行く (iku) 来る (kuru) 飲む (nomu) あげる (ageru)
分かる (wakaru) ある (aru) いる (iru) 聞こえる (kikoeru) 見える (mieru)
降る (furu) 買う (kau)

1. 母は毎朝六時に ＿＿＿＿＿＿。 そしてコーヒーを ＿＿＿＿＿＿。 そして新聞を ＿＿＿＿＿＿。

Haha wa maiasa roku-ji ni _____ Soshite koohii wo _____. Soshite shinbun wo
_____.

2. 私は病気だったので、昨日は学校に＿＿＿＿＿＿。 一日中家に＿＿＿＿＿＿。

Watashi wa byooki datta node, kinoo wa gakkoo ni _____. Ichinichijuu uchi ni
_____.

3. 友達の誕生日だったので、プレゼントを＿＿＿＿＿＿。

Tomodachi no tanjoobi datta node, purezento wo _____.

4. 山田さんはフランス語がよく＿＿＿＿＿＿＿＿＿。

Yamada-san wa furansu-go ga yoku ＿＿＿＿＿＿＿＿.

5. 部屋がうるさくて何も＿＿＿＿＿＿＿＿＿。

Heya ga urusakute nani mo ＿＿＿＿＿＿＿＿.

6. 昨日本屋で雑誌を一さつ＿＿＿＿＿＿＿。

Kinoo honya de zasshi wo issatsu ＿＿＿＿＿＿＿＿.

7. 日本では六月によく雨が＿＿＿＿＿＿＿＿＿。

Nihon de wa rokugatsu ni yoku ame ga ＿＿＿＿＿＿＿＿.

8. 今晩友達が私の家に＿＿＿＿＿＿＿＿＿から、一緒に食事をします。

Konban tomodachi ga watashi no uchi ni ＿＿＿＿＿＿＿＿ kara, issho ni shokuji wo shimasu.

POTENTIAL FORM

Potential verbs express "ability" or "potentiality." This expression is equivalent to "can do such and such" in English.

Formation of potential verbs

1. U verb

The final vowel "**u**" of the dictionary form is replaced by "**-eru**."

Ex. yom-**u** → yom-**eru**   kak-**u** → kak-**eru**

2. Ru verb

The final "**ru**" of the dictionary form is replaced by "**-rareru**."

Ex. tabe-**ru** → tabe-**rareru**   mi-**ru** → mi-**rareru**

3. Irregular verb   **kuru** → **korareru**   **suru** → **dekiru**

In potential sentences the direct object of a transitive verb which usually takes the particle "**wo**" is generally marked by "**ga**," not "**wo**."

1. ニューヨークでおいしいすしが食べられますか？

Nyuuyooku de oishii sushi **ga taberaremasu** ka.

(Can you find good sushi in New York?)

2. 今日は早く家に**帰れません**。

Kyoo wa hayaku uchi ni **kaeremasen**.

(I cannot go home early today.)

3. きのう友達に電話**がかけられませんでした**。

Kinoo tomodachi ni denwa **ga kakeraremasen deshita**.

(I could not call my friend yesterday.)

4. 佐藤さんはテニス**ができます**よ。

Satoo-san wa tenisu **ga dekimasu** yo.

(Mr. Satoo can play tennis, you know.)

5. Change the following sentences into sentences of the potential form.

Ex.   テニスをします。 → テニスができます。

Tenisu wo shimasu.   Tenisu ga dekimasu.

1. 漢字を書きます。   _____

   Kanji wo kakimasu. _____

2. 日本へ行きます。   _____

   Nihon e ikimasu.   _____

3. 日本語で電話をかけません。 _____

   Nihon-go de denwa wo kakemasen. _____

4. 明日九時までに来ません。_____

   Ashita ku-ji made ni kimasen. _____

5. ドイツ語を少し話します。_____

   Doitsu-go wo sukoshi hanashimasu. _____

6. 朝早く起きません。_____

   Asa hayaku okimasen. _____

THE VERBS OF GIVING AND RECEIVING

The verbs "**ageru**" and "**kureru**" mean to "give" in English.   The choice of which one to use depends on who is the giver and who is the recipient.

Ageru

"**Ageru**" is used in the context of "someone gives something to someone else."   It is never used in the context of   "someone gives something to *me* (= 1st person)."

Kureru

"**Kureru**" is used in the context of "someone gives something to *me* or to *my family member*."

1. この本を**あげましょう**か。

   Kono hon wo **agemashoo** ka.

   (Shall I give you this book?)

2. 道子さんは謙さんによく映画の切符を**あげます**。

   Michiko-san wa Ken-san ni yoku eiga no kippu wo **agemasu**.

   (Michiko often gives a movie ticket to Ken.)

3. 誕生日に母がこのかばんを**くれました**。

   Tanjoo-bi ni haha ga kono kaban wo **kuremashita**.

   (My mother gave me this bag on my birthday .)

4. 田中さんは妹にきれいなスカーフを**くれました**。

   Tanaka-san wa imooto ni kirei na sukaafu wo **kuremashita**.

   (Ms. Tanaka gave a beautiful scarf to my younger sister.)

Morau

The verb "**morau**" means "receive" in English, and it is used in the context of "someone receives something from someone else."

1. 良子さんに/から日本のお菓子を**もらいました**。

   Yoshiko-san ni/kara Nihon no okashi wo **moraimashita.**

   (I received Japanese sweets from Yoshiko.)

   C.f. 良子さんが日本のお菓子をくれました。

      Yoshiko-san ga Nihon no okashi wo kuremashita.

      (Yoshiko gave me Japanese sweets.)

2. 妹は太郎さんに/から花を**もらって**喜んでいます。

   Imooto wa Taroo-san ni/kara hana wo **moratte** yorokonde imasu.

   (My little sister is happy to receive flowers from Taroo.)

3. A: きれいなカードですね。誰かに**もらった**んですか。

      Kirei na kaado desu ne. Dareka ni **moratta** n' desu ka.

      (It is a beautiful card isn't it? Did you get it from somebody?)

   B: ええ。友達に**もらった**んです。

      Ee. Tomodachi ni **moratta** n' desu.

      (Yes, I received it from my friend.)

"**Morau**" is not used when the giver of a thing is first person (= "I".)   Therefore, the following sentence is not appropriate.

山田さんは私に/からおみやげをもらいました。

Yamada-san wa watashi ni/kara omiyage wo moraimashita.

(Mr. Yamada received a souvenior from me.)

Honorific and humble expressions

"**Sashiageru**" is the humble expression of "**ageru**" and is used when someone gives something to his or her superior.

"**Kudasaru**" is the honorific expression of "**kureru**" and is used in the context of "someone who is *my* superior gives something to *me* or a member of *my family*."

"**Itadaku**" is the humble expression of "**morau**" and is used when someone receives something from his or her superior.

On the other hand, "**Yaru**" is used instead of "**ageru**" when the speaker gives something to an inferior (e.g. speaker's younger brother, younger sister, and pets), or in a context such as the one when someone waters plants.

1. 私達は先生にお誕生日のプレゼントを**さしあげました**。

   Watashi-tachi wa sensei ni o-tanjoobi no purezento wo **sashiagemashita**.

   (We gave our teacher a birthday present.)

2. 先生が私に日本語の辞書を**くださいました**。

   Sensei ga watashi ni nihon-go no jisho wo **kudasaimashita**.

   (My teacher gave me a Japanese dictionary.)

3. 花子さんのご両親にかぶきの切符を**いただきました**。

   Hanako-san no go-ryooshin ni Kabuki no kippu wo **itadakimashita**.

   (I received a kabuki ticket from Hanako's parents.)

4. 弟にもう読まない本を全部**やった**。

   Otooto ni moo yomanai hon wo zenbu **yatta**.

   (I gave my little brother all the books that I do not read any more.)

5. 毎朝花に水を**やって**います。

   Maiasa hana ni mizu wo **yatte** imasu.

   (I water to the flowers every morning.)

6. Complete the following sentences using an appropriate verb of giving and receiving.

Ex. 私→　妹（かばん）　　　私は<u>妹にかばんをやりました</u>。

watashi →　imooto (kaban)　Watashi wa <u>imotto ni kaban wo yarimashita</u>.

1. 先生 → 私（お手紙）   私は＿＿＿＿＿＿＿＿＿＿＿＿＿＿＿＿
   sensei → watashi (o-tegami)   Watashi wa ＿＿＿＿＿＿＿＿＿＿＿＿＿＿＿

                                  先生は＿＿＿＿＿＿＿＿＿＿＿＿＿＿＿＿

                                  Sensei wa ＿＿＿＿＿＿＿＿＿＿＿＿＿＿＿

2. 私 → 友達（雑誌）   私は＿＿＿＿＿＿＿＿＿＿＿＿＿＿＿＿
   watashi → tomodachi (zasshi) watashi wa ＿＿＿＿＿＿＿＿＿＿＿＿＿＿＿

3. 幸司さん → 敬子さん（時計）   幸司さんは＿＿＿＿＿＿＿＿＿＿＿＿＿＿
   Kooji-san → Keiko-san (tokei) Kooji-san wa ＿＿＿＿＿＿＿＿＿＿＿＿＿＿

                                  敬子さんは＿＿＿＿＿＿＿＿＿＿＿＿＿＿

                                  Keiko-san wa ＿＿＿＿＿＿＿＿＿＿＿＿＿＿

4. 両親 → 私（お金）   私は＿＿＿＿＿＿＿＿＿＿＿＿＿＿＿＿
   ryooshin → watashi (o-kane)   Watashi wa ＿＿＿＿＿＿＿＿＿＿＿＿＿＿＿

                                  両親は＿＿＿＿＿＿＿＿＿＿＿＿＿＿＿＿

                                  Ryooshin wa ＿＿＿＿＿＿＿＿＿＿＿＿＿＿

THE VERBS "NARU" AND "SURU"

The verb "**naru**" corresponds to the English "to become," and this expression means that "something or somebody becomes so and so" or "gets to be so and so."

Formation

Noun: Sensei da → Sensei **ni naru**.

Na-Adjective: Shizuka da → Shizuka **ni naru**.

I-Adjective: Atsui → Atsu-**ku naru**.

1. 来月私は十八才**になります**。

   Raigetsu watashi wa juuhas-sai **ni narimasu**.

   (*I will become eighteen years old next month.*)

2. 父は病気でしたが、もう元気**になりました**。　.

   Chichi wa byooki deshita ga, moo genki **ni narimashita**.

   (*My father was sick but he got well.*)

3. 休みが始まって学校は静か**になりました**。

   Yasumi ga hajimatte, gakkoo wa shizuka **ni narimashita**.

   (*The vacation started and school became quiet.*)

4. 日本語は**難しくなりました**が、楽しいです。

   Nihon-go wa **muzukashiku narimashita** ga, tanoshii desu.

(Japanese has become difficult, but it is fun.)

7. Change the following sentences into ones using the verb "**naru**."

　　Ex. 車は古いです。 → <u>車は古くなりました</u>。

　　　　Kuruma wa furui desu. → <u>Kuruma wa furuku narimashita</u>.

1. 頭が痛いです。 _____

　　Atama ga itai desu. _____

2. スミスさんは医者です。 _____

　　Sumisu-san wa isha desu. _____

3. この部屋はむし暑いです。 _____

　　Kono heya wa mushi-atsui desu. _____

4. この頃ひまです。 _____

　　Kono goro hima-desu. _____

5. 弟はテニスが上手です。 _____

　　Otooto wa tenisu ga joozu desu. _____

6. 私は肉が嫌いです。 _____

　　Watashi wa niku ga kirai desu. _____

　　The verb "**suru**" corresponds to the English "to do," and this transitive expression means to "make someone or something into such and such state" in English.

<u>Formation:</u>

　　Noun: Musuko wa **isha** da.　→ Musuko wo **isha ni suru**.

　　Na-Adjective: Heya wa **kirei** da.　→ Heya wo **kirei ni suru**.

　　I-Adjective: Heya wa **atatakai**.　→ Heya wo **atatakaku suru**.

1. 二つの部屋を広い寝室にしました。

　　Futatsu no heya **wo** hiroi shinshitsu **ni shimashita**.

　　(I made the two rooms into a spacious bedroom.)

2. このスカートを少し短くしてください。

　　Kono sukaato **wo** sukoshi **mijikaku shite** kudasai.

　　(Please make this skirt a little bit shorter.)

　　This pattern is also used as the expression of someone's volitional decision, which means "to decide on."

1. ピクニックは**土曜日にしましょう**。

   Pikunikku wa **doyoobi ni shimashoo**.

   (As for the picnic, let's make it Saturday.)

2. 私は専攻**を政治学にしました**。

   Watashi wa senkoo **wo seijigaku ni shimashita**.

   (I decided to manjor in politics.)

3. (At a restaurant)

   A: 何を食べますか。

       Nani wo tabemasu ka?

       (What will you eat?)

   B: そうですね。私は**パスタにします**。

       Soo desu ne.   Watashi wa pasuta **ni shimasu**.

       (Well, I will have pasta./ Lit. I will make it pasta.)

On the other hand, an expression with "**naru**" indicates that "something is decided."

   Ex.   会議は明日の三時**になりました**。

         Kaigi wa ashita no san-ji **ni narimashita**.

         (It was decided that the meeting will be at 3 o'clock tomorrow.)

V (plain non-past) + koto ni naru   versus   V (plain non-past) + koto ni suru

   "~ **Koto ni naru**" corresponds to "It is decided that ~" or "It turns out that ~" in English. On the other hand, "~ **koto ni suru**" means to "decide to do such and such," and it expresses the speaker's volitional decision.

1. 中国語を**習うことにしました**。

   Chuugoku-go wo **narau koto ni shimashita**.

   (I decided to learn Chinese.)

2. 東京で**働くことになりました**。

   Tookyoo de **hataraku koto ni narimashita**.

   (It has been decided that I will work in Tokyo.)

3. 母と一緒に**旅行することにした**。

   Haha to issho ni **ryokoo suru koto ni shita**.

   (I decided to travel with my mother.)

4. 毎週月曜日に先生と**会うことになった**。

   Maishuu getsu-yoobi ni sensei to **au koto ni natta**.

(It has been decided that I will see my teacher every Monday.)

V (plain non-past) + yoo ni naru   versus   V (plain non-past) + yoo ni suru

"~ **Yoo ni naru**" expresses the gradual change of something or somebody and it corresponds to "come to be that ~" or "reach the point of such and such."   "~ **Yoo ni suru**" indicates the effort or attempt to do something, and it means in English that somebody makes an attempt or effort to do such and such.

1. 日本語が少し**分かるようになりました**。

    Nihon-go ga sukoshi **wakaru yoo ni narimashita**.

    (I came to understand some Japanese.)

2. なるべく早く**来るようにします**。

    Narubeku hayaku **kuru yoo ni shimasu**.

    (I will try to come as early as possible.)

3. 酒はあまり**飲まないようにしています**。

    Sake wa amari **nomanai yoo ni shite imasu**.

    (I've been trying not to drink too much sake.)

4. だれでもコンピューターを**使うようになった**。

    Dare demo konpyuutaa wo **tsukau yoo ni natta**.

    (Everybody has come to use a computer.)

8. Fill the blanks in the following sentences with either "**naru**" or "**suru**".

Ex. 先生は今日のオフィスアワーを少し早く<u>しました</u>。

    Sensei wa kyoo no ofisu awaa (office hour) wo sukoshi hayaku <u>shimashita</u>.

1.   (At a restaurant)

    私はすしに＿＿＿＿＿＿。あなたは何に＿＿＿＿＿＿か。

    Watashi wa sushi ni ＿＿＿＿＿＿. Anata wa nani ni ＿＿＿＿＿＿ ka.

2. 試験は来週の火曜日に＿＿＿＿＿＿と友達が言いました。

    Shiken wa raisyuu no ka-yoobi ni ＿＿＿＿＿＿ to tomodachi ga iimashita..

3. 家族に会いたいので、冬休みに家に帰ることに＿＿＿＿＿＿。

    Kazoku ni aitai node, fuyu-yasumi ni uchi ni kaeru koto ni ＿＿＿＿＿＿.

4. 少し太ったので、甘いものを食べないように＿＿＿＿＿＿。

    Sukoshi futotta node, amai mono wo tabenai yoo ni ＿＿＿＿＿＿.

5. 病気で何もできませんでしたが、少し起きて歩けるように＿＿＿＿＿＿。

    Byooki de nani mo dekimasen deshita ga, sukoshi okite arukeru yoo ni ＿＿＿＿＿＿.

PASSIVE FORM

Formation of the passive verbs

1. U-verbs

   The final vowel "-**u**" of dictionary form is replaced by "-**areru**."

   Ex: tsuka-**u**   →   tsukaw-**areru**   yom-**u** →   yom-**areru**

2. Ru-verbs

   The final syllable "-**ru**" of the dictionary form is replaced by "-**rareru**."

   Ex: mi-**ru**   → mi-**rareru**   tabe-**ru** →   tabe-**rareru**

   Note that the passive and the potential are the same forms in **ru**-verbs

3. Irregular verbs   **kuru**   →   **korareru**   **suru**   →   **sareru**

   All passive verbs are conjugated the same way as **ru**-verbs.

   Ex. taberare-**ru**   →   taberare-**te**

      taberare-**ru**   →   taberare-**nai**

      taberare-**ru**   →   taberare-**masu**

9. Change the following verbs into the passive form.

   Ex. tsukau → <u>tsukawareru</u>

   1. nomu _____

   2. nusumu _____

   3. shiraberu _____

   4. warau _____

   5. tataku _____

   6. hanasu _____

   Japanese passive sentences are divided mainly into two groups, direct and indirect, depending on the context. In the passive structure of "X **wa** Y **ni** V-**rareru**," direct passive indicates that the subject X is directly affected by the action of the agent Y. Indirect passive indicates that the subject X is indirectly affected by the action of the agent Y.

   In general, the Japanese passive sentence, especially indirect passive, reflects the feeling of the subject that heor she is troubled or annoyed by the action of somebody else. Therefore, the indirect passive is often referred to as "suffering passive." In passive sentences the agent who takes the action is marked by the particle "**ni**."

Direct passive

1. けさ早く母に**起こされました**。

   Kesa hayaku haha **ni okosaremashita**.

   (*I was wakened by mother early this morning.*)

2. 宿題を忘れて先生に**しかられました**。

   Shukudai wo wasurete sensei **ni shikararemashita**.

   (*I forgot the homework, and I was scolded by the teacher.*)

Indirect passive

1. 映画館で妹に**泣かれました**。

   Eiga-kan de imooto **ni nakaremashita**.

   (*My sister cried in the movie theater, which bothered me.*)

2. 昨日公園で雨に**降られて**困りました。

   Kinoo kooen de ame **ni furarete** komarimashita.

   (*It rained in the park yesterday and I was troubled by it.*)

3. 山田さんはだれか**に**お金を**ぬすまれました**。

   Yamada-san wa dareka **ni** okane wo **nusumaremashita**.

   (*Mr. Yamada had his money stolen by someone.*)

In Japanese, unlike English, an inanimate thing cannot be the subject of this type of passive sentence. In example 3 above, Mr. Yamada's money was stolen. However, the money is not placed in the subject position but in the object position. Mr. Yamada, who was affected by the incident, takes the subject position .

10. Transform the following sentences into passive structures.

   Ex. 妹が私の車を使いました。 → 私は妹に車を使われました。

   Imooto ga watashi no kuruma wo tsukaimashita. → Watashi wa imooto ni kuruma wo tsukawaremashita.

1. みんなが私を笑いました。_____

   Minna ga watashi wo waraimashita. _____

2. ねこが私の魚を食べました。_____

   Neko ga watashi no sakana wo tabemashita. _____

3. だれかが私の部屋に入りました。_____

   Dareka ga watashi no heya ni hairimashita. _____

4. 母が私をしかりました。 _____

    Haha ga watashi wo shikarimashita. _____

5. 先生が私に質問しました。 _____

    Sensei ga watashi ni shitsumon shimashita. _____

6. 警官が私の住所を聞きました。 _____

    Keikan ga watashi no juusho wo kikimashita. _____

CAUSATIVE FORM

There are two types of causative sentence in Japanese. One is called "make-causative," and the other is called "let-causative."

<u>Formation of causative verbs</u>

1. <u>U-verbs</u>

Replace the final vowel "-**u**" of the dictionary form by "-**aseru**."

Ex. kak-**u** → kak-**aseru**   yom-**u** → yom-**aseru**

2. <u>Ru-verbs</u>

Replace the final "-**ru**" of the dictionary form by "-**saseru**."

Ex. tabe-**ru** → tabe-**saseru**   mi-**ru** → mi-**saseru**

3. <u>Irregular verbs</u>   **kuru** → **kosaseru**   **suru** → **saseru**

All Japanese causative verbs are conjugated the same way as **ru**-verbs.

Ex.   yomase-**ru** → yomase-**te**

       yomase-**ru** → yomase-**nai**

       yomase-**ru** → yomase-**masu**

11. Change the following verbs into the causative form.

    Ex. iku → <u>ikaseru</u>

     1. matsu _____

     2. motte kuru _____

     3. oboeru _____

     4. tetsudau _____

     5. kangaeru _____

     6. kaku _____

7. renshuu-suru _____

8. hanasu _____

Make-causative sentences

The structure of "X **wa** Y **wo** + causative verb/X **wa** Y **ni** + Object **wo** + causative verb" indicates that X makes Y do such and such.　In this structure Y is the agent of the action, and it is marked by "**wo**" or "**ni**" depending on whether the verb takes the direct object or not.

1. 私はよく弟**を泣かせました**。

    Watashi wa yoku otooto **wo nakasemashita**.

    (I often made my little brother cry.)

2. 先生は子供**を**早く家に**帰らせた**。

    Sensei wa kodomo **wo** hayaku uchi ni **kaeraseta**.

    (The teacher made the child go home early)

3. 先生は学生**に**作文**を書かせませす**。

    Sensei wa gakusei **ni** sakubun **wo kakasemasu**.

    (The teacher makes the students write a composition.)

4. 母は妹に部屋**を**そうじ**させました**。

    Haha wa imooto **ni** heya **wo sooji sasemashita**.

    (My mother made my little sister clean up the room.)

12. Change the following sentences into causative structures using the word in parentheses as the person who causes or caused the event.

Ex. 弟が手を洗う。（私）→ 私は弟に手を洗わせます。

    Otooto ga te wo arau. (watashi) → Watashi wa otooto ni te wo arawasemasu.

1. 学生が漢字を覚える。（先生）_____

    Gakusei ga kanji wo oboeru. (sensei) _____

2. 妹が薬を飲んだ。（母）_____

    Imooto ga kusuri wo nonda.　(haha) _____

3. 両親が心配した。（私）_____

    Ryooshin ga shinpai shita.　(watashi) _____

4. 学生が何度もテープを聞く。（先生）_____

    Gakusei ga nando mo teepu wo kiku. (sensei) _____

Let-causative sentences

The structure of "X **wa** Y **ni/wo** + causative-**te** + **ageru/kureru**" means that "X lets/allow Y do such and such." Let-causative is constructed by attaching one of the auxiliary "giving and receiving" verbs to the "**te**-form" of the causative verb.

1. ここで**待たせてください**。

   Koko de **matasete kudasai**.

   (*Please let me wait here.*)

2. 友達に**コンピューターを使わせてあげた**。

   Tomodachi **ni** konpyuutaa **wo tsukawasete ageta**.

   (*I let my friend use my computer.*)

3. 両親は私**を**一人で**出かけさせてくれませんでした**。 .

   Ryooshin wa watashi **wo** hitori de **dekakesasete kuremasen deshita**.

   (*My parents didn't let me go out alone.*)

4. ルームメート**に**新聞**を読ませてもらいました**。

   Ruumumeeto **ni** shinbun **wo yomasete moraimashita.**

   (*I asked my roommate to let me read his or her newspaper. / Lit. I received my roommate's favor of letting me read his or her newspaper.*)

13. Change the following sentences into the let-causative structure by completing the sentences.
   Ex. 私は友達の車を使った。

   Watashi wa tomodachi no kuruma wo tsukatta.

   友達は私に 車を使わせてくれた。

   Tomodachi wa watashi ni kuruma wo tsukawasete kureta.

   私は友達に 車を使わせてもらった。

   Watashi wa tomodachi ni kuruma wo tsukawasete moratta.

1. まり子さんは私の部屋にとまった。

   Mariko-san wa watashi no heya ni tomatta.

   私はまり子さんを _____。

   Watashi wa mariko-san wo _____.

2. 私は今日早く帰った。

   Watashi wa kyoo hayaku kaetta.

   先生は私を_____。

   Sensei wa watashi wo _____.

3. 私は昨日クラスを休んだ。

   Watashi wa kinoo kurasu wo yasunda.

   私は先生に_____。

   Watashi wa sensei ni _____.

4. トムさんは和男さんのノートをコピーした。

   Tomu-san wa Kazuo-san no nooto wo kopii-shita.

   和男さんはトムさんに_____・_____。

   Kazuo-san wa Tomu-san ni _____。

   トムさんは和男さんに_____。

   Tomu-san wa Kazuo-san ni _____.

CAUSATIVE PASSIVE FORM

The structure of "X **wa** Y **ni** (object **wo**) + causative passive verb" means that "X is forced or made to do such and such by Y." It should be noted that only the make-causative form can be transformed into causative passive.

Formation of causative passive verbs

The final syllable "**-ru**" of the causative "**-(s)aseru**" form is replaced by "**-rareru**."

Ex.   tabe-sase-**ru**   →   tabe-sase-**rareru**

       tetsudaw-ase-**ru** →   tetsudaw-ase-**rareru**

       ko-sase-**ru**   →   ko-sase-**rareru**

       sase-**ru**   →   sase-**rareru**

1. 母によく部屋のそうじ**をさせられました**。

   Haha **ni** yoku heya no sooji **wo saseraremashita**.

   (I was often made to clean up the room by my mother.)

2. 学生は先生に毎日漢字**を書かせられます**。

   Gakusei wa sensei **ni** mainichi kanji **wo kakaseraremasu**.

   (The students are made to write kanji by the teacher every day.)

3. 両親は妹に**心配させられました**。

   Ryooshin wa imooto **ni shinpai-saseraremashita**.

   (My parents were made to worry by my little sister.)

4. クラスでは日本語**を話させられます**。

   Kurasu de wa nihon-go **wo hanasaseraremasu**.

(We are forced to speak Japanese in the class.)

14. Change the following verbs into the causative and causative passive.

	causative	**causative passive**
Ex. yomu →	yomaseru	yomaserareru

1. kaku   _____   _____
2. shiraberu   _____   _____
3. oboeru   _____   _____
4. kuru   _____   _____
5. kau   _____   _____
6. matsu   _____   _____
7. suru   _____   _____

15. Change the following causative structures into causative passive structures.

Ex. 先生は学生に辞書を買わせました。 →

Sensei wa gakusei ni jisho wo kawasemashita. →

学生は 先生に辞書を買わせられました。

Gakusei wa sensen ni jisho wo kawaseraremashita.

1. 母は私に野菜を食べさせました。私は_____

   Haha wa watashi ni yasai wo tabesasemashita.Watashi wa _____

2. 友達は私を待たせました。私は_____

   Tomodachi wa watashi wo matasemashita. Watashi wa_____

3. 医者は森さんに酒をやめさせました。森さんは_____

   Isha wa Mori-san ni sake wo yamesasemashita. Mori-san wa _____

4. 母は妹にピアノを練習させます。妹は_____

   Haha wa imooto ni piano wo renshuu sasemasu. Imooto wa _____

TE-FORM

Formation of **te**-form

1. U-verb

   Verbs which end with "-**ku**"

   ka-**ku** → ka-**ite**   ki-**ku** → ki-**ite**   i-**ku** → i-**tte**

Verbs which end with "-**gu**"

oyo-**gu** → oyo-**ide**

Verbs which end with "-**mu**," "-**bu**," and "-**nu**"

yo-**mu** →   yo-**nde**   to-**bu** → to-**nde**   shi-**nu** → shi-**nde**

Verbs which end with "-**u**," "-**tsu**," or "-**ru**"

ma-**tsu** →   ma-**tte**   kae-**ru** → kae-**tte**   ka-**u** →   ka-**tte**

Verbs which end with "-**su**"

hana-**su** →   hana-**shite**

Note: "**Iku** (to go)" is an exception. Its final syllable, "-**ku**," is replaced by "-**tte**,"

2. Ru-verb : The final syllable "**ru**" of the dictionary form is replaced with "**te**."

mi-**ru** → mi-**te**   tabe-**ru** →   tabe-**te**

3. Irregular: **kuru** →   **kite**   **suru** →   **shite**

16. Change the following verbs into their **te**-form.

Ex. au   → <u>atte</u>

1. noru   _____

2. nomu   _____

3. miru   _____

4. motsu   _____

5. oshieru   _____

6. kasu   _____

7. tetsudau   _____

8. shimeru   _____

9. nugu   _____

Sequence of action

The **te**-form refers to the sequence of actions in a sentence. All verbs except for the main verbs which comes at the end of a sentence, take the "**te**-form," and they connect the following verbs as a sequence of action.

1. けさ七時に**起きて**朝ご飯を食べた。

Kesa shichi-ji ni **okite** asagohan wo tabeta.

(*I got up at seven o'clock this morning and ate breakfast .*)

2. 友達に**会って**一緒に映画を見ました。

Tomodachi ni **atte** issho ni eiga wo mimashita.

(I met my friend and we saw a movie together.)

17. State the sequence of the given two actions using the **te**-form.

Ex. 家に帰りました。そして宿題をしました。

Uchi ni kaerimashita. Soshite shukudai wo shimashita.

→ <u>家に帰って宿題をしました。</u>

→ <u>Uchi ni kaette shukudai wo shimashita.</u>

1. 図書館へ行きます。そして本を借ります。 _____

Toshokan e ikimasu. Soshite hon wo karimasu. _____

2. ジムで泳ぎます。そして家に帰ります。 _____

Jimu de oyogimasu. Soshite uch ni kaerimasu. _____

3. 薬を飲みました。そして寝ました。 _____

Kusuri wo nomimashita. Soshite nemashita. _____

4. ご飯を作りました。そして食べました。 _____

Gohan wo tsukurimashita. Soshite tabemashita. _____

5. 酒をやめます。そして運動を始めます。 _____

Sake wo yamemasu. Soshite undoo wo hajimemasu. _____

Reason

Te-form is used to indicate the reason for the statement in the main clause.

1. 雨が**降って**少しすずしくなりました。

Ame ga **futte** sukoshi suzushiku narimashita.

(It became a little bit cool, because it rained.)

2. お金が**なくて**買い物ができませんでした。

O-kane ga **nakute** kaimono ga dekimasen deshita.

(I had no money and I couldn't go shopping.)

3. **食べすぎて**気分が悪いです。

Tabesugite kibun ga warui desu.

(I feel sick, because I ate too much.)

4. へんな日本語を**使って**笑われた。

Hen na nihon-go wo **tsukatte** warawareta.

(I was laughed at because I used funny Japanese.)

In this structure, the statement of the main clause usually refers to an event which is out of of the speaker's control.   Therefore, the expressions of the speaker's intention, requests, desire, etc., do not take place in the main clause. The following two sentences are incorrect because the speaker's intention is given in the main clause.

お金が**なくて**少し貸してください。

O-kane ga **nakute** sukoshi kashite kudasai.

(I have no money, so please lend me some.)

日本語が **難しくなって**やめます。

Nihon-go ga **muzukashiku natte** yamemasu.

(Japanese has become difficult and I will stop trying to learn it.)

18. Connect the given cause-and-effect sentence using the **te**-form.

Ex. テレビが故障しました。ニュースが見られません。

Terebi ga koshoo-shimashita. Nyuusu ga miraremasen.

→ テレビが故障してニュースが見られません。

→ Terebi ga koshoo-shite nyuusu ga miraremasen.

1. 太りました。服が着られません。＿＿＿＿＿＿＿＿＿＿＿＿＿

Futorimashita.   Fuku ga kiraremasen. ＿＿＿＿＿＿＿＿＿＿＿＿

2. 靴が古くなりました。はけません。＿＿＿＿＿＿＿＿＿＿＿＿＿

Kutsu ga furuku narimashita.   Hakemasen. ＿＿＿＿＿＿＿＿＿＿＿

3. 雨がやみました。空が明るくなりました。＿＿＿＿＿＿＿＿＿＿＿

Ame ga yamimashita. Sora ga akaruku narimashita. ＿＿＿＿＿＿＿＿

4. 夏休みが始まりました。うれしいです。＿＿＿＿＿＿＿＿＿＿＿＿

Natsu-yasumi ga hajimarimashita. Ureshii desu. ＿＿＿＿＿＿＿＿＿

5. ねこが死にました。さびしくなりました。＿＿＿＿＿＿＿＿＿＿＿

Neko ga shinimashita. Sabishiku narimashita. ＿＿＿＿＿＿＿＿＿＿＿

Manner

The **te**-form also refers to the manner or means for the action stated in the main clause.

1. いつも**歩いて**学校へ行きます。

Itsumo **aruite** gakkoo e ikimasu.

(I always walk to school.)

2. よくテープを**聞いて**練習してください。

Yoku teepu wo **kiite** renshuu shite kudasai.

(Please practice by listening to tapes carefully.)

3. 何度も**書いて**漢字をおぼえます。

Nando mo **kaite** kanji wo oboemasu.

(I memorize kanji by writing them many times.)

4. インターネットを**使って**切符を見つけました。

Intaanetto wo **tsukatte** kippu wo mitsukemashita.

(I found the ticket by using the Internet.)

Request

The expression of "V-**te kudasai**" corresponds to "please do such and such" in English.

1. ちょっと**待ってください**。

Chotto **matte kudasai**.

(Wait a second, please.)

2. 明日九時に**来てください**。

Ashita ku-ji ni **kite kudasai**.

(Please come here at nine o'clock tomorrow.)

The negative expression "please don't do such and such" is expressed in the form of "negative plain + **de kudasai**."

1. ここでたばこを**吸わないでください**。

Koko de tabako wo **suwanai de kudasai**.

(Please don't smoke here.)

2. このコンピューターは**使わないでください**。

Kono konpyuutaa wa **tsukawanai de kudasai**.

(Please don't use this computer.)

19. Change the following phrases into request.

Ex. 明日来て仕事を手伝う。 → 明日来て仕事を手伝ってください。

  Ashita kite shigoto wo tetsudau. → Ashita kite shigoto to tetsudatte kudasai.

1. よく考える。 _____

  Yoku kangaeru. _____

2. 静かに話す。 _____

  Shizuka ni hanasu. _____

3. 窓を開ける。 ＿＿＿＿＿＿＿＿＿

   Mado wo akeru. ＿＿＿＿＿＿＿＿＿

4. ドアを閉める。 ＿＿＿＿＿＿＿＿

   Doa wo shimeru. ＿＿＿＿＿＿＿＿＿＿

5. ミルクを買ってくる。 ＿＿＿＿＿＿＿＿

   Miruku wo katte kuru. ＿＿＿＿＿＿＿＿＿

6. 本屋へ行って辞書を買う。 ＿＿＿＿＿＿＿＿

   Honya e itte jisho wo kau. ＿＿＿＿＿＿＿＿

Expressions with "V-te iru"

The expression "V-**te iru/imasu**" is used in several contexts as follows.

I. Progressive or habitual action

"V-**te iru**" indicates that someone is doing or has been doing something, or that a certain action is taking place now. It also indicates a habitual action.

1. 弟は今おふろに**入っています**。

   Otooto wa ima o-furo ni **haitte imasu**.

   (My young brother is taking a bath now.)

2. 昨日から雨が**降っています**よ。

   Kinoo kara ame ga **futte imasu** yo.

   (It has been raining since yesterday, you know.)

3. 今晩ご飯を**作っています**。

   Ima ban-gohan wo **tsukutte imasu**.

   (I am making supper now.)

4. 毎朝公園を**歩いています**。

   Maiasa kooen wo **aruite imasu**.

   (I walk in the park every morning.)

II. A state resulting from an action

"V-**te iru**" also expresses a state which results from an action expressed mainly by a motion verb or an intransitive verb.

1. 父はもう家に**帰っています**よ。

   Chichi wa moo uchi ni **kaette imasu** yo.

   (My father is already home.)

2. 山田さんは今ボストンに**行っています**。

Yamada-san wa ima Bosuton ni **itte imasu**.

(Mr. Yamada has gone to Boston and is there now.)

3. 郵便局はまだ**開いています**か。

Yuubin-kyoku wa mada **aite imasu** ka

(Is the post office still open?)

4. このテレビは**こわれています**ね。

Kono terebi wa **kowarete imasu** ne.

(This TV is broken, isn't it?)

20. Choose the right verb from the list and fill in the following blanks with the appropriate progressive expression.

入る (hairu)　聞く (kiku)　書く (kaku)　待つ (matsu)　話す (hanasu)

作る (tsukuru)　する (suru)　飲む (nomu)　寝る (neru)

　Ex. 弟は今、おふろに　<u>入っています</u>。

　　　Otooto wa ima ofuro ni <u>haitte imasu</u>.

1. 父は今仕事を＿＿＿＿＿＿＿＿＿＿。

Chichi wa ima shigoto wo ＿＿＿＿＿＿＿＿＿＿.

2. 母は晩ご飯を＿＿＿＿＿＿＿＿＿＿。

Haha wa ban-gohan wo ＿＿＿＿＿＿＿＿＿＿.

3. 姉は音楽を＿＿＿＿＿＿＿＿＿

Ane wa ongaku wo ＿＿＿＿＿＿＿＿＿＿.

4. 太郎さんは電話で友達と＿＿＿＿＿＿＿＿＿＿。

Taroo-san wa denwa de tomodachi to ＿＿＿＿＿＿＿＿＿＿.

5. 兄はビールを＿＿＿＿＿＿＿＿＿＿。

Ani wa biiru wo ＿＿＿＿＿＿＿＿＿＿.

6. 花子さんは手紙を＿＿＿＿＿＿＿＿＿＿。

Hanako-san wa tegami wo ＿＿＿＿＿＿＿＿＿＿.

　III. <u>Stative verbs</u>

　　The verbs which indicate the state of being of something or somebody rather than an action are usually expressed in "V-**te iru**."

1. 佐藤さんの電話番号を**知っています**か。

Satoo-san no denwa-bangoo wo **shitte imasu** ka.

(Do you know Mr. Satoo's phone number?)

2. 今どこに**住んでいます**か。

Ima doko ni **sunde imasu** ka.

(Where do you live now?)

3. あのレストランはいつも**こんでいます**ね。

Ano resutoran wa itsumo **konde imasu** ne.

(That restaurant is always crowded, isn't it?)

4. まだお腹はあまり**すいていません**。

Mada o-naka wa amari **suite imasen**.

(I am not so hungry yet.)

Expressions with "V-te miru"

The expression "V-**te miru**" means "try doing such and such to see the result or to see how it turns out."

1. 辞書を**引いてみました**が，この言葉はありません。

Jisho wo **hiite mimashita** ga, kono kotoba wa arimasen

(I tried looking in a dictionary, but there is no such a word there.)

2. あの新しいレストランに**入ってみましょう**。

Ano atarashii resutoran ni **haitte mimashoo**.

(Let's go to that new restaurant (to see how it is.)

3. この映画は有名だからぜひ**見てみたい**です．

Kono eiga wa yuumei da kara zehi **mite mitai** desu.

(This movie is famous, so I want to see it (to see how it is.)

Expressions with "V-te oku"

The expression "V-**te oku**" means to "do something in advance for future benefit or future use."   It also means to "leave something in a certain state for a certain period of time."

1. クラスの前にテキストを**読んでおきました**。

Kurasu no mae ni tekisuto wo **yonde okimashita**.

(I read the textbook in advance of the class.)

2. 友達が来るから、部屋を**そうじしておきたい**です．

Tomodachi ga kuru kara, heya wo **sooji shite okitai** desu.

(My friend is coming, so I want to clean up my room beforehand.)

3. 部屋が暑いから、まどを**開けておき**ましょう。

Heya ga atsui kara, mado wo **akete okimasyoo**.

(*The room is hot, so let's leave the window open.*)

Expressions with "V-te shimau"

The expression "V-**te shimau**" is used to express mainly two ideas.   One is the completion of an action, and the other is the speaker's negative feeling such as regret, disappointment, embarrasment, or sorrow and about an event or action.

1. もう宿題を**してしまいました**か。

Moo Shukudai wo **shite shimaimashita** ka.

(*Have you done all the homework yet?*)

2. 今日この本を全部**読んでしまう**つもりです。

Kyoo kono hon wo zenbu **yonde shimau** tsumori desu.

(*I intend to finish reading this entire book today.*)

3. 風邪を**引いてしまって**少し頭が痛いです。

Kaze wo **hiite shimatte** sukoshi atama ga itai desu.

(*I got a cold and I have a headache.*)

4. 電話番号を**忘れてしまって**連絡できません。

Denwa bangoo wo **wasurete shimatte** renraku dekimasen.

(*I forgot the phone number and I cannot contact him or her.*)

21. Rephrase the underlined words using   "V-**te shimau**," "V-**te oku**," or "V-**te miru**".

Ex. このテレビは古く<u>なりました</u>。 →　<u>なってしまいました</u>

Kono terebi wa furuku <u>narimashita</u>. (natte shimaimashita)

1. 友達が来るから、お昼ご飯を<u>作ります</u>。＿＿＿＿＿＿＿＿

Tomodachi ga kuru kara, ohiru-gohan wo <u>tsukurimasu</u>. ＿＿＿＿＿＿＿＿

2. 新しい靴を<u>はきました</u>が、少し小さいです。＿＿＿＿＿＿＿＿

Atarashii kutsu wo <u>hakimashita</u> ga, sukoshi chiisai desu. ＿＿＿＿＿＿＿

3. おもしろそうな本なので、<u>読みます</u>。＿＿＿＿＿＿＿＿

Omoshiro soo na hon na node, <u>yomimasu</u>. ＿＿＿＿＿＿＿＿

4. お金を全部<u>使いました</u>。＿＿＿＿＿＿＿＿

O-kane wo zenbu <u>tsukaimashita</u>. ＿＿＿＿＿＿＿＿

5. 来週のコンサートの切符を今、<u>買います</u>。＿＿＿＿＿＿＿＿

Raishuu no konsaato(concert) no kippu wo ima <u>kaimasu</u>. ＿＿＿＿＿＿＿＿

Expressions with V-te ageru/kureru/morau

Expressions with "V-**te ageru/kureru/morau** (giving and receiving auxiliary verbs)"
are frequently used to refer to somebody's favorable action for somebody else. The use of either
"V-**te** ageru" or "V-**te kureru**" depends on who is the agent of the action and who is the receiver of
its benefit.

"V-**te ageru**" is used in the context of "I (first person) do something for somebody" or
"somebody (second or third person) does something for somebody else."

"V-**te kureru**" is used in the context of "somebody does something *for me* or *for a member of
my family*."

"V-**te morau**" is the alternative expression of the other two expressions, in which the
subject of the sentence is the receiver of the benefit from the action. However, this expression
cannot be used in the context of "I do something for somebody."

1. 友達の仕事を**手伝ってあげるつもり**です。

   Tomodachi no shigoto wo **tetsudatte ageru** tsumori desu.

   (*I intend to help my friend with his job.*)

2. ケンさんはトムさんにお金を**貸してあげ**ました。

   Ken-san wa Tomu-san ni o-kane wo **kashite agemashita**.

   (*Ken lent some money to Tom.*)

   Cf. トムさんはケンさんにお金を**貸してもらい**ました。

   Tomu-san wa Ken-san ni o-kane wo **kashite moraimashita**.

   (*Tom had Ken lend him some money.*)

3. 母はおいしい晩ご飯を**作ってくれ**ました。

   Haha wa oishii ban-gohan wo **tsukutte kuremashita**.

   (*My mother cooked a delicious supper for me.*)

   Cf. 私は母においしい晩ご飯を**作ってもらい**ました。

   Watashi wa haha ni oishii ban-gohan wo **tsukutte moraimashita**.

   (*I asked my mother to make me a delicious supper.*)

4. 兄が私のコンピューターを**直してくれた**。

   Ani ga watashi no konpyuutaa wo **naoshite kuremashita**.

   (*My big brother fixed my computer.*)

   Cf. 私は兄にコンピューターを**なおしてもらった**。

   Watashi wa ani ni konpyuutaa wo **naoshite moratta**.

   (*I asked my big brother to fix my computer.*)

Additional Expressions

"V-**te sashiageru**" replaces "V-**te ageru**" as an humble expression in the context of "someone does something for his or her superior."

"V-**te kudasaru**" replaces "V-**te kureru**" as an honorific expression in a context of "someone who is a superior does something for *me or a member of my family*."

"V-**te itadaku**" is a humble expression of "V-**te morau**" and is used often in the context in which first person receives a benefit from his or her superior.

1. まり子さんのご両親をホテルに**連れて行ってさしあげました**。

   Mariko-san no go-ryooshin wo hoteru ni **tsurete itte sashiagemashita**.

   (I took Mariko's parents to the hotel.)

2. 田中先生に推薦状を**書いていただきました**。

   Tanaka sensei ni suisenjoo wo **kaite itadakimashita**.

   (I asked Prof. Tanaka to write a recommendation for me.)

3. 林さんの奥さんが茶会に**招待してくださいました**。

   Hayashi-san no oku-san ga chakai ni **shootai-shite kudasaimashita**.

   (Mrs. Hayashi invited me to a tea ceremony.)

22. State the following English sentences using the appropriate Japanese expression

"**V-te kureru**," "**V-te morau**," or "**V-te ageru**" as in the example.

Ex. Tom helped me.

→ トムは私を 手伝ってくれました。

   Tomu wa watashi wo tetsudatte kuremashita.

→ 私はトムに 手伝ってもらいました。

   Watashi wa Tomu ni tetsudatte moraimashita.

1. My mother bought me a nice bag.

   母は私に_____

   Haha wa watashi ni _____.

   私は母に_____

   Watashi wa haha ni _____.

2. I found my friend a good part-time job.

   私は友達に_____

   Watashi wa tomodachi ni _____

3. Mariko took me to a famous temple.

まり子さんは私を＿＿＿＿＿＿＿＿＿＿＿＿

Mariko-san wa watashi wo ＿＿＿＿＿＿＿＿＿＿＿＿

私はまり子さんに＿＿＿＿＿＿＿＿＿＿＿＿

Watashi wa Mariko-san ni ＿＿＿＿＿＿＿＿＿＿＿＿

4. Ms. Yamada sent a beautiful kimono to Anne.

山田さんはアンさんに＿＿＿＿＿＿＿＿＿＿＿＿

Yamada-san wa Ann-san ni ＿＿＿＿＿＿＿＿＿＿＿＿

アンさんは山田さんに＿＿＿＿＿＿＿＿＿＿＿＿

Ann-san wa Yamada-san ni ＿＿＿＿＿＿＿＿＿＿＿＿

VOLITIONAL FORM

Volitional form refers to one's intention or plan. The expression "volitional + **to omou**" can be interpreted as to "intend to do such and such" or "think of doing such and such."

Formation of volitional verbs

1. U-verb

The final "-**u**" of the dictionary form is replaced by "-**oo**."

Ex.   kak-**u** → kak-**oo**   yom-**u** → yom-**oo**

2. Ru-verb

The final "-**ru**" of the dictionary form is replaced by "-**yoo**."

Ex.   tabe-**ru** → tabe-**yoo**   ne-**ru** → ne-**yoo**

3. Irregular verb

kuru → koyoo   suru → shiyoo

1. 今晩は薬を飲んで早く**寝よう**と思います。

Konban wa kusuri wo nonde hayaku **neyoo** to omoimasu.

(I think I will take some medicine and go to bed early tonight.)

2. 友達に**手伝ってもらおう**と思っています。

Tomodachi ni **tetsudatte moraoo** to omotte imasu.

(I am thinking of having my friend help me.)

3. よく考えて**決めよう**と思います。

Yoku kangaete **kimeyoo** to omoimasu.

(I think I will consider it carefully and decide.)

4. 姉はアルバイトを**探そう**と思っています。

    Ane wa arubaito wo **sagasoo** to omotte imasu.

    (My big sister is thinking of looking for a part-time job.)

Note: In the statement in which the third person is the subject, volitionatinal forms co-occur always with "**to omotte imasu**" but not with "**to omoimasu**."

    The volitional form is also used as the informal expression of "V-**mashoo**," which corresponds to "let's do such and such." in English.

1. (To a friend)

    「何か**飲もう**。」

    "Nani ka **nomoo**."

    ("Let's drink something.")

2. 友達は「映画を見に**行こう**。」と言いました。

    Tomodachi wa "Eiga wo mi ni **ikoo**." to iimashita.

    (My friend said, "Let's go to see a movie.")

23. Change the following verbs to their volitional forms.

    Ex. miru →   __miyoo__

        1. hanasu   _____

        2. yameru   _____

        3. (uchi wo) deru   _____

        4. (hayaku) kaeru   _____

        5. yasumu   _____

        6. benkyoo suru   _____

        7. tsukuru   _____

        8. tsukau   _____

        9. matsu   _____

        10. mitsukeru   _____

24. Fill in each blank with the appropriate volitional form using the verbs listed below.

    あげる (ageru)、いる (iru)、借りる (kariru), する (suru)、買う (kau)、

    泳ぐ (oyogu)、作る (tsukuru)、読む (yomu)

Ex. 図書館で本を<u>借りよう</u>と思います。

    Toshokan de hon wo <u>kariyoo</u> to omoimasu.

1. 家に帰って本を＿＿＿＿＿＿と思っています。

    Uchi ni kaette hon wo ＿＿＿＿ to omotte imasu.

2. 森さんが、一緒に食事を＿＿＿＿＿＿と言いました。

    Mori-san ga, issho ni shokuji wo ＿＿＿＿＿ to iimashita.

3. 母の誕生日に花を買って＿＿＿＿＿＿と思っています。

    Haha no tanjoobi ni hana wo katte ＿＿＿＿＿ to omotte imasu.

4. 明日は一日中家に＿＿＿＿＿＿と思います。

    Ashita wa ichinichi-juu uchi ni ＿＿＿＿＿ to omoimasu.

5. 兄は新しい車を＿＿＿＿＿＿と思っています。

    Ani wa atarashii kuruma wo ＿＿＿＿＿ to omotte imasu.

6. 暑いので、プールに行って＿＿＿＿＿＿と思います。

    Atsui node, puuru ni itte ＿＿＿＿＿ to omoimasu.

Review

25. Choose the appropriate word from the words goven in parentheses.

1. 今手紙を（書いて、書く、書きます）います。

    Ima tegami wo (kaite, kaku, kakimasu) imasu.

2. コーヒーを（飲んだ、飲みて、飲んで）ください。

    Koohii wo (nonda, nomite, nonde) kudasai.

3. 明日は友達に（会う、会って、会おう）と思っています。

    Ashita wa tomodachi ni (au, atte, aoo) to omotte imasu.

4. この部屋から山が（見ます、見られます、見えます）ね。

    Kono heya kara yama ga (mimasu, miraremasu, miemasu) ne.

5. 姉は今ボストンに（住みます、いています、住んでいます）。

    Ane wa ima Bosuton ni (sumimasu, ite imasu, sunde imasu).

6. お金がないから何も（買ってできません、買えません、買われません）。

    O-kane ga nai kara nani mo (katte dekimasen, kaemasen, kawaremasen).

7. 雨が（降った、降って、降りました）テニスができませんでした。

    Ame ga (futta, futte, furimashita) tenisu ga dekimasen deshita.

8. 日本語が（話せます、話します、話されます）か。

Nihon-go ga (hanasemasu, hanashimasu, hanasaremasu) ka.

9. よし子さんはドイツ語を（知ります、分かります、知っています）。

Yoshiko-san ha doitsu-go wo (shirimasu, wakarimasu, shitte imasu).

10. 新聞はどこに（います、あります、あっています）か。

Shinbun wa doko ni (imasu, arimasu, atte imasu)ka.

11. 弟にワインを全部（飲めました、飲まれました、飲みました）。

Otooto ni wain wo zenbu (nomemashita, nomaremashita, nomimashita).

12. 私は先生に（する、なろう、なって）と思っています。

Watashi wa sensei ni (suru, naroo, natte) to omotte imasu.

13. アルバイトをやめる（ようにした、ようになった、ことにした）。

Arubaito wo yameru (yoo ni shita, yoo ni natta, koto ni shita).

14. 今晩客が来るので、飲み物を買って（おきます、みます、しまいます）。

Konban kyaku ga kuru node, nomimono wo katte (okimasu, mimasu, shimaimasu)

15. 母は台所を新しく（なりました、しました、できました）。

Haha wa daidokoro wo atarashiku (narimashita, shimashita, dekimashita).

16. 初めて日本語で手紙を書いて（みました、おきました、しまいました）。

Hajimete nihon-go de tegami wo kaite (mimashita, okimashita, shimaimashita).

17. 宿題を忘れて（おきました、しまいました、みました）。

Shukudai wo wasurete (okimashita, shimaimashita, mimashita).

18. アメリカでもたくさんの人がすしを食べる（ようになった、ことにした、ことになった）。

Amerika de mo takusan no hito ga sushi wo taberu (yoo ni natta, koto ni shita, koto ni natta).

19. クリスマスに母が私に（もらった、あげた、くれた）セーターはとても暖かい。

Kurisumasu ni haha ga watashi ni (moratta, ageta, kureta) seetaa wa totemo atatakai.

20. 太郎さんのご家族におみやげを（さしあげよう、いただこう、やろう）と思っています。

Taroo-san no go-kazoku ni o-miyage wo (sashiageyoo, itadakoo, yaroo) to omotte imasu.

26. Complete the followng sentences so that the rephrased sentences will have the same meaning as the original ones.

Ex. 妹は私の手紙を読みました。→　私は妹に<u>手紙を読まれました</u>。

Imooto wa watashi no tegami wo yomimashita. →

Watashi wa imooto ni <u>tegami wo yomaremashita</u>.

1. 森さんが日本語を教えてくれました。

   Mori-san ga nihon-go wo oshiete kuremashita.

   　　　　私は森さんに _____

   　　　　Watashi wa Mori-san ni _____

2. メリーはトムにコンサートに連れて行ってもらいました。

   Merii wa Tomu ni konsaato (concert) ni tsurete itte moraimashita.

   　　　　トムはメリーを _____

   　　　　Tomu wa Merii wo _____

3. 和子さんは謙さんに宿題を手伝わせました。

   Kazuko-san wa Ken-san ni shukudai wo tetsudawasemashita.

   　　　　謙さんは和子さんに _____

   　　　　Ken-san wa Kazuko-san ni _____

4. 友達が私を笑いました。

   Tomodachi ga watashi wo waraimashita.

   　　　　私は友達に _____

   　　　　Watashi wa tomodachi ni _____

5. 弟は母にミルクを買って来させられました。

   Otooto wa haha ni miruku wo katte kosaseraremashita.

   　　　　母は弟に _____

   　　　　Haha wa otooto ni _____

6. 私は父に車を使わせてもらいました。

   Watashi wa chichi ni kuruma wo tsukawasete moraimashita.

   　　　　父は私に _____

   　　　　Chichi wa watashi ni _____

7. 山田さんは奥さんを心配させました。

   Yamada-san wa oku-san wo shinpai sasemashita.

   　　　　奥さんは山田さんに _____

   　　　　Oku-san wa Yamada-san ni _____

27. Translate the following English sentences into Japanese.

1. This room is very noisy, and I cannot study.

2. Please call me tonight.

3. I said, "Let's eat something" to Yoshiko.

4. I decided to buy a new bicycle.

5. I hear the sound of rain. (Lit. The sound of rain is audible.)

6. I will write a letter to my friend in Japan beforehand.

7. I am thinking of quitting my current part-time job.

8. Let's go to the new restaurant (to see how it is).

9. I became able to speak some Japanese.

10. Small stores are closed, but large stores are open today.

Chapter 9

Conditional Clauses

TARA

<u>Formation of "~**tara**"</u>

The **tara**-form is formed by attaching "**ra**" to the plain past "**ta**-form."

Ex.		**Plain past**	**Tara-form**
<u>Copula</u>	ame da	ame **datta**	ame **datta-ra**
	ame ja/dewa nai	ame **ja/dewa nakatta**	ame **ja/dewa nakatta-ra**
<u>I-adjective</u>	ookii	ookikat**ta**	ookikat**ta-ra**
	ookiku nai	ookiku nakat**ta**	ookiku nakat**ta-ra**
<u>Na-adjective</u>	hima da	hima **datta**	hima **datta-ra**
	hima ja/dewa nai	hima **ja/dewa nakatta**	hima **ja/dewa nakatta-ra**
<u>U-verb</u>	yomu	yon**da**	yon**da-ra**
	yomanai	yoma**nakatta**	yoma**nakatta-ra**
<u>Ru-verb</u>	miru	mi**ta**	mi**ta-ra**
	minai	mi**nakatta**	mi**nakatta-ra**
<u>Irregular -verbs</u>	suru	**shita**	**shita-ra**
	shinai	shi**nakatta**	shi**nakatta-ra**
	kuru	**kita**	**kita-ra**
	konai	ko**nakatta**	ko**nakatta-ra**

<u>Copula/Adjective-tara</u>

The clause "copula/adjective +**tara**" expresses the speaker's hypothesis regarding something or somebody in the past, the present, or the future and is equivalent to the English "if it is," "if it were," or "if it had been" depending on the context.

I. Copula

1. 英語**だったら**、分かります。

   Ei-go **dattara**, wakarimasu.

   (If it is English, I can understand it.)

2. 私があなた**だったら**、そんな事はしません。

   Watashi ga anata **dattara**, sonna koto wa shimasen.

   (If I were you, I would not do such a thing.)

3. 明日雨**じゃなかったら**、テニスをしませんか。

   Ashita ame **ja nakattara**, tenisu o shimasen ka.

   (If it is not raining tomorrow, won't you play tennis?)

II. I-adjective

1. **暑かったら**、エアコンをつけてください。

   Atsukattara, eakon wo tsukete kudasai.

   (If it is hot, please turn on the air-conditioner.)

2. 新しいビデオカメラが**よくなかったら**、買いません。

   Atarashii bideo kamera ga **yoku nakattara**, kaimasen.

   (If the new video camera is not good, I will not buy it.)

III. Na-adjective

1. **好きじゃなかったら**、食べなくてもいいですよ。

   Suki ja nakattara, tabenakute mo ii desu yo.

   (If you do not like it, you do not have to eat it, you know.)

2. そのお寺が**有名だったら**、見に行ったのですが....。

   Sono o-tera ga **yuumei dattara**, mi ni itta no desu ga....

   (If that temple were famous, I would have gone to see it.)

1. Combine the given two statements by making the first one hypothetical.

   Ex. 明日雨じゃありません。テニスをしましょう。

   Ashita ame ja arimasen.   tenisu wo shimashoo.

   <u>明日雨じゃなかったら、テニスをしましょう。</u>

   <u>Ashita ame ja nakattara, tenisu wo shimashoo.</u>

1.天気が悪いです。出かけたくありません。 _____

  Tenki ga warui desu. Dekaketaku arimasen. _____

2.仕事が簡単です。早くできます。 _____

  Shigoto ga kantan desu. Hayaku dekimasu. _____

3.家が静かじゃありません。図書館で勉強します。 _____

  Uchi ga shizuka ja arimasen. Toshokan de benkyoo shimasu. _____

4.病気です。病院に行った方がいいですよ。 _____

  Byooki desu.　Byooin ni itta hoo ga ii desu yo. _____

IV. <u>Verb</u>

    The clause "V-**tara**" is interpreted as "if ~" or "when~" depending on the context.

1. 家へ**帰ったら**よく休みます。

   Uchi e **kaettara** yoku yasumimasu.

   (When I go home I will rest well.)

2. 明日時間が**あったら**電話してください。

   Ashita jikan ga **attara** denwa shite kudasai.

   (Please call me if you have time tomorrow.)

3. **分らなかったら**聞いてくださいね。

   Wakaranakattara kiite kudasaine.

   (Please ask me if you do not understand, all right?)

If a "V-**tara**" clause that is interpreted as "when" refers to an event or action in the past, the statement in the main clause always refers to an event not under the control of the speaker. In other words, the action based on the speaker's intention does not take place in the main clause. Consequently, the statement often reflects the speaker's surprise, discovery, and so forth, because it refers to an event that the speaker did not expect.

1. 家に**帰ったら**、ドアが開いていた。

   Uchi ni **kaettara**, doa ga aite ita.

   (When I went home, the door was open.)

2. 一日中**勉強したら**、頭が痛くなった。

   Ichinichi-juu **benkyoo shitara**, atama ga itaku natta.

   (When I studied all day, I got a headache.)

2. Complete the following sentences based on the English form given in parentheses.

Ex. (if it rains)

   <u>雨が降ったら</u>　出かけません。

   <u>Ame ga futtara</u>　dekakemasen.

1. (when it becomes one o'clock)

   _____ 昼ご飯を食べましょう。

   _____ hiru-gohan wo tabemashoo.

2. (when I went to the bank)

   _____ 銀行は閉まっていました。

   _____ ginkoo wa shimatte imashita.

3. (if you do not practice)

   _____上手になりませんよ。

   _____ joozu ni narimasen yo.

4. (if my friend can come)

   _____ 一緒に食事ができます。

   _____ issho ni shokuji ga dekimasu.

5. (if you know)

   _____ 教えてください。

   _____ oshiete kudasai.

6. (when the summer vacation starts)

   _____ 何をするつもりですか。

   _____ nani wo suru tsumori desu ka.

BA

The "**~ba**" clause gives a necessary condition for the main clause and corresponds to "if ~" in English. The predicate of the main clause is usually present, unless it is a counter- factual statement.

<u>Formation of "**ba**"</u>

1. Verbs: the final "**u**" of a plain non-past is replaced by "**eba**."

    Ex. ik**u** → ik**eba**

        taber**u** → taber**eba**

2. I-adjectives: the final "**i**" of a plain non-past is replaced by "**kereba**."

Ex. atsui → atsu**kereba**

3. Na-adjectives: the final "**da**" of a plain non-past is replaced by "**nara(ba)**."

Ex.   heta da → heta **nara(ba)**

4. Nouns: Noun + "**nara(ba)**"

Ex.   sensei → sensei **nara(ba)**

(The "**ba**" form of the words such as "**nai**," "**tai**," and   "**hoshii**," is formed in the same way as an I-adjective.)

1. 来週時間が**あれば**、姉とゴルフに行きたいです。

Raishuu jikan ga **areba**, ane to gorufu ni ikitai desu.

(*If I have time next week, I would like to go golfing with my older sister.*)

2. この薬を**飲まなければ**、よくなりませんよ。

Kono kusuri wo **nomanakereba**, yoku narimasen yo.

(*If you do not take this medicine, you will   not get well, you know.*)

3. **暑ければ**、エアコンをつけて下さい。

Atsukereba, eakon wo tsukete kudasai.

(*If it is hot, please turn on the air-conditioner.*)

4. これと同じのが**ほしければ**、まだありますよ。

Kore to onaji no ga **hoshikereba**, mada arimasu yo.

(*If you want the same thing as this, I still have some, you know.*)

5. コンピューターが**好きなら(ば)**、この仕事はおもしろいでしょう。

Konpyuutaa ga suki **nara(ba)**, kono shigoto wa omoshiroi deshoo.

(*If you like computer, this job will probably be   interesting.*)

6. 山田さんは映画の**ことなら(ば)**、何でも知っています。

Yamada-san wa eiga no **koto nara(ba)**, nan demo shitte imasu.

(*When it comes to movies, Mr. Yamada knows everything.*)

3. Make the following two sentences into one, changing the first sentence into a conditional expression of "**ba**."

Ex.   お金があります。旅行をします。 →   お金があれば、旅行をします。

Okane ga arimasu. Ryokoo wo shimasu. → Okane ga areba, ryokoo wo shimasu.

1. 明日雨が降ります。テニスはしません。 _____

Ashita ame ga furimasu. Tenisu wa shimasen. _____

2. 日本へ行きます。日本語が上手になるでしょう。_____

Nihon e ikimasu. Nihon-go ga joozu ni naru deshoo. _____

3. はきやすい靴だ。買いたい。_____

Haki-yasui kutsu da. Kaitai. _____

4. これは嫌いだ。食べなくてもいい。_____

Kore wa kirai da. Tabenakute mo ii. _____

5. 勉強をしません。試験ができません。_____

Benkyoo wo shimasen. Shiken ga dekimasen. _____

6. 夜遅いです。タクシーで帰ります。_____

Yoru osoi desu. Takushii de kaerimasu. _____

TO

The clause "plain non-past + **to**" is an expression which corresponds to "whenever ~," "when ~," or "if ~" in English.   In this structure, the main clause is generally referred to as a natural consequence or effect of the subordinate clause of "**to**."   Therefore, this expression is used to make a statement about a truth, a natural phenomenon, and a common fact.

1. 春になると暖かくなって花が咲き始める。

Haru ni naru **to** atatakaku natte hana ga saki-hajimeru.

(*Whenever spring comes, it gets warm and flowers start to bloom.*)

2. この道をまっすぐ行くと駅に着きますよ。

Kono michi wo massugu iku **to** eki ni tsukimasu yo.

(*If you go straight along this street, you will get to the station.*)

3. 学校が駅に近いと通うのに便利だ。

Gakkoo ga eki ni chikai **to** kayou noni benri da.

(*It is convenient to commute, when the school is near the station.*)

4. 何でも練習をしないと上手にならない。

Nan demo renshuu wo shinai **to** joozu ni naranai.

(*Whatever it is, if we do not practice we will not become good at it.*)

5. 部屋が静かだとよく眠れる。

Heya ga shizuka da **to** yoku nemureru.

(*When the room is quiet, we can sleep well.*)

4. Connect the following sentences with the clause "**to**."

Ex.　運動します。強くなります。 → 　運動すると強くなります。

　　　Undoo-shimasu.　Tsuyoku narimasu. → 　Undoo-suru to tsuyoku narimasu.

1. 書きません。漢字を覚えません。_____

　　Kakimasen.　Kanji wo oboemasen.　_____

2. 十時過ぎです。店は閉まっています。_____

　　Juu-ji sugi desu.　Mise wa shimatte imasu.　_____

3. 声が小さいです。よく聞こえません。_____

　　Koe ga chiisai desu.　Yoku kikoemasen.　_____

4. めがねをかけます。よく見えます。_____

　　Megane wo kakemasu.　Yoku miemasu. _____

Review

5. Transform the underlined words into the conditional form "**tara**," "**ba**," and "**to**."

	たら	ば	と
Ex.　便利だ　→	便利だったら	便利なら（ば）	便利だと
benri da　→	benri dattara	benri nara(ba)	benri dato

1.　早く<u>起きる</u>　　　　_____　　　_____　　　_____
　　hauaku <u>okiru</u>　　　_____　　　_____　　　_____

2.　ひまに<u>なる</u>　　　　_____　　　_____　　　_____
　　hima ni <u>naru</u>　　　_____　　　_____　　　_____

3.　部屋が<u>せまい</u>　　　_____　　　_____　　　_____
　　heya ga <u>semai</u>　　　_____　　　_____　　　_____

4.　仕事が<u>終わる</u>　　　_____　　　_____　　　_____
　　shigoto ga <u>owaru</u>　　_____　　　_____　　　_____

5.　時間が<u>ない</u>　　　　_____　　　_____　　　_____
　　jikan ga <u>nai</u>　　　　_____　　　_____　　　_____

6.　部屋が<u>きれいだ</u>　　_____　　　_____　　　_____
　　heya ga <u>kirei da</u>　　_____　　　_____　　　_____

6. Translate the following sentences into Japanese.

　　1. Whenever I drink coffee at night, I can not sleep. (use "**to**")

2. If it snows a lot, we can go skiing.   (use "**ba**")

3. If you see Mr. Yoshida today, please give this book. (use "**tara**")

4. When I make sushi, I will bring it to your house.   (use "**tara**")

5.If you are not a student, you cannot buy the cheap ticket. (use "**to**")

Chapter 10

Interrogative Words

Nani   what/what thing
Itsu   when
Dare   who
Doko   where/what place
Dotchi/Dochira   which one (of two)
Dore   which one (of more than three or more)
Ikura   how much
Doo   how/what way
Naze/Dooshite   why

1. あの人は**だれ**ですか。

   Ano hito wa **dare** desu ka.

   (Who is that person?)
2. これは**だれの**かばんですか。

   Kore wa **dare no** kaban desu ka.

   (Whose bag is this?)
3. 肉と魚と**どっち**が好きですか。

   Niku to sakana to **dotchi** ga suki desu ka.

   (Which do you like better, meat or fish?)
4. この時計は**いくら**ですか。

   Kono tokei wa **ikura** desu ka.

   (How much is this watch?)

5. **どうして**日本語を勉強していますか。

   Dooshite nihon-go wo benkyoo-shite imasu ka.

   (*Why are you studying Japanese?*)

6. **いつ**大学をそつぎょうしましたか。

   Itsu daigaku wo sotsugyoo-shimashita ka.

   (*When did you graduate from college?*)

7. **どこ**で山本さんに会いましたか。

   Doko de Yamamoto-san ni aimashita ka.

   (*Where did you meet Mr. Yamamoto?*)

8. この漢字は**どう**読みますか。

   Kono kanji wa **doo** yomimasu ka.

   (*How do you read this kanji?*)

9. これは**何**ですか。

   Kore wa **nan** desu ka.

   (*What is this?*)

10. **何を**読んでいますか。

    Nani wo yonde imasu ka.

    (*What are you reading ?*)

1. Fill in the blanks with the appropriate interrogative word based on the answers to the
2.   questions.

   Ex.   _何_ を食べますか。

          Nani wo tabemasu ka.

   1. A: 昨日 _____ に会いましたか。

         Kinoo   _____ ni aimashita ka.

      B: みち子さんに会いました。

         Michiko-san ni aimashita.

      A: _____で会いましたか。

         _____ de aimashita ka.

      B: きっさ店で会いました。

         Kissaten de aimashita.

   2. A: コンサートは_____でしたか。

         Konsaato wa _____ deshita ka.

      B: とてもよかったですよ。

         Totemo yokatta desu yo.

3. A: その時計は_____でしたか。

Sono tokei wa _____ deshita ka.

B: 二万円でした。

Niman-en deshita.

4. A: _____ 日本に行きますか。

_____ Nihon ni ikimasu ka.

B: 来年の二月に行きます。

Rainen no nigatsu ni ikimasu.

5. A: それは _____ という本ですか。

Sore wa _____ to iu hon desu ka.

B: 「こころ」という日本の小説です。

"Kokoro" to iu Nihon no shoosetsu desu.

INTERROGATIVE PHRASES WITH PARTICLES

Interrogative + "demo" in affirmative sentences

This phrase corresponds to "every ~" or "any ~" in English.

1. いつでも電話してください。

   Itsu demo denwa-shite kudasai.

   (*Please call me any time.*)

2. だれでもこの漢字は知っていますよ。

   Dare demo kono kanji wa shitte imasu yo.

   (*Everybody knows this kanji, you know.*)

3. A: どこで食べましょうか。

   Doko de tabemashoo ka.

   (*Where shall we eat ?*)

   B: どこでもいいですよ。

   Doko demo ii desu yo.

   (*Any place is fine.*)

The particles such as "**ni**," "**de**," "**to**,"and "**kara**" are used along with "**demo**" without being dropped.

1 ハンバーガーの店は**どこにでも**あります。

Hanbaagaa no mise wa **doko ni demo** arimsu.

(Hamburger shops are everywhere.)

2 佐藤先生は**だれにでも**親切です。

Satoo sensei wa **dare ni demo** shinsetsu desu.

(Prof. Sato is kind to everybody.)

3 私は**どこで**でも眠れます。

Watashi wa **doko de demo** nemuremasu.

(I can sleep in any place.)

Interrogative + "mo" in negative sentences

This phrase corresponds to " no ~" or " not any ~" in English.

1. **だれも**吉田さんの住所を**知りません**。

   Dare mo Yoshida-san no juusho wo **shirimasen**.

   (Nobody knows Mr. Yoshida's address.)

2. 暗くて**何も見えません**。

   Kurakute **nani mo miemasen**.

   (It is dark and I cannot see anything.)

3. こんな古い車は**どこにもありません**。

   Konna furui kuruma wa **doko ni mo arimasesn**.

   (You do not see this kind of old car anywhere.)

4. 昨日は**だれにも会いませんでした**。

   Kinoo wa **dare ni mo aimasen deshita**.

   (I did not see anybody yesterday.)

Note: The interrogative words "**dore**," "**itsu**," and "**dochira**" occur with "**mo**" in affirmative sentences. They are slightly different in meaning from those which occur with "**demo**" in affirmative sentences.

1.この三冊の小説は**どれも**おもしろいです。

Kono san-satsu no shoosetsu wa **dore mo** omoshiroi desu.

(Every one of these three novels is interesting.)

2. A: すしと天ぷらとどちらが好きですか。

   Sushi to tempura to dochira ga suki desu ka.

(*Which one do you like, sushi or tempura?*)

B: **どちらも**好きです。

Dochira mo suki desu.

(*I like both.*)

3. 私は**いつも**七時に起きます。

Watashi wa **itsu mo** shichi-ji ni okimasu.

(*I always get up at seven o'clock.*)

Interrogative + "ka"

This phrase corresponds to "some ~" or "any ~" in English depending on whether the sentence is affirmative or interrogative.

1. **いつか**日本に行きたいです。

Itsu ka nihon ni ikitai desu.

(*I want to go to Japan some day.*)

2. **どこか**にかぎを置いてきました。

Doko ka ni kagi wo oite kimashita.

(*I left (Lit. placed) my key somewhere.*)

3. A: オフィスに**だれか**いますか。

　　　Ofisu ni **dare ka** imasu ka.

　　　(*Is there someone in the office?*)

B: いいえ、だれもいませんよ。

　　Iie, dare mo imasen yo.

　　(*No, nobody is in the office.*)

4. **何か**聞こえますか。

　Nani ka kikoemasu ka.

　(*Do you hear anything?*)

5. 今晩、家で**何か**作って食べます。

Konban uchi de **nani ka** tsukutte tabemasu.

(*I will make something and eat at home tonight.*)

2. Fill in the blanks with the appropriate phrase using the given interrogative word.

　Ex. 私は <u>何でも 食べられ</u>ます。　　（何）

　　Watashi wa　<u>nan demo</u> taberaremasu.　(nan)

1. _____　一緒に食事をしましょう。（いつ）

_____ issho ni shokuji wo shimashoo.   (itsu)

2. うるさくて_____ 聞こえません。（何）

   Urusakute _____ kikoemasen.   (nani)

3. ここにある本は _____ 安いですよ。（どれ）

   Koko ni aru hon wa _____ yasui desu yo.   (dore)

4. 山田さんは_____いませんね。（どこ）

   Yamada-san wa _____ imasen ne.   (doko)

5. 父は毎日忙しいので _____ 遅く帰ります。（いつ）

   Chichi wa mainichi isogashii node _____ osoku kaerimasu.

6. A: 今日 _____ 行きますか。（どこ）

      Kyoo _____ ikimasu ka.   (doko)

   B: いいえ、_____行きません。（どこ）

      Iie, _____ ikimasen.   (doko)

7. _____に道を聞きましょう。（だれ）

   _____ ni michi wo kikimashoo.   (dare)

Interrogative + V-te mo/I-adj.-te mo / Na.adj- de mo

This phrase is interpreted as "no matter what/how etc." in English.

1. 何を食べても太りません。

   Nani wo **tabete mo** futorimasen.

   (*No matter what I eat, I do not get fat.*)

2. いくら勉強しても日本語が上手になりません。

   Ikura benkyoo **shite mo** nihon-go ga joozu ni narimasen.

   (*No matter how hard I study, I do not become good at Japanese.*)

3. いくら難しくても終わりまで読みます。

   Ikura muzukashikute mo owari made yomimasu.

   (*No matter how hard it is, I will read it to the end.*)

4. いつ電話をかけても忙しそうです。

   Itsu denwa wo **kakete mo** isogashi soo desu.

   (*Whenever I call, she sounds busy.*)

3. Translate the English phrases into Japanese phrases and complete the sentences.

   Ex. このレストランのすしは<u>いつ食べても</u>おいしいですね。   (whenever we eat)

      Kono resutoran no sushi wa <u>itsu tabete mo</u> oishii desu ne.

1. アメリカでは ＿＿＿＿＿＿＿＿＿ チップがいります。(wherever we eat)

    Amerika de wa ＿＿＿＿＿＿＿＿ chippu (tip) ga irimasu.

2. 父は＿＿＿＿＿＿＿＿ 毎週泳ぎに行きます。(no matter how busy he is)

    Chichi wa ＿＿＿＿＿＿＿ maishuu oyogi ni ikimasu.

3. ＿＿＿＿＿＿＿＿＿＿＿答えが分かりません。(no matter how hard I think)

    ＿＿＿＿＿＿＿＿＿＿＿ kotae ga wakarimasen.

4. この仕事は ＿＿＿＿＿＿＿＿＿ 時間がかかりますよ。(no matter who does it)

    Kono shigoto wa ＿＿＿＿＿＿＿＿ jikan ga kakarimasu yo.

Review

4. Write questions with the appropriate interrogative words based on the answers given to the questions.

   Ex. **Q:** だれが教えてくれましたか。　　**A:** 友子さんが教えてくれました。

   　　Dare ga oshiete kuremashita ka.　　Tomoko-san ga oshiete kuremashita.

1. Q: ＿＿＿＿＿＿＿＿＿＿＿＿＿＿　　A: 去年日本へ行きました。

   　　　　　　　　　　　　　　　　　　　　Kyonen Nihon e ikimashita.

2. Q: ＿＿＿＿＿＿＿＿＿＿＿＿＿＿　　A: 私のかばんです。

   　　　　　　　　　　　　　　　　　　　　Watashi no kaban desu.

3. Q: ＿＿＿＿＿＿＿＿＿＿＿＿＿＿　　A: 山田さんはフランスにいますよ。

   　　　　　　　　　　　　　　　　　　　　Yamada-san wa Furansu ni imasu yo.

4. Q: ＿＿＿＿＿＿＿＿＿＿＿＿＿＿　　A: 新聞を読んでいるんです。

   　　　　　　　　　　　　　　　　　　　　Shinbun wo yonde iru n' desu.

5. Q: ＿＿＿＿＿＿＿＿＿＿＿＿＿＿　　A: 日本へ行くから日本語を習っています。

   　　　　　　　　　　　　　　　　　　　　Nihon e iku kara nihon-go wo naratte imasu.

6. Q: ＿＿＿＿＿＿＿＿＿＿＿＿＿＿　　A: このくつは六千円でした。

   　　　　　　　　　　　　　　　　　　　　Kono kutsu wa rokusen-en deshita.

7. Q: ＿＿＿＿＿＿＿＿＿＿＿＿＿＿　　A: ボストンへは車で行きました。

   　　　　　　　　　　　　　　　　　　　　Bosuton e wa kuruma de ikimashita.

5. Translate the following English sentences into Japanese.

1. A: Did you go anywhere yesterday?

   B: No, I did not go anywhere.

2. I did not eat anything last night.

3. No matter where we go, there are Chinese restaurants.

4. A: Which is more difficult, French or German?

   B: Both of them are difficult.

5. I will drink something.

6. I asked my friend when she will return to the United States.

7. Nobody knows why Mr. Satoo did not come to the party.

8. No matter how expensive it is, I will buy it.

Chapter 11

Modification of a Noun

SENTENCE MODIFIER

A sentence which elaborates a noun is called "sentence modifier". It always precedes the modified noun (the head noun). The predicate of a sentence modifier is always in the plain form, and its subject is always marked by "**ga**." The subject marker "**ga**" in the sentence modifier may be interchangeable with "**no**."

1. 私が/の買った本はスペイン語の本です。

   Watashi ga/no katta hon wa supein-go no hon desu.

   (The book I bought is a Spanish book.)

2. リンダさんが/の住んでいる所はあまり静かじゃありません。

   Rinda-san ga/no sunde iru tokoro wa amari shizuka ja arimasen.

   (The place where Linda lives is not so quiet.)

3. 金子さんが/の書いた本を読みましたか。

   Kaneko-san ga/no kaita hon wo yomimashita ka.

   (Did you read the book Mr. Kaneko wrote?)

4. あの先生が/の言う事をよく聞いてください。

   Ano sensei ga/no iu koto wo yoku kiite kudasai.

   (Please listen carefully (Lit. well) to what the teacher says.)

5. 東京から京都まで行く電車に乗りました。

   Tokyo kara Kyoto mede iku densha ni norimashita.

   (I took a train which goes from Tokyo to Kyoto.)

6. 正さんは旅行で会った人と結婚しました。

   Tadashi-san wa **ryokoo de atta** hito to kekkon shimashita.

(*Tadashi married the person whom he met on a trip.*)

7. 酒を飲まない人はジュースを飲んでください。

Sake wo nomanai hito wa juusu wo nonde kudasai.

(*Those who do not drink sake, please have some juice.*)

8. 若いときバレリーナだった人とパーティで話しました。

Wakai toki barerriina datta hito to paatii de hanashimashita.

(*I talked with a person, at a party, who was a ballerina when she was young.*)

9. 目が/の青い猫を見たことがありますか。

Me ga/no aoi neko wo mita koto ga arimasu ka.

(*Have you ever seen a cat with blue eyes?*)

10. ギターが/の上手だったコーエンさんはアメリカに帰りました。

Gitaa ga/no joozu datta Kooen-san wa Amerika ni kaerimashita.

(*Mr. Cohen, who played the guitar well, went back to the United States.*)

1. Write the corresponding Japanese version of the following English phrases.

     Ex.   The computer which my brother bought   <u>兄が買ったコンピューター</u>

                                                            <u>Ani ga katta conpyuutaa</u>

     1. The movie which I saw last year

     2. The park I often go to

     3. The newspaper which was on my desk

     4. The book which my friend borrowed from the library

     5. The teacher who is teaching Japanese

2. Identify the head noun (modified noun) and its sentence modifier for each sentence.

     Ex.   ピアノを弾いている人が野田さんです。

         Piano wo hiite iru hito ga Noda-san desu.

            Head noun   <u>人 (hito)</u>

            Sentence modifier   <u>ピアノを弾いている (Piano wo hiiteiru)</u>

     1. 昨日学校で会った人はとき子さんの妹さんです。

         Kinoo gakoo de atta hito wa Tokiko-san no imooto-san desu.

            Head noun _____

            Sentence modifier _____

2. 母は父にもらった時計を私にくれました。

   Haha wa chichi ni moratta tokei wo watashi ni kuremashita.

        Head noun _____

        Sentence modifier _____ .

3. このカメラはリーさんが日本で買ったものです。

   Kono kamera wa Ree (Lee)-san ga Nihon de katta mono desu.

        Head noun _____

        Sentence modifier _____

4. 先生の言った事を覚えていますか。

   Sensei no itta koto wo oboete imasu ka.

        Head noun _____

        Sentence modifier _____

5. 窓から子供の話す声が聞こえます。

   Mado kara kodomo no hanasu koe ga kikoemasu.

        Head noun _____

        Sentence modifier _____

6. 毎日兄がくれた辞書を使っています。

   Mainichi ani ga kureta jisho wo tsukatte imasu.

        Head noun _____

        Sentence modifier _____

3. Combine the following pairs of sentences using a sentence modifier. The noun in parentheses is a head noun.

    Ex.   母はすしを作りました。(すし)を友達と食べました。

        Haha wa sushi wo tsukurimashita.   (Sushi) wo tomodachi to tabemashita.

        母が作ったすしを友達と食べました。

        <u>Haha ga tsukutta shushi wo tomodachi to tabemashita。</u>

1. 昨日まりさんはデパートへ行きました。(デパート)はとても大きいです。

   Kinoo Mari-san wa depaato e ikimashita. (Depaato) wa totemo ookii desu.

   _____ .

2. 東京で(鈴木さん)に会いました。鈴木さんはI.B.M.につとめています。

   Tokyoo de (Suzuki-san) ni aimashita. Suzuki-san wa I.B.M ni tsutomete imasu.

   _____ .

3. 先週(おもしろい本)を読みました。山田さんはおもしろい本を書きました。

Senshuu (omoshiroi hon) wo yomimashita. Yamada-san wa omoshiroi hon wo kakimashita.

_____.

4. ポールさんはケーキを作ります。(ケーキ)はいつもおいしいです。

Pooru-san wa keeki (cake) wo tsukurimasu. (Keeki) wa itsumo oishii desu.

_____.

5. (アパート)を見に行きました。野中さんは先月アパートを買いました。

(Apaato) wo mi ni ikimashita. Nonaka-san wa sengetsu apaato wo kaimashita.

_____.

6. (エリックさん)を待っています。エリックさんは車のかぎを取りに行きました。

(Erikku-san) wo matte imasu. Erikku-san wa kuruma no kagi wo tori ni ikimashta.

_____.

4. Give the Japanese equivalent to the following English sentences.

1. Please show me the book you bought yesterday.
2. Is this the video that you wanted to watch?
3. I am using the computer which my older brother gave me.
4. Mr. Tomita is working for a company where his father was the president.
5. Kazuo is going to Boston by car, which his younger sister will drive.
6. I think the apple pie which my mother makes is the best.
7. Do you know the person who sent me this letter?

Chapter 12

Nominalization

Japanese verbs can be changed to nouns by attaching "**koto**" or "**no**" to the plain non-past form. "V (plain non-past) + **koto/no**" corresponds to an infinitive or a gerund in English. "**Koto**" and "**no**" are not always interchangeable.

NO

V(plain non-past) + no wa ~(da)

The expression "V(plain non-past) + **no wa** ~(**da**)" corresponds to "to do/doing such and such is ~" or "It is ~ to do such and such" in English.

1. 日本語で**話すのは**あまり難しくない。

   Nihon-go de **hanasu no wa** amari muzukashiku nai.

   (To speak in Japanese is not so difficult.)

2. タバコを**吸うのは**体によくない。

   Tabako wo suu no wa karada ni yoku nai.

   (Smoking is not good for health /Lit. body.)

3. US オープンを**見るのは**おもしろいですね。

   U.S. oopun wo **miru no wa** omoshiroi desu ne.

   (Watching the U.S. Open is interesting, isn't it?)

4. 何時間も**運転するのは**大変です。

   Nan-jikan mo **unten-suru no wa** taihen desu.

   (Driving for many hours is hard.)

155

X wa V(plain non-past) + no ga ~da

The expression "X **wa** V(plain non-past) + **no ga** ~**da**" often takes place with the predicates such as "**suki da**," "**kirai da**," "**joozu da**," "**heta da**," and corresponds to "X likes," "X dislikes," "X is good at ~," and "X is not good at ~" in English.

1. 信子さんは本を**読むのが**嫌いです。

   Nobuko-san wa hon wo **yomu no ga** kirai desu.

   (Nobuko does not like reading.)

2. 太郎さんは絵を**描くのが**上手です。

   Taroo-san wa e wo **kaku no ga** joozu desu.

   (Taroo is good at drawing pictures.)

V(plain non-past) + no wo/ga + V(senses/perception)

The predicate "V(plain non-past) + **no wo/ga** + V" is the verb of senses, perception, etc., such as "**kiku**," "**kikoeru**," "**miru**," "**mieru**."

1. 誰かが歌を歌っ**ているのが**聞こえる。

   Dare ka ga uta to **utatte iru no ga** kikoeru.

   (I can hear someone singing.)

2. 雪江さんが**泣いているのを**見ました。

   Yukie-san ga **naite iru no wo** mimashita.

   (I saw Yukie crying.)

V(plain non-past) + no wo + V(waiting, helping, etc.)

The predicate "V(plain non-past) + **no wo** + V" is the verb of waiting, helping, stopping, discovery, etc., such as "**matsu**," "**tetsudau**," "**yameru**," and "**mitsukeru**."

1. ここで谷さんが**来るのを**待ちましょう。

   Koko de Tani-san ga **kuru no wo** machimashoo.

   (Let's wait here for Mr. Tanaka to come.)

2. 明日友達が新しいアパートに**移るのを**手伝います。

   Ashita tomodachi ga atarashii apaato ni **utsuru no wo** tetsudaimasu.

   (Tomorrow I am going to help my friend move into a new apartment.)

3. 敏江さんは大学に**行くのを**止めて、会社で働いています。

   Toshie-san wa daigaku ni **iku no wo** yamete, kaisha de hataraite imasu.

   (Toshie quit going to college and is working for a company.)

V(plain non-past) + no ni ~

The expression "V(plain non-past) + **no ni** ~" indicates the purpose and is equivalent to "~ in order to do such and such" or "~ for doing such and such" in English. It is often followed by expression of stative nature, such as "**ii**," "**benri da**," "**hitsuyoo da**," and "**kakaru**."

1. この靴は**ジョギングするのに**いい。

   Kono kutsu wa **jogingu suru no ni** ii.

   (These shoes are good for jogging.)

2. その箱は本を**送るのに**ちょうどいい。

   Sono hako wa hon wo **okuru no ni** choodo ii.

   (That box is just right for sending books.)

3. すきやきを作る**のに**何がいりますか。

   Sukiyaki wo tsukuru **no ni** nani ga irimasu ka.

   (What do you need (Lit. what are needed) to make Sukiyaki?)

4. 歴史のレポートを**書くのに**三週間かかりました。

   Rekishi no repooto wo **kaku no ni** san-shuukan kakarimashita.

   (It took three weeks to write a paper on history.)

KOTO

The following are frequently used expressions with "**koto**."

V (plain non-past) + koto ga dekiru

The expression "V (plain non-past) + **koto ga/wa dekiru**" indicates potentiality and is equivalent to "be able to do such and such" in English.

1. 去年の夏あまりお金がなかったので、旅行に**行くことができ**なかった。

   Kyonen no natsu amari o-kane ga nakatta node, ryokoo ni **iku koto ga dekinakatta.**

   (I did not have much money last summer, so I was not able to go on a trip.)

2. 私はフランス語を**話すことはできます**が、**書くことはできません**。

   Watashi wa furansu-go wo **hanasu koto wa dekimasu** ga, **kaku koto wa dekimasnen.**

   (I am able to speak French, but cannot write it.)

3. 自分の国に**帰ることができない**のは悲しいです。

   Jibun no kuni ni **kaeru koto ga dekinai** no wa kanashii desu.

   (It is sad not being able to go back to one's own country.)

4. 昨日は水が出なかったので、**料理することができませんでした**。

Kinoo wa mizu ga denakatta node, ryoori **suru koto ga dekimasen deshita**.

(Since there was no water, I was not able to cook yesterday.)

Note: In the case of verbs which are constructed by attaching "**suru**" to a noun, such as "**benkyoo suru**," "**unten suru**," "**sooji suru**," and "**kaimono suru**", the potential form can be expressed with "noun **ga dekiru**" as well as with "noun **suru koto ga dekiru**." Example: Benkyoo **dekiru** = Benkyoo **suru koto ga dekiru.**

V (plain non-past) + koto ni suru

"V (plain non-past) + **koto ni suru**" corresponds to "a person decides to do such and such" in English.   (Cf. Chapter 8, Verb, pp. 110: V (plain non-past) + koto ni suru)

V(plain non-past) + koto ni naru

"V (plain non-past) + **koto ni naru**" corresponds to "It is decided to/that ~" in English.
(Cf. Chapter 8, Verb, pp. 110: V(plain non-past) + koto ni naru)

1. Select either "**koto**" or "**no**" in order to complete the following sentences.

1. 日本語を勉強する（**こと、の**）はおもしろいけれど、時間がかかります。

Nihon-go wo benkyoo suru (**koto, no**) wa omoshiroi keredo, jikan ga kakarimasu.

2. 兄の家にはプールがあるから.いつでも泳ぐ（**こと、の**）ができます。

Ani no uchi ni wa puuru ga aru kara, itsu demo oyogu (**koto, no**) ga dekimasu.

3. となりの人がピアノを練習している（**こと、の**）が聞こえます。

Tonari no hito ga piano wo renshuu shite iru (**koto, no**) ga kikoemasu.

4. 毎日一時間運動する（**こと、の**）にしています。

Minichi ichi-jikan undoo suru (**koto, no**) ni shite imasu.

5. 日本では一月一日にもちを食べる（**こと、の**）になっている。

Nihon de wa ichi-gatsu tsuitachi ni mochi (rice cake) wo taberu (**koto, no**) ni natte iru.

6. 悟さんは風呂に入る（**こと、の**）が大好きです。

Satoru-san wa furo ni hairu (**koto, no**) ga daisuki desu.

2. Write the corresponding Japanese sentences corresponding to the following English sentences.

1. Are you able to sing in front of people?

2. I decided to take a vacation in September.

3. Kate always helps her mother cooking dinner.

4. A big city is convenient to live.

5. I don't like so much going to a big party.

6. It has been decided that I will work for the Bank of Tokyo from next week.

7. One needs a token in order to ride a subway in Boston.

Chapter 13

Modality

TSUMORI

The noun "**tsumori**" indicates the speaker's intention. "V(plain non-past) + **tsumori da**" is equivalent to "intend to do such and such" in English.

1. 明日は会社に十時ごろ行く**つもりです**。

   Ashita wa kaisha ni juu-ji goro iku **tsumori desu**.

   (I intend to go to work around ten o'clock tomorrow.)

2. 去年スペイン語を勉強する**つもりでした**が、できませんでした。

   Kyonen supein-go wo benkyoo suru **tsumori deshita ga**, dekimasen deshita.

   (I intended to study Spanish last year, but I couldn't do it.)

3. タバコは吸わない**つもりです**。

   Tabako wa suwanai **tsumori desu**

   (I intend not to smoke.)

4. 私は正夫さんと結婚する**つもりはありません**。

   Watashi wa Masao-san to kekkon suru **tsumori wa arimasen**.

   (I have no intention to marry Masao.)

HAZU

The noun "**hazu**" indicates the speaker's expectation concerning something or somebody, but not the speaker himself/herself. The expression "**~ hazu da**" is equivalent to " something or someone is expected to be so and so or to do such and such," "should," etc., in English. The expectation expressed by "**hazu**" does not refer to one's desire, wish, and the like.

<u>Formation of the word preceding "**hazu**"</u>

1. Verbs: V(plain) + "**hazu da**"   Ex.   iku → iku **hazu da**

2. I-adjectives: dictionary form+ "**hazu da**"   Ex.   atsui → atsui **hazu da**

3. Na-adjectives: change the final "**da**" to "**na**" + "**hazu da**"   Ex. rippa **da** → rippa **na hazu da**

4. Nouns: Noun + "**no**" + "**hazu da**"   Ex.   sensei → sensei **no hazu da**

1. あの人は今**四十五才のはずです**。

   Ano hito wa ima **yonjuugo-sai no hazu desu**.

   (She/he is expected to be forty-five years old now.)

2. はなさんは大学を**卒業したはずです**よ。

   Hana-san wa daigaku wo **sotsugyoo shita hazu desu** yo.

   (Hana is supposed to have graduated from a college.)

3. 君江さんは病気だから、**来ないはずです**よ。

   Kimie-san wa byooki da kara, **konai hazu desu** yo.

   (Kimie is expected not to come, since she is sick.)

4. このコンピューターは**簡単なはずです**。

   Kono konpyuutaa wa **kantan na hazu desu**.

   (This computer should be simple.)

5. このケーキは砂糖をあまり入れなかったから、**甘くないはずです**。

   Kono keeki wa satoo wo amai irenakatta kara, **amaku nai hazu desu**.

   (This cake should not be sweet, because I did not put too much sugar in it.)

6. こんな難しい漢字は誰にも**書けないはずです**。

   Konna muzukashii kanji wa dare ni mo **kakenai hazu desu**.

   (It is improbable that anyone can write such a difficult kanji.)

1. Supply either "**tsumori**" or "**hazu**" for the following sentences.

1. 私は来年仕事をさがす _____ です。

   Watashi wa rainen shgoto wo sagasu _____ desu.

2. 図書館にはクーラーがあるから、暑くない _____ です。

   Toshokan ni wa kuuraa ga aru kara, atsuku nai _____ desu.

3. 田中先生の講演はおもしろいから、聴きに行く _____ です。

   Tanaka-sensei no kooen wa omoshiroi kara, kiki ni iku _____ desu.

4. 明日天気がよかったら、私は友達とピクニックをする _____ です。

Ashita tenki ga yokattara, watashi wa tomodachi to pikunikku wo suru _____ desu.

5. スミスさんは医者に止めるように言われたから、タバコは吸わない _____ だ。

Sumisu-san wa isha ni yameru yoo ni iwareta kara, tabako wa suwanai _____ da.

YOO (MITAI)

Conjecture

"~ **Yoo da** " indicates the speaker's conjecture through his or her reasoning process based on his or her observation, or a first-hand information. It is equivalent to "it seems that ~," "It looks like ~," or "it appears to ~" in English. "**Mitai da**" is a colloquial expression of "**yoo da**." When the word preceding "**mitai**" is a **na**- adjective or a noun, "**na**" of "**na**-adjective," or "**no**" following a noun it is dropped.

Formation of the word preceding "**yoo**"

1. Verbs: V(plain) + "**yoo da**"   Ex. iku → iku **yoo da**
2. I-adjectives: dictionary form+ "**yoo da**"   Ex. atsui → atsui **yoo da**
3. Na-adjectives: change the final "**da**" to "**na**" + "**yoo da**"   Ex. rippa **da** → rippa **na yoo da**
4. Nouns: Noun + "**no**" + "**yoo da**"   Ex. sensei → sensei **no yoo da**

1. お母さんが京都にいるから、休みに良子さんは日本へ**行くよう**（**行くみたい**）**です**。

Okaasan ga Kyooto ni iru kara, yasumi ni Yoshiko-san wa Nihon e **iku yoo (iku mitai) desu**.

(It appears that Yoshiko is going to Japan during the holidays, since her mother is in Kyoto.)

2. あのレストランは**おいしいよう**（**おいしいみたい**）**です**よ。いつもたくさん人がいます。

Ano resutoran wa **oishii yoo (oishii mitai) desu** yo. Itsumo takusan hito ga imasu.

(It seems that the restaurant is good. There are always many people there.)

4. 電子辞書は**便利なよう**（**便利みたい**）**です**ね。みんなが使っていますよ。

Denshi-jisho wa benri na **yoo** (benri **mitai**) **desu** ne. Minna ga tsukatte imasu yo.

(It seems that an electronic dictionary is convenient, doesn't it? Everyone is using it.)

5. 一男さんは**病気のよう**（**病気みたい**）**です**が、パーティに来ると思いますか。

Kazuo-san wa byooki no **yoo** (byooki **mitai**) **desu** ga, paatii ni kuru to omoimasu ka.

(It seems that Kazuo is sick, but do you think he will come to the party?)

2. Change the following words into an expression containing "**~ yoo da**" and "**~ mitai da**."

Ex.   行きます → 行くようです → 行くみたいです

Ex.   Ikimasu → <u>iku yoo desu</u> → <u>iku mitai desu</u>

1. 帰ります
   kaerimasu   _____   _____
2. 大きいです
   ookii desu   _____   _____
3. 話します
   hanashimasu   _____   _____
4. 正直です
   shoojiki desu   _____   _____
5. アメリカ人です
   amerika-jin desu _____   _____
6. 安いです
   yasui desu   _____   _____
7. 医者です
   isha desu   _____   _____
8. 好きです
   suki desu   _____   _____

Resemblance

Typically "noun + **no yoo da**" is used as a simile and is equivalent to "~like (noun)" or "look as if (noun)" in English. "**Yoo da**" conjugates the same way as a **na**-adjective.

1. 春さんは**子供のよう**（子供**みたい**）**です**ね。
   Haru-san wa **Kodomo no yoo** (kodomo **mitai**) **desu** ne.
   (Haru is like a child, isn't she?)
2. 川田さんは**アメリカ人のよう**（アメリカ人**みたい**）に英語を話します。
   Kawada san wa **amerika-jin no yoo** (amerika-jin **mitai**) **ni** ei-go wo hanashimasu.
   (Mr. Kawada speaks English like an American.)
3. (It is winter)
   今日は暖かくて、**春のよう**（春**みたい**）**な**日ですね
   Kyoo wa atatakakute, **haru no yoo** (haru **mitai**) **na** hi desu ne.
   (Today, it is warm and like spring, isn't it?)

RASHII

Conjecture

"**~ Rashii**" indicates the speaker's conjecture based on mainly what she or he has heard or read, while "**yoo da**" indicates the speaker's conjecture through his or her reasoning process based on a first-hand information. It is equivalent to "It seems that ~," "it looks like ~," or "it appears to ~" in English.

Cf.   期末試験は難しかった**らしい**。

Kimatsu shiken wa muzukashikatta **rashii**.

(Judging from what I heard from the students, the final test seems to have been difficult.)

期末試験は難しかった**ようだ**。

Kimatsu shiken wa muzukashikatta **yoo da**.

(Judging from the poor results, the final test seems to have been difficult.)

Formation of the word preceding "rahii"

1. Verbs: V(plain) + "**rashii**"   Ex.   iku → iku **rashii**
2. I-adjectives: dictionary form+ "**rashii**"   Ex.   **atsui** → atsui **rashii**
3. Na-adjectives: drop the final "**da**" + "**rashii**"   Ex. rippa **da** → rippa **rashii**
4. Nouns: Noun + "**rashii**"   Ex.   sensei → sensei **rashii**

1. あの会社のサラリーはとても**いいらしい**ですよ。

   Ano kaisha no sararii wa totemo ii **rashii** desu yo.

   (It appears that the pay of that company is very good.)

2. あのピアニストはあまり**上手じゃないらしい**です。

   Ano pianisuto wa amari joozu ja nai **rashii** desu.

   (I understand that the pianist is not very good.)

3. 富田さんの奥さんは静かな**人らしい**。

   Tomita-san no oku-san wa shizuka na **hito rashii**.

   (Mr. Tomita's wife seems quiet /Lit. a quiet person.)

4. 南さんの新しいうちは**立派らしい**ですよ。

   Minami-san no atarashii uchi wa **rippa rashii** desu yo.

   (I understand that Mr. Minami's new residence is magnificent.)

5. 良夫さんと美津子さんは休みにアラスカへ**行ったらしい**。

   Yoshio-san to Mitsuko-san wa yasumi ni Arasuka e **itta rashii**.

   (It seems that Yoshio and Mitsuko went to Alaska on their holiday.)

Typical model

"Noun + **rashii**" signifies a noun that embodies typical or widely accepted ideas associated with that noun. "**Rashii**" conjugates the same way as an **i**-adjective.

1. (It is spring)

   今日は春**らしい**日ですね。

   Kyoo wa haru **rashii** hi desu ne.

   (Today it is really a typical spring day, isn't it?)

2. 星野さんは日本人**らしい**人です。

   Hoshino-san wa nihon-jin **rashii** hito desu.

   (Mrs. Hoshino is a typical Japanese.)

3. 浩は子供**らしくない**。

   Hiroshi wa kodomo **rashiku nai**.

   (Hiroshi doesn't act like a child /Lit. is not like a child.)

3. Fill in the blank lines with the phrase "**yoo**" or "**rashii**" according to the given English phrase.

1. トムさんは日本語がとても上手で、＿＿＿＿＿＿＿＿ (like a Japanese) 話します。

   Tomu –san wa nihon-go ga totemo joozu de, ＿＿＿＿＿＿＿ (like a Japanese) hanashimasu.

2. 今はまだ二月ですが、暖かくて＿＿＿＿＿＿＿ (like spring) です。

   Ima wa mada ni-gatsu desu ga, atatakakute ＿＿＿＿＿＿ (like spring) desu.

3. 桜も咲いて今日は本当に＿＿＿＿＿＿＿ (typical springlike day) ですね。

   Sakura mo saite kyoo wa hontoo ni ＿＿＿＿＿ (typical springlike day) desu ne.

4. 友達から聞きましたが、山田さんは＿＿＿＿＿＿ (seems to get married) です。

   Tomodachi kara kikimashita ga, Yamada-san wa ＿＿＿＿＿＿＿ (seems to get married) desu.

5. 真紀さんはアスピリンを飲んでいましたよ。＿＿＿＿＿＿＿ (appears to have a headache) です。

   Maki-san wa asupirin wo nonde imashita yo. ＿＿＿＿＿＿＿ (appears to have a headache) desu.

SOO

Conjecture

"**Soo**" indicates the speaker's subjective conjecture based on what she or he sees or how she or he feels. It conjugates the same way as a **na**-adjective.

Formation of the word preceding "**soo**"

1. Verbs: V-stem + "**soo da**"   Ex. **naku → naki** masu → **naki soo da**
2. I-adjectives: dictionary form minus the last "**i**" + "**soo da**"   Ex. atsu-i → **atsu soo da**
3. Na-adjectives: drop the final "**da**" + "**soo da**"   Ex. rippa **da** → rippa **soo da**

1. [空を見て]　雨が**降りそうです**ね。

   [Sora wo mite]   Ame ga **furi soo desu** ne.

   [Looking at the sky]   (It looks like it will rain, doesn't it?)
2. [ケーキを見て]　**おいしそうな**ケーキですね。

   [Keeki wo mite]   **Oishi soo na** keeki desu ne.

   [Looking at a piece of cake]   (It looks delicious /Lit. delicious cake, isn't it?)
3. [野田さんに会って]　野田さんは**正直そうな**人ですね。

   [Noda-san ni atte]   Noda-san wa **shoojiki soo na** hito desu ne.

   [Having met Mr. Noda]   (Mr. Noda looks like an honest man.)
4. [本を見て]　面白く**なさそうな**本です。

   [Hon wo mite]   Omoshiroku **nasa soo na** hon desu.

   [Looking at the book]   (It looks like an uninteresting book.)
5. [カメラを見て]　このカメラは**よさそうです**よ。

   [Kamera wo mite]   Kono kamera wa **yosa soo desu** yo.

   [Looking at the camera]   (This camera looks good, you know.)

Note: "looks not ~" → "~**nasa soo da**" and "looks good" → "**yosa soo da**"

Hearsay

"**Soo da**" indicates that the sentence preceding "**soo**" is what the speaker heard.

Formation of the word preceding "**soo**"

1. Verbs: V(plain)+ "**soo da**"   Ex. iku → iku **soo da**
2. I-adjectives: plain form + "**soo da**"   Ex. atsui → atsui **soo da**

3. Na-adjectives: plain form + "**soo da**"   Ex. rippa da → rippa da **soo da**

4. Noun: Noun + "**da**" + "**soo da**"   Ex. sensei **da** → sensei **da soo da**

1. 透さんの犬はおととい**死んだそうです**。

   Tooru-san no inu wa ototoi **shinda soo desu**.

   (I heard that Tooru's dog died the day before yesterday.)

2. ボストンのホテルは**高いそうです**。

   Bosuton no hoteru wa **takai soo desu**.

   (I understand that hotels in Boston are expensive.)

3. ワシントンの桜はとても**きれいだそうです**。

   Washinton no sakura wa totemi **kirei da soo desu**.

   (I have heard that the cherry blossoms in Washington are very beautiful.)

4. 鈴木さんは**セールスマンだったそうです**。

   uzuki-san wa **seerusuman datta soo desu**.

   (I heard that Mr. Suzuki was a salesman.)

4. Change the underlined word(s) into an expression using "**soo**" of conjecture or of hearsay.

   Ex.   このレストランは<u>安いです</u>。 → (hearsay) <u>安いそうです</u>。

   Kono resutoran wa <u>yasui desu</u> → (hearsay) <u>yasui soo desu</u>

   郁子さんはテニスが<u>上手です</u>。 → (conjecture) <u>上手そうです</u>。

   Ikuko-san wa tenisu ga <u>joozu desu</u>. → (conjecture) <u>joozu soo desu</u>.

1. 今晩台風が<u>来ます</u>。   (hearsay) _____.

   Konban taifuu ga <u>kimasu</u>.   (hearsay) _____.

2. あの子供は<u>泣きます</u>。 (conjecture) _____.

   Ano kodomo wa <u>nakimasu</u>.   (conjecture) _____.

3. 敏子さんの時計は<u>高かったです</u>。 (hearsay) _____.

   Toshiko-san no tokei wa <u>takakatta desu</u>.   (hearsay) _____.

4. この本は<u>難しいです</u>。 (conjecture) _____.

   Kono hon wa <u>muzukashii desu</u>.   (conjecture) _____.

5. 友子さんのアパートは<u>静かです</u>。 (hearsay) _____.

   Tomoko-san no apaato wa <u>shizuka desu</u>.   (hearsay) _____.

6. 一男さんの小さい辞書は<u>便利です</u>。 (conjecture) _____.

   Kazuo-san no chiisai jisho wa <u>benri desu</u>.   (conjecture) _____.

NO DA / N' DA

Explanation

"~ **No da** / ~ **n' da**" refers to an explanatory sentence about shared information with the hearer. "~ **no da**" is used in the written Japanese, while "~ **n' da**" is used in spoken Japanese.

1. (B is running)
    A: どうした**んです**か。

    Doo shita **n' desu** ka.

    (What happened to you?)

    B: 授業に遅れそうな**んです**。

    Jugyoo ni okure soo na **n' desu**.

    (I am late for class.)

2. A: いい時計ですね。

    Ii tokei desu ne.

    (It is a nice watch, isn't it?)

    B: そうですか。ヨーロッパで買った**んです**。

    Soo desu ka. Yooroppa de katta **n' desu**.

    (Do you think so? /Lit. is it so?   I bought it in Europe.)

3. A: 明日一緒に映画を見に行きませんか。

    Ashita issho ni eiga wo mi ni ikimasen ka.

    (Won't you go to see a movie with me tomorrow?)

    B: ええと、明日はちょっと都合が悪い**んです**けど。あさってはどうですか。

    Eeto, ashita wa chotto tsugoo ga warui **n' desu** kedo. Asatte wa doo desu ka.

    (Well, tomorrow is not good for me, but how about the day after tomorrow?)

Seeking attention

"~ **No da** / ~ **n' da**" is also used to draw the hearer's attention and to involve him or her in what the speaker is talking about.

1. 頭が痛い**んです**が、帰ってもいいですか。

    Atama ga itai **n' desu** ga, kaette mo ii desu ka.

    (I have a headache. May I go home?)

2. 昨日映画を見た**んです**けど、面白かったですよ。

    Kinoo eiga wo mita **n' desu** kedo, omoshirokatta desu yo.

    (I saw a movie yesterday. It was very interesting.)

3. パーティーでおもしろい人にあった**んです**けど、電話番号を聞きませんでした。

Paatii de omoshiroi hito ni atta **n' desu** kedo, denwa-bangoo wo kikimasen deshita.

(I met an interesting person at a party, but I did not ask for his telephone number.)

4. 私のルームメートはぜんぜんそうじしない**んです**よ。だから部屋はいつもきたないんです。

Watashi no ruumu-meito wa zenzen sooji shinai **n' desu** yo. Dakara heya wa

itsumo kitanai n' desu.

(My roommate doesn't clean at all. That's why our room is always dirty.)

5. Give the Japanese equivalent to the following English sentences, using the expression "**n' desu**."

1. A: Why don't you eat sushi?

   B: I do not like fish.

2. I have two tickets for a concert, won't you go with me?

3. Although this dress was expensive, I bought it because I liked it very much.

4. Where were you? I was looking for you.

Review

6. Complete the following sentences by writing the number from the left-hand phrase in the appropriate blank on the right.

1. 田中さんは日本人 　　　　　　　　　　　　　　　　____ のような人です。

   Tanaka-san wa nihon-jin 　　　　　　　　　　　____ no yoo na hito desu.

2. 新しいラップトップ（lap-top）を見ましたが 　　　　____ つもりです。

   Atarashii rappu-toppu (lap-top) wo mimashita ga, 　　____ tsumori desu.

3. 正子さんの話では、美代さんのアパートは 　　　　　　____ らしい人です。

   Masako-san no hanashi de wa, Miyo-san no apaato wa 　　____ rashii hito desu.

4. 私は結婚しない 　　　　　　　　　　　　　　　　　____ はずです。

   Watashi wa kekkon shinai 　　　　　　　　　　　____ hazu desu.

5. スミスさんは日本人 　　　　　　　　　　　　　　　____ いいそうです。

   Sumisu-san wa nihon-jin 　　　　　　　　　　　　____ ii soo desu.

6. 山田さんは三時になったら、来る 　　　　　　　　　____ 便利そうです。

   Yamada-san wa san-ji ni nattara, kuru 　　　　　　____ benri soo desu.

7. Give the Japanese equivalent to the following English sentences.

1. Kiyoshi should not be able to drive, since he is 15 years old.

2. This vinyl (biniiru) looks like leather.

3. These peaches (momo) look delicious. Let's buy some.

4. Beethoven's sonatas have truly classical sound (are really classical music like), aren't they?

5. I intended to study English and came to the United Sates.

6. Taroo is a child, but he talks like an adult.

7. My father is expected to come from Tokyo today.

8. I heard that Takeda-san is going back to Osaka soon.

Chapter 14

Honorific Expressions

In Japanese there are two ways of expressing your respect to others, especially a person of the higher status or one's seniors. One is the honorific form, and the other is the humble form. The honorific form refers to an action or a state of the person whom the speaker respects, and this humble form refers to an action or a state of the speaker or his or her in-group, such as his or her family.

THE SPECIAL HONORIFIC AND HUMBLE FORMS

Verbs

	Honorific form	Humble form
1. いる * iru * *(to exist)*	いらっしゃる / いらっしゃいます irassharu / irasshaimasu	おる / おります oru / orimasu
2. 行く * iku * *(to go)*	いらっしゃる / いらっしゃいます irassharu / irasshaimasu	参る / 参ります mairu / mairimasu
3. 来る * kuru * *(to come)*	いらっしゃる / いらっしゃいます irassharu / irasshaimasu	参る / 参ります mairu / mairimasu
4. 言う * iu * *(to say)*	おっしゃる / おっしゃいます ossharu / osshaimasu	申す / 申します moosu / mooshimasu

5.	する suru *(to do)*	なさる / なさいます nasaru / nasaimasu	いたす / いたします itasu / itashimasu
6.	食べる taberu *(to eat)*	めしあがる / めしあがります meshiagaru / meshiagarimasu	いただく / いただきます itadaku / itadakimasu
7.	飲む nomu *(to drink)*	めしあがる / めしあがります meshiagaru / meshiagarimasu	いただく / いただきます itadaku / itadakimasu
8.	見る miru *(to see)*	ごらんになる / ごらんになります goran ni naru / goran ni narimasu	拝見する / 拝見します＊＊ haiken suru / haiken shimasu **
9.	知る shiru *(to know)*	ご存知だ / ご存知です gozonji da / gozonji desu	存知る / 存知ます zonjiru / zonjimasu
10.	くれる ＊ kureru * *(to give)*	くださる / くださいます kudasaru / kudasaimasu	_____
11.	あげる ageru *(to give)*	_____	さしあげる / さしあげます sashiageru / sashiagemasu
12.	もらう morau *(to receive)*	_____	いただく / いただきます itadaku / itadakimasu
13.	聞く kiku *(to hear, to ask)*	_____	伺う / 伺います ukagau / ukagaimasu
14.	会う au *(to meet)*	_____	お目にかかる / お目にかかります ome ni kakaru / ome ni kakarimasu

* The honorific form of the verbs with asterisked (*) above conjugates as a **u**-verb, except for the **masu**-form, in which the "**r**" of "-**r**imasu" is dropped: irassha**rimasu** → irassha**imasu**

  ** An object of "**haiken suru**" has to be something which belongs to a person whom the speaker respects: **Sensei no o-tegami** wo haiken shimashita.

Copula

Honorific form	Humble form

~ だ   ~ でいらっしゃる / ~ でいらっしゃいます   ~ でござる / ~ でございます

~ da   ~ de irassharu / de irasshaimasu   ~ de gozaru / ~ de gozaimasu

(to be)

Note: The honorific form and humble forms of copula "**da**" conjugate as a **u**-verb, except for the **masu**-form, in which "**r**" of "**-r**imasu" is dropped: ~ de irassha**rimasu** → ~ de irassha**imasu**

1. 伊藤先生、明日学校に**いらっしゃいます**か。

   Itoo-sensei, ashita gakkoo ni **irasshaimasu** ka

   (Professor Itoo, are you coming to school tomorrow?)

2. 良子さんのお母さんに東京で**お目にかかりました**。

   Yoshiko-san no okaasan ni Tookyoo de **ome ni kakarimashta**.

   (I met Yoshiko's mother in Tokyo.)

3. 明日は家に**おります**。

   Ashita wa uchi ni **orimasu**.

   (I will be at home tomorrow.)

4. 日本で何を**なさいました**か。

   Nihon de nani wo **nasaimashita** ka.

   (What did you do in Japan?)

5. どうぞ**めしあがって**ください。

   Doozo **meshiagatte** kudasai.

   (Please have something to ear or drink.)

6. あの方が野口先生**でいらっしゃいます**か。

   Ano kata ga Noguchi-sensei **de irasshaimasu** ka.

   (Is that person Dr. Noguchi?)

7. 初めまして。私は新田と**申します**。

   Hajimemashite. Watashi wa Nitta to **mooshimasu**.

   (How do you do. I am Nitta.)

8. 黒沢の「七人の侍」を**ごらんになりました**か。

   Kurosawa no "Shichi-nin no samurai" wo **goran ni narimashita** ka.

   (Did you see Kurosawa's "Seven Samurai"?)

9. ちょっと**伺いたい**ことがあります。

   Chotto **ukagaitai** koto ga arimasu.

(There is something I would like to ask you.)

10. 先生に教科書を**貸していただきました**。

Sensei ni kyookasho wo **kashite itadakimashita**.

(I had my teacher lend me his textbook.)

11. 日本語の新聞を毎日**読んでいらっしゃいます**か。

Nihon-go no shinbun wo mainichi **yonde irasshaimasu** ka.

(Do you read (Lit. are you reading) a Japanese newspaper every day?)

12. 私は韓国語を少し**存じております**が、とても難しいです。

Watashi wa kankoku-go wo sukoshi **zonjite orimasu** ga, muzukashii desu.

(I know Korean a little, but it is difficult.)

1. Give the honorific equivalent of the underlined words, maintaining their original forms (e.g., plain, polite).

Ex.   学校へ<u>行った</u>。   →   学校へ<u>いらっしゃった</u>。

Gakkoo e <u>itta</u>. → Gakkoo e <u>irasshatta.</u>

1. ビールを<u>飲みます</u>。 _____

Biiru wo <u>nomimasu</u>. _____

2. 写真を<u>見る</u>。 _____

Shashin wo <u>miru</u> _____

3. 散歩を<u>します</u>。 _____

Sanpo wo <u>shimasu</u>. _____

4. 家に<u>来た</u>。 _____

Uchi ni <u>kita</u>. _____

5. 会社に<u>いる</u>。 _____

Kaisha ni <u>iru</u>. _____

6. プレゼントを<u>くれました</u>。 _____

Purezento wo <u>kuremashita</u>. _____

7. 京都に行くと<u>言った</u>。 _____

Kyooto ni iku to <u>itta</u>. _____

8. ヨーロッパをよく<u>知っています</u>。 _____

Yooroppa wo yoku <u>shitte imasu</u>. _____

2. Answer the following questions with a humble form.

Ex.   A: 明日十時に<u>いらっしゃいます</u>か。

Ashita juu-ji ni irasshaimasu ka.

B: はい、参ります。

   Hai, mairimasu.

1. A: 今お昼をめしあがりますか。

   Ima ohiru wo meshiagarimasu ka

   B: はい、＿＿＿＿＿＿＿＿＿＿＿＿＿＿＿。

   Hai, ＿＿＿＿＿＿＿＿＿＿＿＿＿＿＿

2. A: 吉田さんでいらっしゃいますか。

   Yoshida-san de irasshaimasu ka.

   B: はい、<u>そう</u>＿＿＿＿＿＿＿＿＿＿＿＿＿。

   Hai, <u>soo</u>＿＿＿＿＿＿＿＿＿＿＿＿＿

3. A: 津田先生の絵をごらんになりましたか。

   Tsuda-sensei no e wo goran ni narimashita ka.

   B: いいえ、＿＿＿＿＿＿＿＿＿＿＿＿＿＿。

   Iie, ＿＿＿＿＿＿＿＿＿＿＿＿＿＿＿

4. A: 赤い紙を二・三枚いただけますか。

   Akai kami wo ni, san-mai itadakemasu ka.

   B: はい、＿＿＿＿＿＿＿＿＿＿＿＿＿＿。

   Hai, ＿＿＿＿＿＿＿＿＿＿＿＿＿＿.

5. A: 広島をご存知ですか。

   Hiroshima wo go-zonji desu ka.

   B: はい、＿＿＿＿＿＿＿＿＿＿＿＿＿＿。

   Hai, ＿＿＿＿＿＿＿＿＿＿＿＿＿＿＿

OTHER HONORIFIC AND HUMBLE FORMS

Verbs

	Honorific forms	**Humble forms**
"**ru**" and "**u**"-verbs	"**o** + V-stem + **ni naru**"	"**o** + V-stem + **suru**"

1. これを**お買いになります**か。

   Kore wo **o-kai ni narimasu** ka.

   (Are you going to buy this?)

2. 山下先生が**お書きになった**本を読みました。

Yamashita-sensei ga **o-kaki ni natta** hon wo yomimashita.

(I read the book Professor Yamashita wrote.)

3. ここで**お待ちしております**。

Koko de **o-machi shite orimasu**.

(I will be waiting for you here.)

4. 先生に**お借りした**本を今日**お返しする**つもりです。

Sensei ni **o-kari shita** hon wo kyoo **o-kaeshi suru** tsumori desu.

(Today I intend to return the book I borrowed from the teacher.)

Note: The humble form "**o** + V-stem + **suru**" is used only when the speaker's action involves the person being respected by the speaker: Toshokan ni hon wo **kaeshimasu**. *(I will return the book to the library.)* Sensei ni hon wo **o-kaeshi shimasu**. *(I will return the book to the teacher.)* O-cha wo **ireru**. *(I make tea.)* O-cha wo **o-ire suru**. *(I make tea for someone.)*

3. Give the honorific or humble equivalent of the underlined words, maintaining their original forms (e.g., plain, polite).

Ex.　先生が話します　→　先生がお話しになります。

Sensei ga <u>hanashimasu</u>. → Sensei ga <u>o-hanashi ni narimasu</u>

1. 先生が本を<u>読みます</u>。　＿＿＿＿＿＿＿＿＿＿＿＿＿＿

Sensei ga hon wo <u>yomimasu</u>.　＿＿＿＿＿＿＿＿＿＿＿＿＿＿

2. 社長のかばんを<u>持ちます</u>。　＿＿＿＿＿＿＿＿＿＿＿＿＿

Shachoo no kaban wo <u>mochimasu</u>　＿＿＿＿＿＿＿＿＿＿＿＿

3. 友達のお父さんが<u>買う</u>。　＿＿＿＿＿＿＿＿＿＿＿＿＿

Tomodachi no otoosan ga <u>kau</u>.　＿＿＿＿＿＿＿＿＿＿＿＿

4. 田中さんは朝ニュースを<u>聞きます</u>。　＿＿＿＿＿＿＿＿＿＿＿＿

Tanak-san wa asa nyuusu wo <u>kikimasu</u>.　＿＿＿＿＿＿＿＿＿＿

5. 先生にビデオを<u>送った</u>。　＿＿＿＿＿＿＿＿＿＿＿＿＿

Sensei ni bideo wo <u>okutta</u>.　＿＿＿＿＿＿＿＿＿＿＿

Nouns

Honorific/polite form

"**o** / **go**" + noun (usually prefix "**o**" is attached to a Japanese word and "**go**" to a Sino-Japanese word.)

1. 本   ご本
   hon   go-hon
   (book)

2. 病気   ご病気
   byooki   go-byooki
   (illness)

3. 名前   お名前
   namae   o-namae
   (name)

4. 手紙   お手紙
   tegami   o-tegami
   (letter)

Family terms

There are two sets of family terms, plain and honorific. The plain forms are used when one talks about his or her own family to outsiders and carry the general meaning of the word as well. The honorific forms are used in referring to the members of the other families. However, the asterisked terms in the following list are used for addressing the members of one's own family.

Plain forms	Honorific forms
father: 父(chichi)	お父さん(o-too-san)*
mother: 母(haha)	お母さん(o-kaa-san)*
older brother: 兄(ani)	お兄さん(o-nii-san)*
older sister: 姉(ane)	お姉さん(o-nee-san)*
younger brother: 弟(otooto)	弟さん(otooto-san)
younger sister: 妹(imooto)	妹さん(imooto-san)
husband: 夫(otto) / 主人(shujin)	ご主人(go-shujin)
wife: 妻(tsuma) / 家内(kanai)	奥さん(okusan)
child: 子供(kodomo)	お子さん(o-ko-san)
parents: 両親(ryooshin)	ご両親(go-ryooshin)

siblings: 兄弟(kyoodai)   ご兄弟(go-kyoodai)

couple: 夫婦(fuufu)   ご夫婦(go-fuufu)

relative: 親類(shinrui) /親戚(shinseki)   ご親類(go-shinrui)/ご親戚(go-shinseki)

grandfather: 祖父(sofu)   おじいさん(o-jii-san)*

grandmother: 祖母(sobo)   おばあさん(o-baa-san)*

uncle: おじ(oji)   おじさん(oji-san)*

aunt: おば(oba)   おばさん(oba-san)*

cousin: いとこ(itoko)   おいとこさん(o-itoko-san)

1. **ご家族**はお元気でいらっしゃいますか。

   Go-kazoku wa o-genki de irasshaimasu ka.

   (Are your family well?)

2. 昨日友達の**ご両親**から**お手紙**をいただきました。

   Kinoo tomodachi no **go-ryooshin** kara **o-tegami** wo itadakimashita.

   (I received a letter from my friend's parents.)

3. 新聞で**ご主人**の**お写真**を拝見しました。

   Shinbun de **go-shujin** no **o-shashin** wo haiken shimashita.

   (I saw your husband's picture in a newspaper.)

4. **ご兄弟**は何人いらっしゃいますか。

   Go-kyoodai wa nan-nin irasshaimasu ka.

   (How many brothers and sisters do you have?)

5. **お母さん**、**お父さん**から電話ですよ。

   O-kaa-san, **o-too-san** kara denwa desu yo.

   (Mother, it is a call from Father.)

6. 子供は両親のすることをよく見ている。

   Kodomo wa ryooshin no suru koto wo yoku mite iru.

   (Children carefully watch what their parents do.)

I-adjectives and Na-adjectives

Honorific/polite form

"**o**" + i-adjective, "**o**"/"**go**" + na-adjective

1. 若い   お若い

   wakai   o-wakai

   (young)

2. 忙しい   お忙しい

   isogashii   o-isogashii

   (busy)

3. やさしい   おやさしい

   yasashii   o-yasashii

   (gentle)

4. きれいだ   おきれいだ

   kirei da   o-kirei da

   (pretty, clean)

5. 上手だ   お上手だ

   joozu da   o-joozu da

   (skillful)

6. 親切だ   ご親切だ

   shinsetsu da   go-shinsetsu da

   (kind)

7. 立派だ   ご立派だ

   rippa da   go-rippa da

   (magnificent)

1. 美代子さんのおじさんはゴルフが**お上手です**ね。

   Miyoko-san no ojisan wa gorufu ga **o-joozu desu** ne.

   (Miyoko's uncle is good at playing golf, isn't he?)

2. **おひまな**時、一緒に公園にいらっしゃいませんか。

   O-hima na toki, issho ni kooen ni irasshaimasen ka.

   (If you have time, won't you come to the park with us?)

3. 高橋先生はこの頃**お忙しい**そうです。

   Takahashi sensei wa kono goro **o-isogashii** soo desu.

   (I heard that Dr. Takahashi is busy these days.)

4. 吉田さんは**お若い**時から将棋がお上手ですね。

   Yoshida-san wa **o-wakai** toki kara shoogi ga o-joozu desu ne.

   (Mr. Yoshida has been good at playing Japanese chess since he was young, hasn't he?)

4. Change the underlined words in the following sentences into honorific or humble forms, depending on the context.

Ex.   大木さんは私の貸した本を読んだでしょうか。お貸しした，　お読みになった

Ooki-san wa watashi no **kashita** hon wo yonda deshoo ka.   o-kashishita, oyomininatta

1. 先生は大きいアパートに<u>住んでいます</u>。 _____

   Sensei wa ookii apaato ni <u>sunde imasu</u>. _____

2. ゆうべ友達の<u>両親</u>と<u>話しました</u>。 _____, _____

   Yuube tomodachi no <u>ryooshin</u> to <u>hanashimashita</u>. _____, _____

3. 鈴木先生の<u>描いた</u>絵を<u>見ました</u>。 _____, _____

   Suzuki-sensei no <u>kaita</u> e wo <u>mimashita</u>. _____, _____

4. <u>旅行</u>で<u>疲れました</u>か。 _____, _____

   <u>Ryokoo</u> de <u>tsukaremashita</u> ka. _____, _____

5. グリーンさんは<u>忙しい</u>ので、まだ家に<u>帰りません</u>。 _____, _____

   Guriin (Green)-san wa <u>isogashii</u> node, mada uchi ni <u>kaerimasen</u>. _____, _____

Review

5. Give the honorific equivalent of the given words, maintaining their original form (e.g., plain, polite).

   Ex.   子供   → <u>お子さん</u>、   読んだ → <u>お読みになった</u>

            Kodomo → <u>okosan,</u>   yonda → <u>o-yomi ni natta</u>

   1. 行く   _____

      iku   _____

   2. 見た   _____

      mita   _____

   3. します   _____

      shimasu   _____

   4. 妻   _____

      tsuma   _____

   5. やさしい   _____

      yasashii   _____

   6. 両親   _____

      ryooshin   _____

   7. 知っていました   _____

      shitte imashita   _____

   8. 買ってくれる   _____

      katte kureru   _____

9. 立派だ _____

   rippa da _____

10. 飲む _____

    nomu _____

6. Change some words in the following sentences into honorific or humble expressions. If it is appropriate, change not only the predicates but also the nouns and adjectives.

   Ex.   先生は部屋にいます。 → 先生はお部屋にいらっしゃいます。

        Sensei wa heya ni imasu. → Sensei wa o-heya ni irasshaimasu.

1. 奥さんは今電話をしています。 _____

   Okusan wa ima denwa wo shite imasu. _____

2. 先生の子供はギターが上手ですね。 _____

   Sensei no kodomo wa gitaa (guitar) ga joozu desu ne. _____

3. 小野さんの主人に会いました。 _____

   Ono-san no shujin ni aimashita. _____

4. テーラー先生に英語のレポートを見てもらいます。 _____

   Teeraa (Taylor)-sensei ni ei-go no repooto wo mite moraimasu. _____

5. 福島さんの若い時の写真が見たいですね。 _____

   Fukushima-san no wakai toki no shashin ga mitai desu ne. _____

6. 星野さんのお父さんが日本の地図をくれるといいました。 _____

   Hoshino-san no otoosan ga Nihon no chizu wo kureru to iimashita. _____

7. The following paragraph is a description of your karate teacher. Rewrite the sentences in Japanese with the appropriate honorific expressions.

I met my karate teacher three years ago.

_____.

He (the teacher) is forty-five years old, but he started leaning karate when he was very young.

_____.

He (the teacher) lives in Nagoya with his wife and three children.

_____.

His parents also live nearby.

_____.

Every day he (the teacher) eats fruit in the morning.

_____.

He (the teacher) teaches karate for four hours and rests thirty minutes after lunch.

_____.

I sometimes help him clean his gym.

_____.

I like to listen to his talk, because it is always interesting.

_____.

I heard that he is writing a book on karate now.

_____.

I would like (want) to see it.

_____.

Chapter 15

Useful Expressions

COMPARISON

In Japanese there is no comparative form equivalent to "~er" or "more" in English. The structure "X **hoo ga** Y **yori** ~" is equivalent to "X is more or less ~ than Y. "Y **yori**" may be omitted when it is understood from the context.

<u>Formation of X and Y</u>

1. Verbs: V(plain non-past) + "**hoo ga**"/"**yori**"

    Ex. **iku** → **iku** hoo ga ,   **kuru** → **kuru** yori

2. I-adjective: dictionary form + "**hoo ga**"/"**yori**",

    Ex. **atsui** → **atsui** hoo ga,   **samui** → **samui** yori

3. Na-adjective: change the final "**da**" to "**na**" + "**hoo ga**"/"**yori**",

    Ex. **benri da** → **benri na** hoo ga,   **fuben da** → **fuben** (**na**) yori

4. Noun: noun + "**no**" + "**hoo ga**",   noun + "**yori**"

    Ex.   **sensei** → **sensei no** hoo ga,   **gakusei** → **gakusei** yori

1. Talking to Yoshiki: 芳樹さんは野球とバスケットボールとどちら（の方）が好きですか。

    Yoshiki-san wa yakyuu to basukettobooru to dochira (no hoo) ga suki desu ka.

    (Yoshiki, which do you prefer baseball or basketball?)

    Yoshiki: **バスケットボールの方が（野球より）**好きです。

    Basukettobooru no hoo ga (yakyuu yori) suki desu.

    (I prefer basketball (to baseball).)

2. 弘さんもまりさんもピアノが弾けますが、**まりさんの方が**（弘さんより）上手です。

Hiroshi-san mo Mari-san mo piano ga hikemasu ga , **Mari-san no hoo ga (Hiroshi-san yori)**
joozu desu.

(Both Hiroshi and Mari can play the piano, but Mari is better (than Hiroshi).)

3. デパートで大きい時計と小さい時計を見ました。姉は**大きい方が**いいと言いますが、

Depaato de ookii tokei to chiisai tokei wo mimashita. Ane wa **ookii hoo ga** ii to
私は**小さい方が**ほしいです。

iimasu ga, watashi wa **chiisai hoo ga** hoshii desu.

*(I saw a small watch and a large one at a department store. My older sister says that a
larger one is better , but I want a smaller one.)*

4. 町は**にぎやかな方が静かなより**いい。

Machi wa **nigiyaka na hoo ga shizuka na yori** ii.

(Lively town is better than a quiet one.)

5. 京都に行く時は新幹線で**行く方が飛行機で行くより**楽しい。

Kyooto e iku toki wa shinkansen de **iku hoo ga hikooki de iku yori** tanoshii.

(When one goes to Kyoto, it is more enjoyable going by Brett Train than by plane.)

1. Answer the following questions.

Ex.

Q: エベレストとモンブランとどちら/どっち（の方）が高いですか。

Eberesuto (Mt. Everest) to Monburan (Mont Blanc) to dochira / dotchi (no hoo) ga takai
desu ka.

A: エベレストの方がモンブランより高いです。

Eberesuto no hoo ga Monburan yori takai desu.

1. Q: アラスカとメインとどちら/どっち（の方）が大きいですか。

Arasuka to Mein to dochira / dotchi (no hoo) ga ookii desu ka.

A: _____.

2. Q: アメリカと中国とどちら/どっち（の方）が新しいですか。

Amerika to Chyuugoku to dochira/dotchi (no hoo) ga atarashii desu ka.

A: _____.

3. Q: アパートは便利なのと大きいのとどちら/どっち（の方）がいいですか。

Apaato wa benri na no to ookii no to dochira/dotchi (no hoo) ga ii desu ka.

A: _____.

4. Q: ワインは新しいのと古いのとどちら/どっち（の方）がおいしいですか。

Wain wa atarashii no to furui no to dochira / dotchi (no hoo) ga oishii desu ka.

A: _____.

5. Q: 漢字で書くのとひらがなで書くのとどちら/どっち（の方）が難しいですか。

Kanji de kaku no to hiragana de kaku no to dochira/dotchi (no hoo) ga muzukashii desu

Ka.

A: _____.

SUPERLATIVE

In Japanese there is no superlative form equivalent to "~est" or "most" in English. The
adverbial phrase "**ichiban ~**" is equivalent to " ~ est" or "~ the most."

1. 私の友達の中で太郎さんが**一番頭がいい**。

Watashi no tomodachi no naka de Taroo-san ga **ichiban atama ga ii**.

(Taro is the brightest among my friends.)

2. 太田さんはビートルズの歌が**一番好きだ**そうです。

Oota-san wa biitoruzu no uta ga **ichiban suki da** soo desu.

(I heard that Ms. Ota likes the Beetles' songs the best.)

3. 島田さんと林さんと森さんの中で、誰が**一番ゴルフが上手ですか**。

Shimada-san to Hayashi-san to Mori-san no naka de dare ga **ichiban gorufu ga
joozu desu** ka.

(Among Mr. Shimada, Mr. Hayashi, and Mr. Mori, who plays the golf the best?)

4. 私はローマに**一番行きたい**です。

Watashi wa Rooma ni **ichiban ikitai** desu.

(I want to go to Rome the most.)

5. けさは佐野さんが**一番早く**クラスに来ました。

Kesa wa Sano-san ga **ichiban hayaku** kurasu ni kimashita.

*(Mr. Sano was the first one to come to class this morning /Lit. came to class the
earliest.)*

6. メトロポリタン美術館へ行くのはバスが**一番便利だ**と思いますよ。

Metoroporitan bijutsukan e iku no wa basu ga **ichiban benri da** to omoimasu yo.

(I think the bus is the most convenient way to go to the Metropolitan Museum.)

7. エベレストは世界で**一番高い**山だ。

Eberesuto wa sekai de **ichiban takai** yama da.

(Mt. Everest is the highest mountain in the world.)

2. Change the English phrases to the corresponding Japanese phrases.

Ex.   the largest department store   → _一番大きいデパート (ichiban ookii depaato)_

1. the coldest room
2. the youngest person
3. the prettiest park
4. to study the most
5. to be the nearest
6. to speak the slowest
7. to want to buy the most

3. Give the Japanese equivalent to the English questions and then write either superlative or comparative answers in Japanese using the clues in parentheses.

Ex.   Q: What do you want to eat now?

今何が食べたいですか。

Ima nani ga tabetai desu ka.

A: (delicious sushi) おいしいすしが一番食べたいです。

(delicious sushi) Oishii sushi ga ichiban tabetai desu.

1. Q: Where do you want to go now?

   _____.

   A: (quiet place) _____.

2. Q: Who is the tallest among your friends?

   _____.

   A: (Mr. Nakano) _____.

3. Q: Which is cheaper, gold or silver?

   _____.

   A: (Silver) _____.

4. Q: Who is the best tennis player in your family?/Lit. Who is best at tennis in your family?

   _____.

   A: (my older brother) _____.

5. Q: What is your favorite thing to do? /Lit. What would you like to do the most?

   _____.

   A: (to listen to music) _____.

6. Q: Who (Lit. Which one) plays tennis more often, Mr. Yoshida or Ms. Iida?

    _____.

    A: (Mr. Yoshida) _____.

7. Q: Which is more interesting, reading books or watching TV?

    _____.

    A: (reading books) _____.

8. Q: Whom do you want to see now the most?

    _____.

    A: (the friends in high school) _____.

9. Q: Which airplane is the fastest?

    _____.

    A: (Concord) _____.

10. Q: Who is the richest person in this town?

    _____.

    A: (Mr. Smith) _____.

NEGATVE TE-FORM

The expression "V-**nai de**" corresponds to "without doing such and such" or "instead of doing such and such" in English depending on the context.

Formation of "**nai de**" form

Add "**de**" to the plain negative non-past form of a verb.

Ex.   行く → 行か**ない** → 行か**ない**＋**で**

ik-**u** → ik-**anai** → ik-**anai** + **de**

食べる → 食べ**ない** → 食べ**ない**＋**で**

tabe-**ru** → tabe-**nai** → tabe-**nai** + **de**

1. 明日は図書館に**行かないで**うちで勉強をしようと思います。

    Ashita wa toshokan ni **ikanai de** uchi de benkyoo wo shiyoo to omimasu.

    (I am thinking of studying at home tomorrow instead of going to the library.)

2. 遅く起きたので、朝ご飯を**食べないで**会社に行きました。

    Osoku okita node, asa-gohan wo **tabenai de** kaisha ni ikimashita.

    (I went to work without eating breakfast, because I got up late.)

3. 地下鉄にもバスにも**乗らないで**歩いて来ました。

Chikatetsu ni mo busu ni mo **noranai de** aruite kimashita.

(I walked instead of riding either the subway or the bus.)

4. ゆうべはぜんぜん**寝ないで**レポートを書きました。

Yuube wa zenzen **nenai de** repooto wo kakimashita.

(Last night I wrote a report without sleeping at all.)

5. アパートは高いから、**買わないで**借りることにしました。

Apaato wa takai kara, **kawanai de** kariru koto ni shimashita.

(I decided to rent the apartment instead of buying it, because it is expensive.)

4. Change the following verbs into the "**nai de**" form.

Ex.   食べる　→　食べ**ないで**

       Tabe-**ru**　→　<u>tabe-**nai de**</u>

1. 置く _____
   ok-u _____
2. 読む _____
   yom-u _____
3. 使う _____
   tsuka-u _____
4. 起きる _____
   oki-ru _____
5. 話す _____
   hanas-u _____
6. 飛ぶ _____
   tob-u _____
7. 立つ _____
   tats-u _____
8. 教える _____
   oshie-ru _____
9. 帰る _____
   kaer-u _____
10. 泳ぐ _____
    oyog-u _____

5. Change the words in parentheses into a phrase using the "**nai de**" form. Supply a particle if necessary.

　　Ex.　マリさんの家へ行ったけれど、（お母さん、会う）<u>お母さんに会わないで</u>帰って

　　　　Mari-san no uchi e itta keredo, (okaasan, au) <u>okaasan ni awanai de</u>, kaette

　　　　来てしまいました。

　　　　kite shimaimashita.

1. 時間がないから（あるく）＿＿＿＿＿＿＿＿＿、地下鉄にのりましょう。

　　Jikan ga nai kara (aruku) ＿＿＿＿＿＿＿＿, chikatetsu ni norimashoo.

2. 昨日は（デパート、行く）＿＿＿＿＿＿＿＿＿＿、映画をみました。

　　Kinoo wa (depaato, iku) ＿＿＿＿＿＿＿,＿＿＿ eiga wo mimashita.

3. ジムさんはいつも（英語、話す）＿＿＿＿＿＿＿＿、日本語を使います。

　　Jim-san wa itsumo (ei-go, hanasu) ＿＿＿＿＿＿, nohon-go wo tsukaimasu.

4. 今日は（肉、買う）＿＿＿＿＿＿＿＿＿＿、魚にしました。

　　Kyoo wa (niku, kau) ＿＿＿＿＿＿＿＿, sakana ni shimashita.

5. この日本語の本は（辞書、使う）＿＿＿＿＿＿＿、読めました。

　　Kono nihon-go no hon wa (jisho, tsukau) ＿＿＿＿＿＿＿＿, yomemashita.

COMPOUND VERBS

Certain Japanese verbs, such as "**hajimeru**," "**owaru**," and "**sugiru**," can form compound verbs when they are attached to another verb. In a compound verb the first verb always takes the form of a verb stem.

V-stem + hajimeru

"V-stem + **hajimeru**" is equivalent to "begin or start to do such and such" or "begin to be in a certain state" in English.

1. いつから日本語を**習い始めました**か。

　　Itsu kara nihon-go wo **narai-hajimemashita** ka.

　　(When did you start to study Japanese?)

2. 飯田さんは来月からレストランで**働き始める**そうだ。

　　Iida-san wa raigetsu kara restoran de **hataraki-hajimeru** soo da.

　　(I heard that Mr. Iida will begin to work at a restaurant next month.)

3. レポートを**書き始めたら**、コンピューターが故障してしまいました。

   Repooto wo **kaki-hajimetara**, konpyuutaa ga koshoo shite shimaimashita.

   (My computer broke down, when I began to write a report.)

4. 昨日から暑く**なり始めました**ね。

   Kinoo kara atsuku **nari-hajimemashita** ne.

   (It has become hot since yesterday, hasn't it?)

V-stem + owaru

"V-stem + **owaru**" is equivalent to "finish doing such and such" in English.

1. その本を**読み終わったら**、貸してください。

   Sono hon wo **yomi-owattara**, kashite kudasai.

   (When you finish reading the book, please lend it to me.)

2. みんながご飯を**食べ終わった**から、かたずけ始めましょう。

   Minna ga gohan wo **tabe-owatta** kara, katazuke-hajimemashoo.

   (Since everyone has finished eating, let's start to clean up.)

3. このレポートは**書き終わった**けれど、もう一つ他のを書かなければいけません。

   Kono repooto wo **kaki-owatta** keredo, moo hitotsu hoka no wo kakanakereba ikemasen.

   (Although I finished writing this report, I have to write another one.)

V-stem/Adj-stem + sugiru

"V-stem/Adj-stem + **sugiru**" corresponds to "do such and such excessively" or "be too much such and such" in English.

1. 昨日**飲みすぎて**今日は頭が痛い。

   Kinoo **nomi-sugite** kyoo wa atama ga itai.

   (I drank too much yesterday and I have a headache today.)

2. このインド料理はおいしいけれど、子供には**からすぎる**。

   Kono Indo ryoori wa oishii keredo, kodomo ni wa **kara-sugiru**.

   (This Indian dish is delicious, but too spicy for children.)

3. 兄はみんなに**正直すぎる**と言われます。

   Ani wa minna ni **shoojiki-sugiru** to iwaremasu.

   (My older brother is told by everybody that he is too honest.)

6. Change the underlined words into an appropriate compound verb using "**~hajimeru**," "**~owaru**," or "**~sugiru**."

Ex.　昼ご飯を**食べたので**、まだお腹がいっぱいだ → 食べ過ぎたので

Hiru-gohan wo **tabeta node**, mada onaka ga ippai da. → <u>tabe-sugita node</u>

1. このネックレスは**高くて**、買えません。　_____

Kono nekkuresu (necklace) wa **takakute**, kaemasen.　_____

2. その手紙を**書いたら**、散歩に行きませんか。　_____

Sono tegami wo **kaitara**, sanpo ni ikimasen ka.　_____

3. 中村さんがコンピューターを**使ったら**、私が使いたいです。　_____

Nakamura-san ga konpyuutaa wo <u>tsukattara</u>, watashi ga tsukaitai desu.　_____

4. 来年から日本語を**習おうと**思っています。　_____

Rainen kara nihon-go wo **naraoo to** omotte imasu.　_____

5. 今日は**運動して**、疲れてしまいました。　_____

Kyoo wa **undooo shite**, tsukarete shimaimashita.　_____

6. この皿は**立派で**、家では使えません。　_____

Kono sara wa **rippa de**, uchi de wa tsukaemasen.　_____

7. 子供は一才になったら、**歩きます**。　_____

Kodomo wa issai ni nattara, **arukimasu**.　_____

COMPOUND NOUNS

V-stem + kata

"**Kata**" is a suffix which indicates "the way / manner" and this noun phrase corresponds to "how to do such and such" or "the way one does such and such" in English.

1. この辞書の**使い方**がよく分かりません。

Kono jisho no **tsukai-kata** ga yoku wakarimasen.

(I do not know how to use this dictionary.)

2. 人によって**考え方**は違います。

Hito ni yotte **kangae-kata** wa chigaimasu

(The way of thinking varies depending on the person.)

3. 駅への**行き方**を教えてくれませんか。

Eki e no **iki-kata** wo oshiete kuremasen ka?

(Would you please tell me how to go to the station?)

4. インターネットでの買い**物**の**し方**を知っていますか。

   Intaanetto de no kaimono no **shi-kata** wo shitte imasu ka

   (Do you know how to shop on the Internet?)

7. Change the given verb phrases into noun phrases using "~**kata**".

   Ex. 漢字を読む。 → <u>漢字の読み方</u>

   　　Kanji wo yomu → <u>kanji no yomi-kata</u>

1. 言葉をおぼえる。　　_____

   Kotoba wo oboeru.　　_____

2. おいしいすしを作る。　　_____

   Oishii sushi wo tsukuru.　　_____

3. 日本語で手紙を書く。　　_____

   Nihon-go de tegami wo kaku.　　_____

4. ボストンから来る。　　_____

   Bosuton kara kuru.　　_____

QUOTED SENTENCES

V(plain non-past) + yoo ni tanomu and V(plain non-past) + yoo ni iu

The expressions "V(plain non-past) + **yoo ni tanomu**" and "V(plain non-past) + **yoo ni iu**" indicate "quoted sentences" and are equivalent to "ask someone to do something" and "tell someone to do something," respectively, in English.

1. 母は弟に毎晩十時までに**帰って来るように言いました**。

   Haha wa otooto ni maiban juu-ji made ni **kaette kuru yoo ni iimashita**.

   (My mother told my younger brother to come home by ten o'clock every night.)

2. 学生に宿題を月曜日に**持って来るように言います**。

   Gakusei ni shukudai wo getsuyoobi ni **motte kuru yoo ni iimasu**.

   (I will tell the students to bring their homework on Monday.)

3. 友達に休みの間犬の世話を**してくれるように頼みました**。

   Tomodachi ni yasumi no aida inu no sewa wo **shite kureru yoo ni tanomimashita**.

   (I asked my friend to take care of my dog for me during the holidays.)

4. 良子さんに一緒に旅行に**行くように頼みましょう**。

   Yoshiko-san ni issho ni ryokoo ni **iku yoo ni tanomimashoo**.

(Let's ask Yoshiko to go on a trip with us.)

5. 忠夫さんにこの部屋でタバコを**吸わないように言ってください**。

Tadao-san ni kono heya de tabako wo **suwanai yoo ni itte kudasi**.

(Please tell Tadao not to smoke in this room.)

6. となりの人に家の前に車を**止めないように頼んでみます**。

Tonari no hito ni uchi no mae ni kuruma wo **tomenai yoo ni tanonde mimasu**.

(I will try asking the people next door not to park a car in front of our house.)

~ to iu / omou / kangaeru / shinjiru, etc.

The expressions "**~ to iu/omou/kangaeru/shinjiru**," etc., indicate a "quoted sentence" and correspond to "say/think/consider/believe that ~" in English. "**Omou**"/"**kangaeru**"/"**shinjiru**" take place in the form "V-te + **iru**" when the subject in a main clause is in the third person.

1. 日本の友達がもうすぐ香港へ行く**と言いました**。

Nihon no tomodachi ga moo sugu Honkon e iku **to iimashita**.

(My friend in Japan said that he is going to Hong Kong soon.)

2. 外国語を習うのはとてもおもしろい**と思います**。

Gaikoku-go wo narau no wa totemo omoshiroi **to omoimasu**.

(I think that learning a foreign language is very interesting.)

3. テレビは子供によくない**と考える**人がたくさんいます。

Terebi wa kodomo ni yoku nai **to kangaeru** hito ga takusan imasu..

(There are many people who consider that TV is no good for children.)

4. 小さい子供達はサンタクロースがいる**と信じています**。

Chiisai kodomo-tachi wa Santakuroosu (Santa Claus) ga iru **to shinjite imasu**.

(Young (Lit. small) children believe that there is Santa Claus.)

8. Give the Japanese equivalent to the following English sentences.

1. I told Mitsuko to wait for 10 minutes.
2. My father considers that the family is important.
3. Ms. Okada believes that sugar is not good.
4. I asked Jiroo to write a letter in Japanese for me.
5. Do you think that department stores in Chicago are open on Sundays?
6. Mr. Tani's wife said that she was born in the United States.

CONJECTURE

The expression "~ **kamoshirenai**" indicates "conjecture" and it corresponds to "may ~" in English.

<u>Formation</u>

　1. Verb: V(plain) + **kamoshirenai**　Ex. **iku** → **iku** kamoshirenai.

　2. I-adjective: plain form + **kamoshirenai**　　Ex. **atsui** → **atsui** kamoshirenai

　3. Na-adjective: plain form minus "**da**" + **kamoshirenai**　Ex. **benri da** → **benri** kamoshirenai

　4. Noun: noun + **kamoshirenai**　　Ex. **sensei** → **sensei** kamoshirenai

　1. 明日雨が**降るかもしれない**。

　　 Ashita ame ga **furu kamoshirenai**.

　　 (It may rain tomorrow.)

　2. 石田さんはもう大学を**卒業したかもしれません**。

　　 Ishida-san wa moo daigaku wo **sotsugyoo shita kamoshiremasen**.

　　 (Miss Ishida may have graduated from a college already.)

　3. あのレストランは**よくないかもしれません**よ。

　　 Ano restoran wa **yoku nai kamoshiremasen** yo.

　　 (That restaurant may not be good, you know.)

　4. この辺に住んだら、**便利かも**しれませんね。

　　 Kono hen ni sundara, **benri kamoshiremasen** ne.

　　 (If you live around here, it may be convenient.)

9. Change the following underlined words into expressions using "**kamoshirenai**".

　　 Ex.　明日は雪が<u>降ります</u>。 → <u>降るかもしれません</u>

　　　　 Ashita wa yuki ga <u>furimasu</u>. → <u>furu kamoshiremasen</u>

　1. 美智子さんはもうすぐ<u>結婚します</u>。　＿＿＿＿＿＿＿＿＿＿

　　 Michiko-san wa moo sugu <u>kekkon shimasu</u>.　＿＿＿＿＿＿＿＿＿＿

　2. この辺は車があまり通らないから、<u>静かだ</u>。　＿＿＿＿＿＿＿＿＿＿

　　 Kono hen wa kuruma ga amari tooranai kara, <u>shizuka da</u>.　＿＿＿＿＿＿＿＿

　3. 頭が痛かったから、試験はよく<u>できませんでした</u>。　＿＿＿＿＿＿＿＿

　　 Atama ga itakatta kara, shiken wa yoku <u>dekimasendeshita</u>.　＿＿＿＿＿＿＿＿

　4. 先週作ったケーキはまずかったけれど、今日のは<u>おいしいです</u>。＿＿＿＿＿＿

　　 Senshuu tsukutta keeki wa mazukatta keredo, kyoo no wa <u>oishii desu</u>.　＿＿＿＿

PARTIAL LISTING OF ACTIONS

"**V-tari V-tari suru**" is used to enumerate a few actions among others and   means to "do this, do that, and so on" in English. The phrase "**V-tari**" is formed simply by attaching "**ri**" to the plain past "**-ta**" form of verbs.

Ex.   yomu → yon-**da** → yon-**dari**   taberu → tabe-**ta** → tabe-**tari**

1. 今日は家で本を**読んだり**テレビを**見たりする**つもりです。

  Kyoo wa uchi de hon wo **yondari** terebi wo **mitari suru** tsumori desu.

  (Today, I am going to read a book, watch TV,   and so on, at home .)

2. きのうは銀行に**行ったり**買い物を**したりしました**。

  Kinoo wa ginkoo ni **ittari** kaimono wo **shitari shimashita**.

  (Yesterday, I went to the bank, did some shopping, and so on.)

3. テキストを**読んだり**テープ**聞いたりして**日本語を勉強しています。

  Tekisuto wo **yondari** teepu wo **kiitari shite** nihon-go wo benkyoo shite imasu.

  (I am studying Japanese by reading the textbook, listening to the tape, and so on.)

This expression also refers to alternating repeated actions or states, and it means "sometimes ~, some other times ~" in English.   "Adjective-**tari**" is formed by attaching "**ri**" to the plain past of   I/Na-adjective as well as V-**tari**.

Ex.   takai → taka-**katta** → taka-**kattari**

       shizuka da → shizuka **datta** → shizuka **dattari**

1. 今日は一日中雨が**降ったりやんだり**しました。

  Kyoo wa ichinichi-juu ame ga **futtari yandari shimashita**.

  (It rained on and off all day today.)

2. 日本語のクラスは**おもしろかったりおもしろくなかったり**します。

  Nihon-go no kurasu wa **omoshirokattari omoshiroku nakattari shimasu**.

  (The Japanese class is sometimes interesting and sometimes it is not.)

3. 最近会社では**忙しかったりひまだったり**します。

  Saikin kaisha de wa **isogashikattari himadattari shimasu**.

  (Lately sometimes I am busy at the office and sometimes I am not.)

10. Combine the pairs of sentences using the expression "**~tari~tari suru**."

  Ex. 手紙を書く。料理を作る。 → 手紙を書いたり料理を作ったりします。

     Tegami wo **kaku**.   Ryoori wo **tsukuru**. → Tegami wo kaitari ryoori wo tsukuttari shimasu.

1. 映画を見る。友達に会う。 _____

　Eiga wo miru.　Tomodachi ni au. _____

2. ジムで泳いだ。公園を歩いた。 _____

　Gimu (Gym) de oyoida.　Kooen wo aruita. _____

3. 図書館で本を借りる。宿題をする。 _____

　Toshokan de hon wo kariru.　Shukudai wo suru. _____

4. 天気はいい。（天気は）悪い。 _____

　Tenki wa ii.　(Tenki wa) warui. _____

5. 部屋は静かだ。（部屋は）うるさい。 _____

　Heya wa shizuka da.　(Heya wa) urusai. _____

PERMISSION

　　The expression "V/Adj.+ **te mo ii**" indicates "permission" and it is interpreted as "one may ~" or "It is all right to ~" in English.　This phrase is formed by attaching "**mo ii**" to the **te**-form of both verbs and adjectives.

　　Ex.　nomu → no**nde** → no**nde mo ii**

　　　　neru → ne**te** → ne**te mo ii**

　　　　kuru → **kite** → **kite mo ii**

　　　　furui → furu**kute** → furu**kute mo ii**

1. ここでたばこを**吸ってもいい**ですか。

　Koko de tabako wo **sutte mo ii desu** ka.

　(Is it all right to smoke / May I smoke here?)

2. 今日は早く家に**帰ってもいい**ですよ。

　Kyoo wa hayaku uchi ni **kaette mo ii** desu yo.

　(It is all right for you to go home early today, you know.)

3. [To a waiter at a restaurant]

　テーブルは**小さくてもいい**です。

　Teeburu wa **chiisakute mo ii desu**.

　(A small table is fine./ Lit. It is all right that a table is small.)

　　"V/Adj. + **nakute mo ii**" means that "It is all right that one does not ~" or "do not have to ~" in English.　This phrase is formed with "**-nakute** (**te**-form of negative non-past plain)" + "**mo ii**."

Ex.	**non-past neg.**		**te-form + mo ii**
taberu	→	tabe-**nai** →	tabe-**nakute mo ii**
iku	→	ika-**nai** →	ika-**nakute mo ii**
kuru	→	**konai** →	ko-**nakute mo ii**

1. 今すぐにお金を**払わなくてもいい**です。

    Ima suguni o-kane wo **harawanakute mo ii** desu.

    (You do not have to pay the money right now.)

2. この本はまだ図書館に**返さなくてもいいです**。

    Kono hon wa mada toshokan ni **kaesanakute mo ii** desu.

    (I still do not have to return this book to the library.)

3. 妹は元気になったので,もう**薬を飲まなくてもいい**そうです。

    Imooto wa genki ni natta node, moo kusuri wo **nomanakute mo ii** soo desu.

    (I heard that my sister does not have to take the medicine any more, since she recovered.)

11. Change the following phrases into ones using the expression "~ **te mo ii desu**"

   Ex. 酒を飲む。 → 酒を飲んでもいいです。

       Sake wo nomu. → <u>Sake wo nonde mo ii desu.</u>

   1. 英語で話す。 _____

       Eigo de hanasu. _____

   2. 辞書を使う。 _____

       Jisho wo tsukau. _____

   3. おかしを食べる。 _____

       Okashi wo taberu. _____

   4. ペンで書く。 _____

       Pen de kaku . _____

   5. エアコンをつける。 _____

       Ea-kon (air- conditioner) wo tsukeru. _____

12. Change the following phrases into ones using the expression "~ **nakute mo ii desu**."

   Ex.　お金を払う。 → <u>お金を払わなくてもいいです。</u>

       Okane wo harau.　 → <u>Okane wo harawanakute mo ii desu.</u>

   1. 仕事を早くする。 _____

       Shigoto wo hayaku suru. _____

2. 明日ここに来る。＿＿＿＿＿＿＿＿＿＿＿＿＿＿＿＿

   Ashita koko ni kuru. ＿＿＿＿＿＿＿＿＿＿＿＿＿＿＿＿

3. 急ぐ。＿＿＿＿＿＿＿＿＿＿＿

   Isogu. ＿＿＿＿＿＿＿＿＿＿＿

4. 早く起きる。＿＿＿＿＿＿＿＿＿＿＿

   Hayaku okiru. ＿＿＿＿＿＿＿＿＿＿＿

5. 買い物に行く。＿＿＿＿＿＿＿＿＿＿＿

   Kaimono ni iku. ＿＿＿＿＿＿＿＿＿＿＿＿＿

6. 晩ご飯を作る。＿＿＿＿＿＿＿＿＿＿＿＿＿

   Ban-gohan wo tsukuru. ＿＿＿＿＿＿＿＿＿＿＿＿＿＿

PROHIBITION

The expression "V/Adj.-**te wa ikenai**" indicates "prohibition" and means that "one must not do such and such" or "something must not be so and so" in English.

1. ここでたばこを**吸ってはいけない**そうです。

   Koko de tabako wo **sutte wa ikenai** soo desu.

   (I heard that one must not smoke here.)

2. 授業中に何か食べたり飲んだり**してはいけません**。

   Jugyoo-chuu ni nani ka tabetari nondari **shite wa ikemasen**.

   (You must not eat, drink, and so on, during the class.)

3. クラスに**遅れてはいけません**よ。

   Kurasu ni **okurete wa ikemasen** yo.

   (You must not be late for the class, you know.)

4. 作文はあまり**長くてはいけません**。

   Sakubun wa amari **nagakute wa ikemasen.**

   (The composition must not be too long.)

13. Change the following phrases into ones using the expression   " ~ **te wa ikemasen**."

   Ex.   まんがをたくさん読む。 →   まんがをたくさん読んではいけません。

   Manga wo takusan yomu.   Manga wo takusan yonde wa ikemasen.

   1. うそを言う。＿＿＿＿＿＿＿＿＿＿＿＿＿＿＿＿

      Uso wo iu. ＿＿＿＿＿＿＿＿＿＿＿＿＿＿＿＿

2. 一日中テレビを見る。 _____

   Ichinichi-juu terebi wo miru. _____

3. 酒を飲み過ぎる。 _____

   Sake wo nomi-sugiru. _____

4. ここで写真をとる。 _____

   Koko de shashin wo toru. _____

5. 約束を忘れる。 _____

   Yakusoku wo wasureru. _____

6. 図書館で話す。 _____

   Toshokan de hanasu. _____

OBLIGATION

The double negative expression "V-**nakute wa/nakereba ikenai**" means that "one must/has to do such and such" in English.

1. 今晩母に電話を**かけなくては/かけなければいけない**。

   Konban haha ni denwa wo **kakenakute wa/kakanakereba ikenai**..

   (I have to call my mother tonight.)

2. レポートを**書かなくては/書かなければいけない**ので,今日は出かけられません。

   Repooto wo kakanakute wa/*kakanakereba ikenai* node, kyoo wa dekakeraremasen.

   (I have to write a paper, so I can not go out today.)

3. 父の仕事を**手伝わなくては/手伝わなければいけません**でした。

   Chichi no shigoto wo **tetsudawanakute wa/tetsudawanakereba ikemasen** deshita.

   (I had to help my father with his work.)

4. A: まだ病院に**行かなくては/行かなければいけない**んですか。

      Mada byooin ni **ikanakute wa/ikanakereba ikenai** n' desu ka.

      (Do you still have to go to the hospital?)

   B: いいえ、もう行かなくてもいいんですよ。

      Iie, moo ikanakute mo ii n' desu yo.

      (No, I do not have to go any more, you know.)

14. Change the underlined verbs in the following sentences into the form "~ **nakute wa/ ~ nakereba ikemasen**."

Ex. 急ぐ。 → <u>急がなくては / 急がなければいけません</u>。

   Isogu.   →   <u>Isoganakute wa / isoganakereba ikemasen.</u>

1. 早く家を<u>出る</u>。 _____
   Hayaku uchi wo <u>deru</u>. _____

2. 二時までに駅に<u>着く</u>。 _____
   Niji made ni eki ni <u>tsuku</u>. _____

3. バスを<u>待つ</u>。 _____
   Basu wo <u>matsu</u>. _____

4. 日本語で<u>話す</u>。 _____
   Nihon-go de <u>hanasu</u>. _____

5. よく<u>考える</u>。 _____
   Yoku <u>kangaeru</u>. _____

6. ルームメートを<u>見つける</u>。 _____
   Ruumu meeto (room mate) wo <u>mitsukeru</u>. _____

15. Change the following sentences into a question-and-answer form which corresponds to the English "Do you have to~?" and "No, I do not have to~."

   Ex. 宿題をする。

      Shukudai wo suru.

      Q: <u>宿題をしなくては/しなければいけませんか</u>。

         (<u>Syukudai wo shinakute wa /shinakereba ikemasen ka.</u>)

      A: <u>いいえ、しなくてもいいです</u>

         (<u>Iie, shinakute mo ii desu.</u>)

1. 早く帰る。   Q: _____ A: _____
   Hayaku kaeru.

2. 日本語で手紙を書く。 Q: _____ A: _____
   Nihon-go de tegami wo kaku.

3. かさを持って行く。 Q: _____ A: _____
   Kasa wo motte iku.

4. 一日中家にいる。 Q: _____ A: _____
   Ichinichi-juu uchi ni iru.

5. 今晩出かける。 Q: _____ A: _____
   Konban dekakeru.

6. 今このレポートを読む。 Q: _____ A: _____

Ima kono repooto(report) wo yomu.

EXPERIENCE

The phrase "V-**ta** (plain past) **koto ga aru**" refers to "experience" and means "someone has the experience of doing such and such" or "someone has done such and such before" in English.

1. 日本へ**行ったことがあります**か。

   Nihon e **itta koto ga arimasu** ka.

   (Have you ever been to Japan?)

2. かぶきを**見たことがない**ので、見てみたいです。

   Kabuki wo **mita koto ga nai** node, mite mitai desu.

   (I have never seen Kabuki, so I would like to see it.)

3. トムさんは日本で英語を**教えたことがある**そうだ。

   Tomu-san wa Nihon de ei-go wo **oshieta koto ga aru** soo da.

   (I heard that Tom has taught English in Japan.)

4. そんな変な話は**聞いたことがない**。

   Sonna henna hanashi wa **kiita koto ga nai**.

   (I have never heard such a weird story.)

16. Change the following phrases into ones using the expression "**~ta koto ga aru**."

   Ex. 日本の映画を見る。 → 日本の映画を見たことがあります。

   Nihon no eiga wo miru. → Nihon no eiga wo mita koto ga arimasu.

1. アサヒビールを飲む。 _____

   Asahi biiru wo nomu.   _____

2. ラテン語を習う。 _____

   Laten-go (Latin) wo narau. _____

3. 新幹線に乗る。 _____

   Shinkansen ni noru. _____

4. 海で泳ぐ。 _____

   Umi de oyogu. _____

5. 着物を着る。 _____

   Kimono wo kiru. _____

6. ゴルフをする。＿＿＿＿＿＿＿＿＿＿＿＿＿＿＿＿＿＿

Gorufu (Golf) wo suru. ＿＿＿＿＿＿＿＿＿＿＿＿＿＿＿＿

ADVICE

The phrase "V-**ta** (plain past) **hoo ga ii**" indicates "advice," and it corresponds to "it is better to do such and such" or "had better do such and such" in English.

1. 風邪だったら、早く**寝た方が**いいですよ。

   Kaze dattara, hayaku **neta hoo ga ii** desu yo.

   (If it is a cold, you had better go to bed early, you know.)

2. 雨が降りそうだから、かさを**持って行った方が**いいです。

   Ame ga furi soo da kara, kasa wo **motte itta hoo ga ii** desu.

   (It looks like it is going to rain, so you had better to take an umbrella.)

3. 食べた後で歯を**みがいた方が**いいです。

   Tabeta ato de ha wo **migaita hoo ga ii** desu.

   (It is better to brush your teeth after you eat.)

4. レストランに行く前に**予約しておいた方が**いい。

   Resutoran ni iku mae ni **yoyaku shite oita hoo ga ii.**

   (We had better make a reservation before we go to the restaurant.)

The expression "V-**nai** (plain negative non-past) + **hoo ga ii**," on the other hand, corresponds to the English "it is better not to do such and such."

1. この辺はあぶないから夜**歩かない方が**いいですよ。

   Kono hen wa abunai kara yoru **arukanai hoo ga ii** desu yo.

   (It is dangerous in this neighborhood, so you had better not walk at night, you know.)

2. **働き過ぎない方が**いいです。

   Hataraki-suginai hoo ga ii desu.

   (It is better not to work too much.)

3. 両親をあまり**心配させない方が**いいですよ。

   Ryooshin wo amari **shinpai sasenai hoo ga ii** desu yo.

   (You had better not make your parents worry too much, you know.)

4. たばこは**吸わない方が**いいと医者に言われました。

   Tabako wa **suwanai hoo ga ii** to isha ni iwaremashita.

(I was told by the doctor that I had better not smoke.)

5. 寝る前には**何も食べない方がいい**です。

Neru mae ni wa nani mo **tabenai hoo ga ii** desu.

(It is better not to eat anything before we go to bed.)

17. Change the underlined verbs in the following phrases using the expression "~**ta hoo ga ii**" or "~**nai hoo ga ii**" according to the examples.

Ex.   急ぎます。 → 急いだ方がいいです。

Isogimasu.   →   Isoida hoo ga ii desu.

遅くまでテレビを見ません。 → 見ない方がいいです。

Osoku made terebi wo mimasen. → <u>Minai hoo ga ii desu</u>.

1. 先生に質問<u>します</u>。 _____

Sensei ni shitsumon <u>shimasu</u>. _____

2. 静かに<u>話します</u>。 _____

Shizuka ni <u>hanashimasu</u>. _____

3. クラスを<u>休みません</u>。 _____

Kurasu wo <u>yasumimasen</u>. _____

4. この川で<u>泳ぎません</u>。 _____

Kono kawa de <u>oyogimasen</u>. _____

5. レポートを<u>書き始めます</u>。 _____

Repooto (report) wo <u>kaki-hajimemasu</u>. _____

6. あまりたくさん<u>買いません</u>。 _____

Amari takusan <u>kaimasen</u>. _____

7. 友達にお金を<u>返します</u>。 _____

Tomodachi ni o-kane wo <u>kaeshimasu</u>. _____

Review

18. Give personal answers to the following questions.

1. 中国語とヘブライ語とどちらの方が難しいと思いますか。

Chuugoku-go to heburai-go (Hebrew) to dochira no hoo ga muzukashii to omoimasu ka?

A: _____.

2. 果物の中で何が一番好きですか。

Kudamono (fruites) no naka de nani ga ichiban suki desu ka.

A: _____.

3. テニスとゴルフとどちらの方が面白いですか。

Tenisu to gorufu to dochira no hoo ga omoshiroi desu ka.

A: _____.

4. 世界のどこに一番行きたいですか。

Sekai no doko ni ichiban ikitai desu ka.

A: _____.

5. マックとピーシィーとどちらが使いやすいですか。

Makku (Mac) to PC to dochira ga tsukai-yasui desu ka.

A: _____.

6. ご家族の中でだれが一番せが高いですか。

Go-kazoku no naka de dare ga ichiban se ga takai desu ka.

A: _____.

19. Complete the following sentences by writing the number from the left-hand phrase in the appropriate blank on the right.

1. 田中さんは人は皆同じだ   _____ 友達と会うひまがない。

   Tanaka-san wa hito wa mina onaji da   _____ tomodachi to au hima ga nai.

2. とても寒くなったから、   _____ と思います。

   Totemo samuku nattta kara,   _____ to omoimasu.

3. 日本語を習い始めた時は   _____ 雪が降るかもしれません。

   Nihon-go wo narai-hajimeta toki wa   _____ yuki ga furu kamo shiremasen.

4. 忙しくて   _____ と考えています。

   Isogashiku te   _____ to kangaete imasu.

Ex.5. 子供が病気なので、   _____ ひらがなしか書けませんでした。

Ex.5. Kodomo ga byooki na node,   _____ hiragana shika kakemasen deshita.

  6. 医者に毎日ビタミンを飲む   _____ように頼んでみます。

     Isha ni mainichi bitamin wo nomu   _____ yoo ni tanonde mimasu.

  7. 宿題をしないで   _____ように言われました。

     Shukudai wo shinaide   _____ yoo ni iwaremashita

  8. ミラノはきれいな町だ   _____ 会社に遅れてしまいました。

    Mirano wa kirei na machi da   _____ kaisha ni okurete shimaimashita.

9. 今朝は寝すぎて
   Kesa wa nesugite

10. ルームメイトにラジオの音を大きくしない
    Ruumu-meeto ni rajio no oto wo ookiku shinai

5. 今日は早く帰ります。
5. kyoo wa hayaku kaerimasu.

_____ 学校へ行きました。
_____ gakkoo e ikimashita

20. Give the Japanese equivalent to the following English sentences.

1. Our friend has gone back to Canada without saying good-bye to us.
2. Those shoes look nice (good), but they are too big for me.
3. Mr. Noro is the latest to arrive at the office (comes to the office the latest) every day.
4. Please tell Emiko to talk about Kyoto in class on Monday.
5. If one does exercise (sports) without eating sweets, one may become thin.
6. Which do you prefer, to live in a city or to live in the country?

21. Complete the following sentences by filling in the blanks with the proper form of one of the verbs given below.

飲む(nomu)、聞く(kiku)、見せる(miseru)、食べる(taberu)、かける(kakeru)、洗う(arau)、
出る(deru)、会う(au)、なおす(naosu)、書く(kaku)、捨てる(suteru: _throw away_)

Ex. こんな変な料理は<u>食べた</u>ことがありません。

Konna henna ryoori wa <u>tabeta</u> koto ga arimasen.

1. 家でＣＤを_____り手紙を_____りするつもりです。
   Uchi de CD wo _____ri tegami wo _____ri suru tsumori desu.

2. 古くなった薬は_____方がいいですよ。
   Furuku natta kusuri wa _____ hoo ga ii desu yo.

3. これはアダルトビデオだから、子供に_____はいけません。
   Kore wa adaruto (adult) bideo da kara, kodomo ni _____ ikemasen.

4. 明日の朝はクラスがないので、早く家を_____もいい。
   Ashita no asa wa kurasu ga nai node, hayaku uchi wo _____mo ii.

5. 小川さんには_____ことがないので、よく知りません。
   Ogawa-san ni wa _____ koto ga nai node, yoku shirimasen.

6. 野菜は料理する前によく_____はいけませんよ。
   Yasai wa ryoori-suru mae ni yoku _____wa ikemasen yo.

7. 子供の時よく両親に知らない人と_____はいけないと言われました。
   Kodomo no toki yoku ryooshin ni shiranai hito to _____wa ikenai to iwaremashita.

8. この雑誌は古いから、_____もいいですよ。
   Kono zasshi wa furui kara, _____ mo ii desu yo.

22. Translate the following English sentences into Japanese.

    1. I have never sung songs at a karaoke bar.

    2. I have to give the ticket to my little sister.

    3. It is better to close the window.

    4. I do not have to bring the homework tomorrow.

    5. The Japanese class is sometimes big and sometimes small.

    6. I talked with my friend while having tea, eating lunch, and so on.

    7. You had better not go out all alone late at night.

    8. If you do not have a car, you may use mine.

Answers to Exercises

Chapter 1

1.　1. 母じゃない (haha ja nai)

　　2. 火曜日でした (ka-yoobi deshita)

　　3. 日本人じゃありませんでした (nihon-jin ja arimasen deshita)

　　4. 大きいビルで (ookii biru de)

　　5. 田中さんじゃありません (Tanaka-san ja arimasen)

　　6. 魚だった (sakana datta)

　　7. イタリアの映画じゃなかった (Itaria no eiga ja nakatta)

2.　1. です (desu)

　　2. じゃありません (ja arimasen)

　　3. でした (deshita)、です (desu)

　　4. で (de)

　　5. です (desu)

　　6. です (desu)

　　7. じゃありませんでした (ja arimasen deshita)

　　8. で (de)

　　9. です (desu)

Chapter 2

1.　1. 大きくない (ookiku nai)

　　2. 暑くなかったです (atsuku nakatta desu)

　　3. きれいじゃなかった (kirei ja nakatta)

　　4. 若くなかった (wakaku nakatta)

　　5. 簡単じゃない (kantan ja nai)

　　6. 好きじゃありませんでした (suki ja arimasen deshita)

　　7. 寒くない (samuku nai)

　　8. 上手じゃありません (joozu ja arimasen)

　　9. 高くない (takaku nai)

　　10. 正直じゃありませんでした (shoojiki ja arimasen deshita)

2.　1. 高かったです (takakatta desu)

　　2. よくありません (yoku arimasen)

　　3. 面白くありませんでした (omoshiroku arimasen deshita)

　　4. 上手じゃありません (joozu ja arimasen)

　　5. きれいだった (kirei datta)

3.　1. 高い (takai)

　　2. きれいに (kirei ni)

　　3. 早く (hayaku)

4. 簡単な (kantan na)

5. 長い (nagai)

6. 好きな (suki na)

7. 有名に (yuumei ni)

4. 1. このお茶はとても熱くて飲めません。(Kono ocha wa totemo atsukute nomemasen.)

2. 岡田さんは正直でいい人です。(Okada-san wa shoojiki de ii hito desu.)

3. あのレストランは天ぷらが有名で、いつもこんでいます。(Ano resutoran wa tenpura ga yuumei de, itsumo konde imasu.)

4. きのうは忙しくて友達のパーティーに行けませんでした。(Kinoo wa isogashikute tomodachi no paatii ni ikemasen deshita.)

5. このカメラは安くて使いやすいです。(Kono kamera wa yasukute tsukai-yasui desu.)

5. 1. 話したい (hanashi-tai)

2. 行きやすい (iki-yasui)

3. 帰りにくい (kaeri-nikui)

4. 食べにくくない (tabe-nikuku nai)

5. 来たかった (ki-takatta)

6. 読みやすくない (yomi-yasuku nai)

7. したくなかった (shi-taku nakatta)

8. 見やすくなかった (mi-yasuku nakatta)

9. 使ってほしい/もらいたい (tsukatte hoshii/moraitai)

6. 1. 私は小さいラジオがほしいです。(Watashi wa chiisai rajio ga hoshii desu.)

2. 今晩は酒は飲みたくありません。(Konban wa sake wa nomi-taku arimasen)

3. この漢字は覚えにくいです。(Kono kanji wa oboe-nikui desu.)

4. この間買ったくつははきやすいです。(Kono aida katta kutsu wa haki-yasui desu.)

5. 子供の時、私は警官になりたかったです。(Kodomo no toki, watashi wa keikan ni naritakatta desu.)

6. 日本の母と話したくて、アメリカから電話をかけました。(Nihon no haha to hanashitakute, Amerika kara denwa wo kakemashita.)

7. 1. 寒いです。(samui desu)

2. この安いペンは書きやすいです。(Kono yasui pen wa kaki-yasui desu.)

3. おそい電車 (osoi densha)

4. その男の人は若くなかったです。(Sono otoko no hito wa wakaku nakatta desu.)

5. 私が一番住みたい所 (watashi ga ichiban sumi-tai tokoro)

6. 便利な店 (benri na mise)

7. 敏子さんに家へ来てほしかった/もらいたかった (Toshiko-san ni uchi e kite hoshikatta/morai-takatta)

8. その建物はりっぱでした。(Sono tatemono wa rippa deshita.)

9. 先生の声は聞きにくかったです。(Sensei no koe wa kiki-niku katta desu.)

8. 1. 暑くて (atsukute)

2. 静かで (shizuka de)

3. ほしくて (hoshikute)
4. したくて (shitakute)
5. きれいで (kirei de)
6. はきにくくて (haki-nikukute)

9. 1. 遅く (osoku)
2. 有名な (yuumei na)
3. 難しくなかった (muzukashiku nakatta)
4. 親切な (shinsetsu na)
5. 行きたい (iki-tai)
6. 上手に (joozu ni)
7. よくありません (yoku arimasen)
8. 便利じゃありませんでした (benri ja arimasen deshita)
9. 使いやすい (tsukai-yasui)
10. したくありません (shi-taku arimasen)

Chapter 3

1. 1. まだ (mada)
2. まだ, もう (mada, moo)
3. まだ、もう (mada, moo)
4. もう、まだ (moo, mada)

2. 1. 私はウィスキーはぜんぜん飲みません。 (Watashi wa uisukii wa zenzen nomimasen.)
2. たいてい家で勉強しますが時々図書館でします。 (Taitei uchi de benkyoo shimasu ga, tokidoki toshokan de shimasu.)
3. 今日は天気があまりよくありません。 (Kyoo wa tenki ga amari yoku arimasen.)
4. 毎日この花に水をやっていますが、なかなか咲きません. (Mainichi kono hana ni mizu wo yatte imasu ga, nakanaka sakimasen.)
5. 江口さんは歌がなかなか上手です。 (Eguchi-san wa uta ga nakanaka joozu desu.)

3. 1. あまり (amari)
2. もう (moo)
3. ぜんぜん (zenzen)
4. まだ (mada)
5. 時々 (tokidoki)
6. なかなか (nakanaka)

4. 1. ぜんぜん、まだ (amari, mada)
2. あまり、時々 (amari, tokidoki)
3. なかなか (nakanaka)
4. もう、まだ /ぜんぜん (moo, mada / zenzen)

Chapter 4

1. 1. その (sono)

2. あの (ano)

3. これ (kore), あなたがよく使うの (anata ga yoku tsukau no), ここ (koko)

2. 1. あの (ano)

2. それ (sore), あの (ano)

3. そこ (soko)

4. どんな (donna)

3. 1. この食べ物は何ですか。(Kono tabemono wa nan desu ka),　日本のおかしです。(Nihon no okashi desu.)

2. 日本の銀行につとめてそこで家内に会いました。(Nihon no ginkoo ni tsutomete soko de kanai ni aimashita.)

3. どんな車がほしいですか。(Donna kuruma ga hoshii desu ka),　清水さんが小さくて赤いのを持っていますね。(Shimizu-san ga chiisakute akai no wo motte imasu ne.) あんなの/車がほしいです。(Anna no/kuruma ga hoshii desu.)

Chapter 5

1. 1. ni-juu-yon

2. hachi-juu-kyuu

3. hyaku-kyuu-juu-hachi

4. san-byaku-go-juu-roku

5. hap-pyaku-hachi-juu-ichi

6. rop-pyaku-san-juu

7. kyuu-sen-san

8. ichi-man-san-zen-ni-hyaku

9. go-man

2. 1. yo-ji jup-pun

2. go-ji juugo-fun

3. ku-ji sanjup-pun

4. hachi-ji gojup-pun

5. shichi-ji yonjuugo-fun

6. ni-ji yonjup-pun

7. ichi-ji go-fun

8. juuni-ji nijup-pun

4. 1. 十本 (jup-pon)

2. 何人 (nan-nin)

3. 二匹 (ni-hiki)

4. 何枚 (nan-mai)

5. 二つ (futa-tsu)、三本 (san-bon)

6. 二十本 (nijup-pon)

7. いくつ (ikutsu)

8. 四枚 (yon-mai)

    9. 三ばい (san-bai)

   10. 一人 (hitori)

5. 1.   san-ji yonjuu go-fun

    2.   ku-ji jup-pun

    3.   roku-gatsu sanjuu-nichi

    4.   ichi-gatsu tsuitachi

    5.   juuichi-gatsu mikka

    6.   roppyaku-juu-mai

    7.   juu-rop-pai

    8.   jup-piki

    9.   nanatsu

   10.   sen-sanbyaku-kyuujuu-ni-nin

   11.   kyuujup-pon

6. 1. 今日は何日ですか。(Kyoo wa nan-nichi desu ka.),　十月十六日、月曜日です。(Juu-gatsu juuroku-nichi, getsu-yoobi desu.)

    2. 今何時ですか。(Ima nan-ji desu ka.),　四時五十分です。(Yo-ji gojup-pun desu.)

    3. ゆうべケーキを三つ食べました。(Yuube keeki wo mittsu tabemashita.)

    4. 四月十一日から九月三十日まで日本にいます。(Shi-gatsu juuichi-nichi kara ku-gatsu san-juu-nichi made Nihon ni imasu.)

    5. 図書館に日本の雑誌が八さつあります。(Toshokan ni Nihon no zasshi ga has-sa tsu arimasu.)

    6. 時計をいくつ持っていますか。(Tokei wo ikutsu motte imasu ka.),　二つしか持っていません。(Futatsu shika motte imasen.)

    7. 昨日ビールを六本飲みました。(Kinoo biiru wo rop-pon nomimashita.)

Chapter 6

1. 1. が (ga)

   2. は (wa)

   3. は (wa)

   4. が (ga)

   5. が (ga)

2.   は(wa)、が(ga)/の(wa)、は(wa)、は(wa)、が(ga)、は(wa)、が(ga)、は(wa)

3. 1. に (ni)

   2. で (de)

   3. に (ni)、を (wo)

   4. で (de)

   5. に (ni)/へ (e)

   6. で (de)

   7. に (ni)

   8. を (wo)

   9. で (de)

10. を (wo)、に (ni)、へ (e)/に (ni)
11. を (wo)、に (ni)
12. で (de)

4. に(ni)、へ(e)/に(ni)、で(de)、を(wo)、に(ni)、へ(e)/に(ni)、に(ni)、に(ni)、を(wo)、で(de)、を(wo)、で(de)、で(de)、に(ni)、を(wo)

5. ね(ne)、か(ka)、よ(yo)、か(ka)、ね(ne)、よ(yo)、ね(ne)、か(ka)、か(ka)、よ(yo)、か(ka)、か(ka)、よ(yo)、ね(ne)、か(ka)、ね(ne)

6. 1. の (no)
   2. も (mo)
   3. と (to)
   4. や (ya)、や (ya)
   5. の (no)
   6. も (mo)
   7. と (to)
   8. と (to)
   9. の (no)
   10. の (no)
   11. と (to)
   12. も (mo)、も (mo)
   13. と (to)

7. の(no)、と(to)、や(ya)、や(ya)、も(mo)、と(to)、の(no)、が(ga)/ の(no)、も(mo)、の(no)、と(to)、と(to)、と(to)

8. 1. までに (made ni)
   2. から (kara)
   3. から (kara)
   4. から (kara)、まで (made)

9. から(kara)、までに(made ni)、まで(made)、から(kara)、まで(made)、までに(made ni)、まで(made)、までに(made ni)

10. 1. ほど (hodo)
   2. しか (shika)
   3. しか (shika)
   4. ほど (hodo)
   5. より (yori)

11. しか(shika)、より(yori)、ほど(hodo)、しか(shika)、だけ(dake)、ほど(hodo)、より(yori)

12. 1. に (ni)、が (ga)

2. を (wo)

3. を (wo)、に (ni)、へ (e)

4. の (no)、か (ka)

5. が (ga)

6. で (de)、の (no)、を (wo)

7. で (de)、が (ga)

8. で (de)

9. を (wo)、と (to)

10. しか (shika)

11. も (mo)、も (mo)

12. ほど (hodo)

13. まで (made)

14. に (ni)、までに (made·ni)

13. は(wa)、に(ni)/へ(e)、に(ni)、に(ni)/へ(e)、を(wo)、を(wo)、を(wo)、を(wo)、は(wa)、や(ya)、、や(ya)、や(ya)、が(ga)、を(wo)、も(mo)、が(ga)/の(no)、が(ga)、しか(shika)、は(wa)、より (yori)、と(to)、の(no)、で(d)、を(wo)、に(ni)、で(de) 、を(wo)、に(ni)、を(wo)、から(kara)、を(wo)、に(ni)、と(to)

Chapter 7

1. 1. 本を借りる時 ID を見せました。(Hon wo kariru toki ID wo misemashita.)

2. 車に乗る時は酒を飲みません。(Kuruma ni noru toki wa sake wo nomimasen.)

3. 先生に会った時質問します。(Sensei ni atta toki shitsumon shimasu.)

4. 日本へ行った時かぶきが見たいです。(Nihon e itta toki kabuki ga mitai desu.)

2. 1. 図書館へ行った時本を借ります。(Toshokan e itta toki hon wo karimasu.)

2. 忙しい時は早く家に帰れません。(Isogashii toki wa hayaku uchi ni kaeremasen.)

3. 家を出る時電話します。(Uchi wo deru toki denwa shimasu.)

4. かばんと靴を買った時クレディットカードを使いました。(Kaban to kutsu wo katta toki kureditto kaado(credit card) wo tsukaimashita.

3. 1. 手紙を書いた後で郵便局へ行きます。(Tegami wo kaita ato de yuubinkyoku e ikimasu.)

2. 日本へ行く前に東京のホテルに予約しておきます。(Nihon e iku mae ni Tookyoo no hoteru ni yoyaku shite okimasu.)

3. ジョギングした後でシャワーをあびます。(Jogingu (jogging) shita ato de shawaa (shower) wo abimasu.)

4. 食事をした後でデザートを食べます。(Shokuji wo shita ato de dezaato wo tabemasu.)

4. 1. 試験の前に漢字を練習します。(Shiken no mae ni kanji wo renshuu shimasu.)

2. 宿題をした後で出かけます。(shukudai wo shita ato de dekakemasu.)

3. 中国へ行く前に友達に電話しました。(Chuugoku e iku mae ni tomodachi ni denwa shimashita.)

4. おふろに入った後で寝るつもりです。(O-furo ni haitta ato de neru tsumori desu.)

5. 1. 飛行機に乗っている間に映画を二つ見ました。(Hikooki ni notte iru aida ni eiga wo futatsu mimashita.)

    2. セールがある間店がこんでいます。(Seeru ga aru aida mise ga konde imasu.)

    3. 日本にいる間に富士山が見たいです。(Nihon ni iru aida ni Fujisan ga mitai desu.)

    4. 学校が休みの間ジムは閉まっています。(Gakkoo ga yasumi no aida jimu (gym) wa shimatte imasu.)

6. 1. セールがある間にコートが買いたいです。(Seeru ga aru aida ni kooto (coat) ga

       kai-tai desu.)

    2. 冬の間このビーチは静かです。(Fuyu no aida kono biichi(beach) wa shizuka desu.)

    3. 父は私が寝ている間に家を出ました。(Chichi wa watashi ga nete iru aida ni uchi wo demashita.)

7. 1. 部屋がきたないからそうじをしてください。(Heya ga kitanai kara sooji wo shite kudasai.)

    2. 時間がないから急いでください。(Jikan ga nai kara isoide kudasai.)

    3. みんなが勉強しているから静かに話しましょう。(Minna ga benkyoo shite iru kara shizuka ni

       hanashimashoo.)

    4. 試験が終わったから遊びに行きたいです。(Shiken ga owatta kara asobi ni ikitai desu.)

8. 1. 両親が来るから出かけられません。(Ryooshin ga kuru kara dekakeraremasen.)

    2. あなたの誕生日だからパーテイをしましょう。(Anata no tanjoobi da kara paatii (party) wo

       shimashoo.

    3. 安くて速いからいつも地下鉄に乗ります。(Yasukute hayai kara itsumo chikatetsu ni norimasu.)

    4. 新しいコンピューターを買ったからお金がありません。(Atarashii konpyuutaa (computer) wo

       katta kara o-kane ga arimasen.)

9. 1. 宿題を忘れたので先生にしかられました (Shukudai wo wasureta node sensei ni

       shikararemashita.)

    2. 歌が嫌いなのにカラオケで歌わされました。(Uta ga kirai na noni karaoke de utawasaremashita.)

    3. この寺は有名なのでだれでも知っています。(Kono tera wa yuumei na node dare demo shitte

       imasu.)

    4. 古いアパートなのに家ちんが高いです。(Furui apaato na noni yachin ga takai desu.)

    5. 勉強しなかったのに試験はやさしかったです。(Benkyoo shinakatta noni shiken wa yasashikatta

       desu.)

10. 1. 吸いながら (suinagara)

    2. 飲みながら (nominagara)

    3. 歌いながら (utainagara)

    4. 食べながら (tabenagara)

11. 1. 手紙を書きながら昼ご飯を食べました。(Tegami wo kakinagara hiru-gohan wo tabemashita.)

    2. ラジオを聞きながら晩ご飯を作りました。(Rajio wo kikinagara ban-gohan wo tsukurimashita.)

    3. 先生はクラスでいつも歩きながら教えます。(Sensei wa kurasu de itsmo arukinagara oshiemasu.)

12. 1. 七時半までに (shichiji-han made ni)

    2. 暗くなるまで (kuraku naru made)

    3. ニュースを聞くまで (nyuusu wo kiku made)

    4. 休みが終わるまでに (yasumi ga owaru made ni)

    5. 三十才までに (sanjus-sai made ni)

    6. 家を出るまでに (uchi wo deru made ni)

13. 1. テレビを見ながら (terebi wo minagara)

    2. あなたの家へ行く前に (anata no uchi e iku mae ni)

    3. 電車に乗っている間に (densha ni notte iru aida ni)

    4. 病気の間 (byooki no aida)

    5. 手紙を書いている時 (tegami wo kaite iru toki)

    6. テニスをした後で (tenisu wo shita ato de)

    7. 元気に/よくなるまで (genki ni/yoku naru made)

    8. 日本人なのに (nihon-jin na noni)

    9. 明日は母の誕生日なので/だから (ashita wa haha no tanjoobi na node/da kara)

   10. お金がないから (o-kane ga nai kara)

14. 1. 音楽を聞き (ongaku wo kiki)

    2. 部屋のそうじをする (heya no sooji wo suru)

    3. 部屋のそうじをした (heya no sooji wo shita)

    4. 地下鉄に乗っている (chikatetsu ni notte iru)

    5. 佐々木さんと会議をしている (Sasaki-san to kaigi wo shite iru)

    6. きっさ店に行った (kissa-ten ni itta)

    7. 会社を出た (kaisha wo deta)

    8. 家に帰る (uchi ni kaeru)

Chapter 8

1. 1. aruku, aruita, arukanai, arukanakatta

    2. shinu, shinda, shinanai, shinanakatta

    3. nomu, nonda, nomanai, nomanakatta

    4. kaku, kaita, kakanai, kakanakatta

    5. kaeru, kaetta, kaeranai, kaeranakatta

    6. asobu, asonda, asobanai, asobanakatta

    7. tatsu, tatta, tatanai, tatanakatta

    8. hajimeru, hajimeta, hajimenai, hajimenakatta

    9. suru, shita, shinai, shinakatta

   10. suu, sutta, suwanai, suwanakatta

2. 1. moraimasu

    2. kikimasu

    3. machimasu

    4. hanashimasu

    5. tsukurimasu

    6. demasu

    7. agemasu

3. 1. に、が、あります (ni, ga, arimasu), ありません(arimasen)

  2. に、が、います (ni, ga, imasu)

  3. は、に、あります(wa, ni, arimasu)

  4. に、が、います(ni, ga, imasu)

  5. は、に、いました(wa, ni, imashita)

4. 1. 起きます、飲みます、読みます (okimasu, nomimasu, yomimasu)

  2. 行きませんでした、いました (ikimasen deshita, imashita)

  3. あげました (agemashita)

  4. 分かります (wakarimasu)

  5. 聞こえません (kikoemasen)

  6. 買いました (kaimashita)

  7. 降ります (furimasu)

  8. 来る (kuru)

5. 1. 漢字が書けます。(Kanji ga kakemasu.)

  2. 日本へ行けます。(Nihon e ikemasu.)

  3. 日本語で電話がかけられません。(Nihon-go de denwa ga kakeraremasen.)

  4. 明日九時までに来られません。(Ashita ku-ji made ni koraremasen.)

  5. ドイツ語が少し話せます。(Doitsu-go ga sukoshi hanasemasu.)

  6. 朝早く起きられません。(Asa hayaku okiraremasen.)

6. 1. 先生にお手紙をいただきました。(sensei ni o-tegami wo itadakimashita.)
     私にお手紙をくださいました。(watashi ni o-tegami wo kudasaimashita.)

  2. 友達に雑誌をあげました。(tomodachi ni zasshi wo agemashita.)

  3. 敬子さんに時計をあげました。(Keiko-san ni tokei wo agemashita.)
     幸司さんに時計をもらいました。(Kooji-san ni tokei wo moraimashita.)

  4. 両親にお金をもらいました。(ryooshin ni o-kane wo moraimashita.)
     私にお金をくれました。(watashi ni o-kane wo kuremashita.)

7. 1. 頭が痛くなりました。(Atama ga itaku narimashita.)

  2. スミスさんは医者になりました。(Sumisu-san wa isha ni narimashita.)

  3. この部屋はむし暑くなりました。(Kono heya wa mushi-atsuku narimashita.)

  4. この頃ひまになりました。(Kono goro hima ni narimashita.)

  5. 弟はテニスが上手になりました。(Otooto wa tenisu ga joozu ni narimashita.)

  6. 私は肉が嫌いになりました。(Watashi wa niku ga kirai ni narimashita.)

8. 1. します、します (shimasu, shimasu)

  2. なった (natta)

  3. しました (shimashita)

  4. します (shimasu)

  5. なりました (narimashita)

9. 1. nomareru

  2. nusumareru

   3. shiraberareru

   4. warawareru

   5. tatakareru

   6. hanasareru

10. 1. 私はみんなに笑われました。(Watashi wa minna ni warawaremashita.)

    2. 私はねこに魚を食べられました。(Watashi wa neko ni sakana wo taberaremashita.)

    3. 私はだれかに部屋に入られました。(Watashi wa dareka ni heya ni hairaremashita.)

    4. 私は母にしかられました。(Watashi wa haha ni shikararemashita.)

    5. 私は先生に質問されました。(Watashi wa sensei ni shitsumon saremashita.)

    6. 私は警官に住所を聞かれました。(Watashi wa keikan ni juusho wo kikaremashita.)

11. 1. mataseru

    2. motte-kosaseru

    3. oboesaseru

    4. tetsudawaseru

    5. kangaesaseru

    6. kakaseru

    7. renshuu-saseru

    8. hanasaseru

12. 1. 先生は学生に漢字を覚えさせます。(Sensei wa gakusei ni kanji wo oboesasemasu.)

    2. 母は妹に薬を飲ませました。(Haha wa imooto ni kusuri wo nomasemashita.)

    3. 私は両親を心配させました。(Watashi wa ryooshin wo　shinpai sasemashita.)

    4. 先生は学生に何度もテープを聞かせます。(Sensei wa gakusei ni nando mo teepu wo kikasemasu.)

13. 1. 部屋にとまらせてあげた　(heya ni tomarasete ageta)

    2. 今日早く帰らせてくれた/くださった　(kyoo hayaku kaerasete kureta/kudasatta)

    3. 昨日クラスを休ませてもらった/いただいた　(kinoo kurasu wo yasumasete moratta/itadaita)

    4. ノートをコピーさせてあげた, ノートをコピーさせてもらった(nooto wo kopii sasete ageta),(nooto wo kopii sasete moratta)

14. 1. kakaseru, kakaserareru

    2. shirabesaseru, shirabesaserareru

    3. oboesaseru, oboesaserareru

    4. kosaseru, kosaserareru

    5. kawaseru, kawaserareru

    6. mataseru, mataserareru

    7. saseru, saserareru

15. 1. 母に野菜を食べさせられました。(Haha ni yasai wo tabesaseraremashita.)

    2. 友達に待たせられました。(Tomodachi ni mataseraremashita.)

    3. 医者に酒をやめさせられました。(Isha ni sake wo yamesaseraremashita.)

    4. 母にピアノを練習させられます。(Haha ni piano wo renshuu saseraremasu.)

16.   1. notte
        2. nonde
        3. mite
        4. motte
        5. oshiete
        6. kashite
        7. tetsudatte
        8. shimete
        9. nuide

17.   1. 図書館へ行って本を借ります。(Toshokan e itte hon wo karimasu.)
        2. ジムで泳いで家に帰ります。(Jimu de oyoide uchi ni kaerimasu.)
        3. 薬を飲んで寝ました。(Kusuri wo nonde nemashita.)
        4. ご飯はんを作って食べました。(Gohan wo tsukutte tabemashita.)
        5. 酒をやめて運動を始めます。(Sake wo yamete undoo wo hajimemasu.)

18.   1. 太って服が着られません。(Futotte fuku ga kiraremasen.)
        2. 靴が古くなってはけません。(Kutsu ga furuku natte hakemasen.)
        3. 雨がやんで空が明るくなりました。(Ame ga yande sora ga akaruku narimashita.)
        4. 夏休みが始まって嬉しいです。(Natsu-yasumi ga hajimatte ureshii desu.)
        5. ねこが死んでさびしくなりました。(Neko ga shinde sabishiku narimashita.)

19.   1. よく考えてください。(Yoku kangaete kudasai.)
        2. 静かに話してください。(Shizuka ni hanashite kudasai.)
        3. 窓を開けてください。(Mado wo akete kudasai.)
        4. ドアを閉めてください。(Doa wo shimete kudasai.)
        5. ミルクを買ってきてください。(Miruku wo katte kite kudasai.)
        6. 本屋へ行って辞書を買ってください。(Hon-ya e itte jisho wo katte kudasai.)

20.   1. しています (shite imasu)
        2. 作っています (tsukutte imasu)
        3. 聞いています (kiite imasu)
        4. 話しています (hanashite imasu)
        5. 飲んでいます (nonde imasu)
        6. 書いています (kaite imasu)

21.   1. 作っておきます (tsukutte okimasu)
        2. はいてみました (haite mimashita)
        3. 読んでみます (yonde mimasu)
        4. 使ってしまいました (tsukatte shimaimashita)
        5. 買っておきます (katte okimasu)

22.   1. いいかばんを買ってくれました。(Ii kaban wo katte kuremashita.)
          いいかばんを買ってもらいました。(Ii kaban wo katte moraimashita.)

2. いいアルバイトを見つけてあげました。(Ii arubaito wo mitsukete agemashita.)

3. 有名な寺に連れて行ってくれました。(Yuumei na tera ni tsurete itte kuremashita.)
   有名な寺に連れて行ってもらいました。(Yuumei na tera ni tsurete itte moraimashita.)

4. きれいな着物を送ってあげました。(Kirei na kimono wo okutte agemashita.)
   きれいな着物を送ってもらいました。(Kirei na kimono wo okutte moraimashita.)

23.
1. hanasoo
2. yameyoo
3. deyoo
4. kaeroo
5. yasumoo
6. benkyoo shiyoo
7. tsukuroo
8. tsukaoo
9. matoo
10. mitsukeyoo

24.
1. 読もう (yomoo)
2. しよう (shiyoo)
3. あげよう (ageyoo)
4. いよう (iyoo)
5. 買おう (kaoo)
6. 泳ごう (oyogoo)

25.
1. 書いて (kaite)
2. 飲んで (nonde)
3. 会おう (aoo)
4. 見えます (miemasu)
5. 住んでいます (sunde imasu)
6. 買えません (kaemasen)
7. 降って (futte)
8. 話せます (hanasemasu)
9. 知っています (shitte imasu)
10. あります (arimasu)
11. 飲まれました (nomaremashita)
12. なろう (naroo)
13. ことにした (koto ni shita)
14. おきます (okimasu)
15. しました (shimashita)
16. みました (mimashita)
17. しまいました (shimaimashita)
18. ようになった (yoo ni natta)
19. くれた (kureta)
20. さしあげよう (sashiageyoo)

26.   1. 日本語を教えてもらいました。(nihon-go wo oshiete moraimashita.)

     2. コンサートに連れて行ってあげました。(konsaato ni tsurete itte agemashita.)

     3. 宿題を手伝わせられました。(shukudai wo tetsudawaseraremashita.)

     4. 笑われました。(warawaremashita.)

     5. ミルクを買って来させました。(miruku wo katte kosasemashita.)

     6. 車を使わせてくれました。(kuruma wo tsukawasete kuremashita.)

     7. 心配させられました。(shinpai saseraremashita.)

27.   1. この部屋はうるさくて勉強ができません。(Kono heya wa urusakute benkyoo ga dekimasen.)

     2. 今晩、電話してください。(Konban, denwa shite kudasai.)

     3. よしこさんに何か食べよう、と言いました。(Yoshiko-san ni nani ka tabeyoo, to iimashita.)

     4. 新しい自転車を買うことにしました。(Atarashii jitensha wo kau koto ni shimashita.)

     5. 雨の音が聞こえます。(Ame no oto ga kikoemasu.)

     6. 日本の友達に手紙を書いておきます。(Nihon no tomodachi ni tegami wo kaite okimasu.)

     7. 今のアルバイトをやめようと思っています。(Ima no arubaito wo yameyoo to omotte imasu.)

     8. 新しいレストランへ行ってみましょう。(Atarashii resutoran e itte mimashoo.)

     9. 日本語が少し話せるようになりました。(Nihon-go ga sukoshi hanaseru yoo ni narimashita.)

    10. 今日小さい店は閉まっていますが、大きい店は開いています。(Kyoo chiisai mise wa shimatte imasu ga ooki mise wa aite imasu.)

Chapter 9

1.   1. 天気が悪かったら、出かけたくありません。(Tenki ga warukattara, dekaketaku arimasen.)

     2. 仕事が簡単だったら。早くできます。(Shigoto ga kantan dattara, hayaku dekimasu.)

     3. 家が静かじゃなかったら、図書館で勉強します。(uchi ga shizuka ja nakattara, toshokan de benkyoo shimasu.)

     4. 病気だったら、病院に行った方がいいですよ。(Byooki dattara, byooin ni itta hoo ga ii desu yo.)

2.   1. 一時になったら (ichi-ji ni nattara)

     2. 銀行に行ったら、(ginkoo ni ittara)

     3. 練習しなかったら(renshuu shinakattara)

     4. 友達が来たら (tomodachi ga kitara)

     5. 知っていたら (shitte itara)

     6. 夏休みが始まったら (natsu yasumi ga hajimattara)

3.   1. 明日雨が降れば、テニスはしません。(Ashita ame ga fureba, tenisu wa shimasen.)

     2. 日本へ行けば、日本語が上手になるでしょう。(Nihon e ikeba, nihon-go ga joozu ni naru deshoo.)

     3. はきやすい靴なら（ば）買いたい。(Haki-yasui kutsu nara(ba), kai-tai.)

     4. これが嫌いなら（ば）、食べなくてもいい。(Kore ga kirai nara(ba), tabenakutemo ii.)

     5. 勉強しなければ、試験ができません。(Benkyoo shinakereba, shiken ga dekimasen.)

     6. 夜遅ければ、タクシーで帰ります。(Yoru osokereba, takushii de kaerimasu.)

4.   1. 書かないと漢字を覚えません。(Kakanai to kanji wo oboemasen.)

     2. 十時過ぎだと店は閉まっています。(Juu-ji sugi da to mise wa shimatte imasu.)

     3. 声が小さいとよく聞こえません。(Koe ga chiisai to yoku kikoemasen.

4. めがねをかけるとよく見えます。(Megane wo kakeru to yoku mimemasu.)

5. 1. 起きたら、起きれば、起きると　(okitara, okireba, okiru to)

2. なったら、なれば、なると　(nattara, nareba, naru to)

3. せまかったら、せまければ、せまいと　(semakattara, semakereba, semai to)

4. 終わったら、終われば、終わると　(owattara, owareba, owaru to)

5. なかったら、なければ、ないと　(nakattara, nakereba, nai to)

6. きれいだったら、きれいなら（ば）、きれいだと　(kirei dattara, kirei nara(ba), kirei da to)

6. 1. 夜コーヒーを飲むと眠れません。(Yoru koohii wo nomu to nemuremasen,)

2. 雪がたくさん降れば、スキーに行けます。(Yuki ga takusan fureba, sukii ni ikemasu.)

3. 今日吉田さんに会ったら、この本をあげてください。(Kyoo Yoshida-san ni attara, kono hon wo agete kudasai.)

4. すしを作ったら家に持って行ってあげます。(Sushi wo tsukuttara, uchi ni motte itte agemasu.)

5. 学生じゃないと安い切符は買えません。(Gakusei ja nai to yasui kippu wa kaemasen.)

Chapter 10

1. 1. だれ (dare)、どこ (doko)

2. どう (doo)

3. いくら (ikura)

4. いつ (itsu)

5. 何 (nan)

2. 1. いつか (itsu ka)

2. 何も (nani mo)

3. どれも (dore mo)

4. どこにも (doko ni mo)

5. いつも (itsu mo)

6. どこかに/かへ (doko ka ni/ka e)　どこにも/へも (doko ni mo/e mo)

7. だれか (dare ka)

3. 1. どこで食べても (doko de tabete mo)

2. いくら忙しくても (ikura isogashikute mo)

3. いくら考えても (ikura kangaete mo)

4. だれがやっても (dare ga yatte mo)

4. 1. いつ日本へ行きましたか。(Itsu nihon e ikimashita ka.)

2. だれのかばんですか。(Dare no kaban desu ka.)

3. 山田さんはどこにいますか。(Yamada-san wa doko ni imasu ka.)

4. 何を読んでいるんですか。(Nani wo yonde iru n desu ka.)

5. どうして日本語を習っていますか。(Dooshite nihon-go wo naratte imasu ka.)

6. このくつはいくらでしたか。(Kono kutsu wa ikura deshita ka.)

7. ボストンへ何で行きましたか。(Bosuton e nan de ikimashita ka.)

5. 1. きのうどこかへ行きましたか。(Kinoo doko ka e ikimashita ka.)

いいえ、どこへも行きませんでした。(Iie, doko e mo ikimasen deshita.)

2. ゆうべは何も食べませんでした。(Yuube wa nani mo tabemasen deshita.)

3. どこへ行っても中国のレストランがあります。(Doko e itte mo Chuugoku no resutoran ga arimasu.)

4. フランス語とドイツ語とどちら（の方）が難しいですか。(Furansu-go to doitsu-go to dochira (no hoo) ga muzukashii desu ka.),　どちらも難しいです。(Dochira mo muzukashii desu.)

5. 何か飲みます。(Nani ka nomimasu.)

6. 友達にいつアメリカに帰るか聞きました。(Tomodachi ni itsu Amerika ni kaeru ka kikimashita.)

7. どうして佐藤さんがパーティに来なかったかだれも知りません。(Dooshite Satoo-san ga paatii (*party*) ni konakatta ka dare mo shirimasen)

8. いくら高くても買います。(Ikura takakute mo kaimasu.)

Chapter 11

1. 1. 去年私が/の見た映画 (kyonen watashi ga/no mita eiga)

2. 私が/のよく行く公園 (watashi ga/no yoku iku kooen)

3. 私の机の上にあった新聞 (watashi no tsukue no ue ni atta shinbun)

4. 私の友達が図書館で借りた本 (watashi no tomodachi ga toshokan de karita hon)

5. 日本語を教えている先生 (nihon-go wo oshiete iru sensei)

2. 1. 人 (hito)、　きのう学校で会った (kinoo gakkoo de atta)

2. 時計 (tokei)、父にもらった (chichi ni moratta)

3. もの (mono)、リーさんが日本で買った (Rii-san ga nihon de katta)

4. 事 (koto)、先生の言った (sensei no itta)

5. 声 (koe)、子供の話す (kodomo no hanasu)

6. 辞書 (jisho)、兄がくれた (ani ga kureta)

3. 1. 昨日まりさんが/の行ったデパートはとても大きいです。(Kinoo Mari-san ga/no itta depaato wa totemo ookii desu.)

2. 東京でI.B.M.につとめている鈴木さんに会いました。(Tokyoo de I.B.M. ni tsutomete iru Suzuki-san ni aimashita.)

3. 先週山田さんが/の書いたおもしろい本を読みました。(Senshuu Yamada-san ga/no kaita omoshiroi hon wo yomimashita.)

4. ポールさんが/の作るケーキはいつもおいしいです。(Pooru-san ga/no tsukuru keeki wa itsumo oishii desu.)

5. 野中さんが/の先月買ったアパートを見に行きました。(Nonaka-san ga/no sengetsu katta apaato wo mi ni ikimashita.)

6. 車のかぎを取りに行ったエリックさんを待っています。(Kuruma no kagi wo tori ni itta Erikku-san wo matte imasu.)

4. 1. きのう買った本を見せてください。(Kinoo katta hon wo misete kudasai.)

2. これはあなたが/の見たかったビデオですか。(Kore wa anata ga/no mitakatta bideo desu ka.)

3. 兄が/のくれたコンピューターを使っています。(Ani ga/no kureta konpyuutaa wo tsukatte imasu.)

4. 富田さんはお父さんが社長だった会社に勤めています。(Tomita-san wa otoo-san ga shachoo datta

kaisha ni tsutomete imasu.)

5. かずおさんは妹さんが/の運転する車でボストンに行きます。(Kazuo-san wa imooto-san ga/no unten-suru kuruma de Bosuton ni ikimasu.)

6. 私は母が/の作るアップルパイが一番おいしいと思います。(Watashi wa haha ga/no tsukuru appuru-pai ga ichiban oishii to omoimasu.)

7. この手紙を私に送った人を知っていますか。(Kono tegami wo watashi ni okutta hito wo shitte imasu ka.)

Chapter 12

1. 1. の (no)

2. こと (koto)

3. の (no)

4. こと (koto)

5. こと (koto)

6. の (no)

2. 1. 人の前で歌を歌うことができますか。(Hito no mae de uta wo utau koto ga dekimasu ka.)

2. 9月に休みをとることにしました。(Ku-gatsu ni yasumi wo toru koto ni shimashita.)

3. ケイトはいつもお母さんがばんごはんを作るのを手伝います。(Keito wa itsumo okaa-san ga ban-gohan wo tsukuru no wo tetsudaimasu.)

4. 大きいまちは住むのに便利です。(Ookii machi wa sumu no ni benri desu.)

5. 私は大きいパーティーに行くのはあまり好きじゃありません。(Watashi wa ookii paatii ni iku no wa amari suki ja arimasen.)

6. 私は来週から東京銀行で働くことになりました。(Watashi wa raishuu kara Tookyoo Ginkoo de hataraku koto ni narimashita.)

7. ボストンの地下鉄に乗るのにはトークンがいります。(Bosuton no chikatetsu ni noru no ni wa tookun ga irimasu.)

Chapter 13

1. 1. つもり (tsumori)

2. はず (hazu)

3. つもり (tsumori)

4. つもり (tsumori)

5. はず (hazu)

2. 1. 帰るようです(kaeru yoo desu)、帰るみたいです (kaeru mitai desu)

2. 大きいようです (ookii yoo desu)、大きいみたいです (ookii mitai desu)

3. 話すようです (hanasu yoo desu)、話すみたいです (hanasu mitai desu)

4. 正直なようです (syoojiki na yoo desu)、正直みたいです (shoojiki mitai desu)

5. アメリカ人のようです (amerika-jin no yoo desu)、アメリカ人みたいです (america-jin mitai desu)

6. 安いようです (yasui yoo desu)、安いみたいです (yasui mitai desu)

7. 医者のようです (isha no yoo desu)、医者みたいです (isha mitai desu)

8. 好きなようです (suki na yoo desu)、好きみたいです(suki mitai desu)

3. 1. 日本人のように (nihon-jin no yoo ni)

2. 春のよう (haru no yoo)

3. 春らしい日 (haru rahsii hi)

4. 結婚するらしい (kekkon-suru rashii)

5. 頭が痛いよう (atama ga itai yoo)

4. 1. 来るそうです (kuru soo desu)

2. 泣きそうです (naki soo desu)

3. 高かったそうです (takakatta soo desu)

4. 難しそうです (muzukashi soo desu)

5. 静かだそうです (shizuka da soo desu)

6. 便利そうです (benri soo desu)

5. 1. どうしてすしを食べないんですか。(Dooshite sushi wo tabenai n' desu ka.)

魚が好きじゃないんです。(Sakana ga suki ja nai n' desu.)

2. コンサートの切符を二枚持っているんですが、一緒に行きませんか。(Konsaato no kippu wo ni-mai motte iru n' desu ga, issho ni ikimasen ka.)

3. この洋服は高かったんですが、とても好きだったから買いました。(Kono yoofuku wa takakatta n' desu ga, suki datta kara kaimashita.)

4. どこにいたんですか。探していたんですよ。(Doko ni ita n' desu ka. Sagashite ita n' desu yo.)

6. 5, 4, 1, 6, 3, 2

7. 1. 清は十五才だから、車は運転できないはずです。(Kiyoshi wa juugo-sai da kara, kuruma wa unten dekinai hazu desu.)

2. このビニールは皮のようです。(Kono biniiru wa kawa no you desu.)

3. この桃はおいしそうです。買いましょう。(Kono momo wa oishi soo desu. Kaimashoo.)

4. ベートーベンのソナタはクラシックらしい音楽ですね。(Beetooben no sonata wa kurashikku rashii ongaku desu ne.)

5. 私は英語を勉強するつもりでアメリカに来ました。(Watashi wa eigo wo benkyoo-suru tsumori de Amerika ni kimashita.)

6. 太郎は子供ですが、大人のように話します。(Taroo wa kodomo desu ga, otona no yoo ni hanashimasu.)

7. 父は今日東京から来るはずです。(Chichi wa kyoo Tookyoo kara kuru hazu desu.)

8. 竹田さんはもうすぐ大阪に帰るそうです。(Takeda-san wa moo sugu Oosaka ni kaeru soo desu.)

Chapter 14

1. 1. めしあがります (meshiagarimasu)

2. ごらんになる (goran ni naru)

3. なさいます (nasaimasu)

4. いらっしゃった (irasshatta)

5. いらっしゃる (irassharu)

6. くださいました (kudasaimashita)

7. おっしゃった (osshatta)

8. ご存知です (gozonji desu)

2. 1. いただきます (itadakimasu)
2. そうでございます (soo de gozaimasu)
3. 拝見しませんでした (haiken shimasen deshita)
4. さしあげます (sashiagemasu)
5. 存じております (zonjite orimasu)

3. 1. お読みになります (o-yomi ni narimasu)
2. お持ちします (o-mochi shimasu)
3. お買いになる (o-kai ni naru)
4. お聞きになります (o-kiki ni narimasu)
5. お送りした (o-okurishita)

4. 1. 住んでいらっしゃいます (sunde irasshaimasu)/お住みになっています (o-sumi ni natte imasu)
2. ご両親 (go-ryooshin)、お話しました (o-hanashi shimashita)
3. お描きになった (o-kaki ni natta)、拝見しました (haiken shimashita)
4. ご旅行 (go-ryokoo)、お疲れになりました (o-tsukare ni narimashita)
5. お忙しい (o-isogashii)、お帰りになりません (o-kaeri ni narimasen)

5. 1. いらっしゃる (irassharu)
2. ごらんになった (goran ni natta)
3. なさいます (nasaimasu)
4. 奥さん (oku-san)
5. おやさしい (o-yasashii)
6. ご両親 (go-ryoushin)
7. ご存知でした (go-zonji deshita)
8. 買ってくださる (katte kudasaru)
9. ごりっぱだ (go-rippa da)
10. 召し上がる (meshiagaru)/お飲みになる (o-nomi ni naru)

6. 1. 奥さんは今お電話をなさっています。(Okusan wa ima o-denwa wo nasatte imasu.)
2. 先生のお子さんはギターがお上手ですね。(Sensei no okosan wa gitaa ga ojoozu desu ne.)
3. 小野さんのご主人にお会いしました。(Ono-san no go-shujin ni o-ai shimashita.)
4. テーラー先生に英語のレポートを見ていただきます。(Teeraa sensei ni eigo no repooto wo mite itadakimasu.)
5. 福島さんのお若い時のお写真を拝見したいですね。(Fukushima-san no o-wakai toki no o-shashin wo haiken shitai desu ne.)
6. 星野さんのお父さんが日本の地図をくださるとおっしゃいました。(Hoshino-san no otoo-san ga chizu wo kudasaru to osshaimashita.)

7. 私は３年前に空手の先生にお会いしました。(Watashi wa san-nen mae ni karate no sensei ni o-ai shimashita.)
先生は四十五才でいらっしゃいますが、お若いときに空手をお始めになりました。(Sensei wa yonjuu-go-sai de irasshaimasu ga, o-wakai toki ni karate wo o-hajime ni narimashita.)
奥さんと三人のお子さんと一緒に名古屋に住んでいらっしゃいます。(Oku-san to san-nin no o-ko-san to

issho ni Nagoya ni sunde irasshaimasu.)

ご両親もお近くに住んでいらしゃいます。(Go-ryooshin mo o-chikaku ni sunde irasshaimasu.)

先生は毎日朝果物を召し上がります。(Sensei wa mainichi asa kudamono wo meshiagarimasu.)

四時間空手をお教えになって、お昼の後三十分お休みになります。(Yo-jikan karate wo o-oshie ni natte, o-hiru no ato sanju-pun o-yasumi ni narimasu.)

私は時々ジムの掃除をお手伝いします。(Watashi wa tokidoki jimu no sooji wo o-tetsudai-shimasu.)

先生のお話はいつもおもしろいので、うかがうのが好きです。(Sensei no o-hanashi wa itsumo omoshiroi node, ukagau no ga suki desu.)

先生は今空手の本を書いていらっしゃるとうかがいました。(Sensei wa ima karate no hon wo kaite irassharu to ukagaimashita.)

それを拝見したいです。(Sore wo haiken shitai desu.)

Chapter 15

1. 1. アラスカの方がメインより大きいです。(Arasuka no hoo ga Mein yori ookii desu.)

2. アメリカの方が中国より新しいです。(Amerika no hoo ga Chuugoku yori atarashii desu.)

3. アパートは便利な方が大きいのよりいいです。(Apaato wa benri na hoo ga ookii no yori ii desu.)

4. ワインは古い方が新しいのよりおいしいです。(Wain wa furui hoo ga atarashii no yori oishii desu.)

5. 漢字で書くほうがひらがなで書くより難しいです。(Kanji de kaku hoo ga hiragana de kaku yori muzukashii desu.)

2. 1. 一番寒い部屋 (ichiban samui heya)

2. 一番若い人 (ichiban wakai hito)

3. 一番きれいな公園 (ichiban kirei na kooen)

4. 一番(よく)勉強する (ichiban <yoku> benkyou suru)

5. 一番近い (ichiban chikai)

6. 一番おそく話す (ichiban osoku hanasu)

7. 一番買いたい (ichiban kai-tai)

3. 1. 今一番どこに行きたいですか。(Ima ichiban doko ni iki-tai desu ka.)

静かな所に一番行きたいです。(Shizuka na tokoro ni ichiban iki-tai desu.)

2. 友達の中で誰が一番背が高いですか。(Tomodachi no naka de dare ga ichiban se ga takai desu ka.)

中野さんが一番背が高いです。(Nakano-san ga ichiban se ga takai desu.)

3. 金と銀とどちらが安いですか。(Kin to gin to dochira ga yasui desu ka.)

銀の方が(金より)安いです。(Gin no hoo ga <kin yori> yasui desu.)

4. 家族の中で誰が一番テニスが上手ですか。(Kazoku no naka de dare ga ichiban tenisu ga joozu desu ka.)

兄が一番上手です。(Ani ga ichiban joozu desu.)

5. 何をするのが一番好きですか。(Nani wo suru no ga ichiban suki desu ka.)

音楽をきくのが一番好きです。(Ongaku wo kiku no ga ichiban suki desu.)

6. 吉田さんと飯田さんとどちらがよくテニスをしますか。(Yoshida-san to Iida-san to dochira ga yoku tenisu wo shimasu ka.)

吉田さんの方が(飯田さんより)よくテニスをします。(Yoshida-san no hoo ga <Iida-san yori> yoku tenisu wo shimasu.)

7. 本を読むのとテレビを見るのと、どちらがおもしろいですか。(Hon wo yomu no to terebi wo miru no to, dochira ga omoshiroi desu ka.)

本を読む方が(テレビを見るより)、おもしろいです。(Hon wo yomu hoo ga <terebi wo miru yori> omoshiroi desu.)

8. 今、誰に一番会いたいですか。(Ima, dare ni ichiban ai-tai desu ka.)
高校の友達に一番会いたいです。(Kookoo no tomodachi ni ichiban ai-tai desu.)

9. どの飛行機が一番早いですか。(Dono hikooki ga ichiban hayai desu ka.)
コンコルドが一番早いです。(Konkorudo ga ichiban hayai desu.)

10. この町で誰が一番お金持ちですか。(Kono machi de dare ga ichiban o-kanemochi desu ka.)
スミスさんが一番お金持ちです。(Sumisu-san ga ichiban o-kanemochi desu.)

4.
1. 置かないで (okanai de)
2. 読まないで (yomanai de)
3. 使わないで (tsukawanai de)
4. 起きないで (okinai de)
5. 話さないで (hanasanai de)
6. 飛ばないで (tobanai de)
7. 立たないで (tatanai de)
8. 教えないで (oshienai de)
9. 帰らないで (kaeranai de)
10. 泳がないで (oyoganai de)

5.
1. 歩かないで (arukanai de)
2. デパートに行かないで (depaato ni ikanai de)
3. 英語を話さないで (eigo wo hanasanai de)
4. 肉を買わないで (niku wo kawanai de)
5. 辞書を使わないで (jisho wo tukawanai de)

6.
1. 高すぎて (taka-sugi te)
2. 書き終わったら (kaki-owattara)
3. 使い終わったら (tsukai-owattara)
4. 習い始めようと (narai-hajimeyoo to)
5. 運動しすぎて (undoo-shi-sugite)
6. 立派すぎて (rippa-sugite)
7. 歩き始めます (aruki-hajimemasu)

7.
1. 言葉の覚え方 (kotoba no oboe-kata)
2. おいしいすしの作り方 (oishii sushi no tsukuri-kata)
3. 日本語での手紙の書き方 (nihon-go de no tegami no kaki-kata)
4. ボストンからの来方 (Bosuton kara no ki-kata)

8.
1. みつこに十分待つように言いました。(Mitsuko ni jup-pun matsu yoo ni iimashita.)
2. 父は家族は大事だと思っています。(Chichi wa kazoku wa daiji da to omotte imasu.)
3. 岡田さんは砂糖はよくないと信じています。(Okada-san wa satoo wa yoku nai to shinjite imasu.)
4. 私は次郎さんに日本語で手紙を書いてくれるように頼みました。(Watashi wa Jiroo-san ni nihon-go de tegami wo kaite kureru yoo ni tanomimashita.)

5. シカゴのデパートは日曜日に開いていると思いますか。(Shikago no depaato wa nichi-yoobi ni aite iru to omoimasu ka.)

6. 谷さんの奥さんはアメリカで生まれたと言っていました。(Tani-san no okusan wa Amerika de umareta to itte imashita.)

9. 1. 結婚するかもしれません (kekkon suru kamo shiremasen)
    2. 静かかもしれません (shizuka kamo shiremasen)
    3. できなかったかもしれません (dekinakatta kamo shiremasen)
    4. おいしいかもしれません (oishii kamo shiremasen)

10. 1. 映画を見たり友達に会ったりします。(Eiga wo mitari tomodachi ni attari shimasu.)
    2. ジムで泳いだり公園を歩いたりしました。(Jimu(gym) de oyoidari kooen wo aruitari shimasu.)
    3. 図書館で本を借りたり宿題をしたりします。(Toshokan de hon wo karitari shukudai wo shitari shimasu.)
    4. 天気はよかったり悪かったりします。(Tenki wa yokattari warukattari shimasu.)
    5. 部屋は静かだったりうるさかったりします。(Heya wa shizuka dattari urusakattari shimasu.)

11. 1. 英語で話してもいいです。(Eigo de hanashite mo ii desu.)
    2. 辞書を使ってもいいです。(Jisho wo tsukatte mo ii desu.)
    3. おかしを食べてもいいです。(Okashi wo tabete mo ii desu.)
    4. ペンで書いてもいいです。(Pen de kaite mo iidesu.)
    5. エアコンをつけてもいいです。(Eakon wo tsukete mo ii desu.)

12. 1. 仕事を早くしなくてもいいです。(Shigoto wo hayaku shinakute mo ii desu.)
    2. 明日ここに来なくてもいいです。(Ashita koko ni konakute mo ii desu.)
    3. 急がなくてもいいです。(Isoganakute mo ii desu.)
    4. 早く起きなくてもいいです。(Hayaku okinakute mo ii desu.)
    5. 買い物に行かなくてもいいです。(Kaimono ni ikanakute mo ii desu.)
    6. 晩ごはんを作らなくてもいいです。(Ban-gohan wo tsukuranakute mo ii desu.)

13. 1. うそを言ってはいけません。(Uso wo itte wa ikemasen.)
    2. 一日中テレビを見てはいけません。(Ichinichi-juu terebi wo mite wa ikemasen.)
    3. 酒を飲み過ぎてはいけません。(Sake wo nomi-sugite wa ikemasen.)
    4. ここで写真をとってはいけません。(Koko de shashin wo totte wa ikemasen.)
    5. 約束を忘れてはいけません。(Yakusoku wo wasurete wa ikemasen.)
    6. 図書館で話してはいけません。(Toshokan de hanashite wa ikemasen.)

14. 1. 出なくては/ 出なければいけません。(denakute wa/ denakereba ikemasen.)
    2. 着かなくては/ 着かなければいけません。(tsukanakute wa/ tsukanakereba ikemasen.)
    3. 待たなくては/ 待たなければいけません。(matanakute wa /matanakereba ikemasen.)
    4. 話さなくては/ 話さなければいけません。(hanasanakute wa / hanasanakereba ikemasen.)
    5. 考えなくては/ 考えなければいけません。(kangaenakute wa /kangaenakereba ikemasen.)
    6. 見つけなくては/ 見つけなければいけません。(mitsukenakute wa /mitsukenakereba ikemasen.)

15. 1. 早く帰らなくては/ 帰らなければいけませんか。(Hayaku kaeranakute wa / kaeranakereba
　　　ikemasen ka.)
　　　いいえ、早く帰らなくてもいいです。(Iie, hayaku kaeranakute mo ii desu.)

　　2. 日本語で手紙を書かなくては/ 書かなければいけませんか。(Nihon-go de tegami wo kakanakute
　　　wa/ kakanakereba ikemasen ka.)
　　　いいえ、書かなくてもいいです。(Iie, kakanakute mo ii desu.)

　　3. かさを持って行かなくては/ 行かなければいけませんか。(Kasa wo motte ikanakute wa/ ikanakereba
　　　ikemasen ka.)
　　　いいえ、持って行かなくてもいいです。(Iie, motte ikanakute mo ii desu.)

　　4. 一日中家にいなくては/ いなければいけませんか。(Ichinichi-juu uchi ni inakute wa/ inakereba
　　　ikemasen ka.)
　　　いいえ、いなくてもいいです。(Iie, inakute mo ii desu.)

　　5. 今晩出かけなくては/ 出かけなければいけませんか。(Kon-ban dekakenakute wa/ dekakenakereba
　　　ikemasen ka.) いいえ、出かけなくてもいいです。(Iie, dekakenakute mo ii desu.)

　　6. 今このレポートを読まなくては/ 読まなければいけませんか。(Ima kono repooto wo yomanakute wa/
　　　yomanakereba ikemasen ka.)
　　　いいえ、読まなくてもいいです。(Iie, yomanakute mo ii desu.)

16. 1. アサヒビールを飲んだことがあります。(Asahi biiru wo nonda koto ga arimasu.)
　　2. ラテン語を習ったことがあります。(Raten-go(Latin) wo naratta koto ga arimasu.)
　　3. 新幹線に乗ったことがあります。(Shinkansen ni notta koto ga arimasu.)
　　4. 海で泳いだことがあります。(Umi de oyoida koto ga arimasu.)
　　5. 着物を着たことがあります。(Kimono wo kita koto ga arimasu.)
　　6. ゴルフをしたことがあります。(Gorufu wo shita koto ga arimasu.)

7. 1. 先生に質問した方がいいです。(Sensei ni shitsumon shita hoo ga ii desu.)
　　2. 静かに話した方がいいです。(Shizuka ni hanashita hoo ga ii desu.)
　　3. クラスを休まない方がいいです。(Kurasu wo yasumanai hoo ga ii desu.)
　　4. この川で泳がない方がいいです。(Kono kawa de oyoganai hoo ga ii desu.)
　　5. レポートを書き始めた方がいいです。(Repooto wo kaki-hajimeta hoo ga ii desu.)
　　6. あまりたくさん買わない方がいいです。(Amari takusan kawanai hoo ga ii desu.)
　　7. 友達にお金を返した方がいいです。(Tomodachi ni o-kane wo kaeshita hoo ga ii desu.)

18. 1. 中国語（ヘブライ語）の方が、ヘブライ語（中国語）より難しいと思います。 (Chuugoku-go <heburai-
　　　go> no hoo ga , heburaoi-go <chuugoku-go> yori muzukashii to omoimasu.)
　　2. （りんご）が一番好きです。(<Ringo ga> ichiban suki desu.)
　　3. テニス（ゴルフ）の方がゴルフ（テニス）よりおもしろいです。(Tenisu <gorufu> no hoo ga gorufu
　　　<tenisu> yori omoshiroi desu.)
　　4. （タヒチ）に一番行きたいです。(<Tahit>i ni ichiban ikitai desu.)
　　5. マック（ピィーシー）の方がピィーシー（マック）より使いやすいです。(Makku<PC> no hoo ga
　　　PC<makku> yori tsukai yasui desu.)
　　6. （兄）が一番背が高いです。(<Ani> ga ichiban se ga takai desu.)

19. 　4,　8,　2,　1,　3,　10,　6,　9,　(5),　7

20. 1. 友達はさよならと言わないでカナダに帰ってしまいました。(Tomodachi wa sayonara to iwanai de Kanada ni kaette shimaimashita.)

 2. この靴はよさそうですが、私には大きすぎます。(Kono kutsu wa yosa soo desu ga, watashi ni wa ooki-sugimasu.)

 3. 野呂さんは毎日一番遅く会社に来ます。(Noro-san wa mainichi ichiban osoku kaisha ni kimasu.)

 4. えみ子さんに月曜日、クラスで京都について話すように言ってください。(Emiko-san ni getsuyoo-bi, kurasu de Kyooto ni tsuite hanasu yoo ni itte kudasai.)

 5. 甘いものを食べないで運動したら、やせるかもしれません。(Amai mono wo tabenai de undoo-shitara, yaseru kamo shiremasen.)

 6. 町に住むのと田舎に住むのと、どちらがいいですか。(Machi ni sumu no to inaka ni sumu no to, dochira ga ii desu ka.)

21. 1. 聞いた (kiita)、書いた (kaita)
 2. 飲まない (nomanai)
 3. 見せては (misete wa)
 4. 出なくて (denakute)
 5. 会った (atta)
 6. 洗わなくて (arawanakute)
 7. 話して (hanashite)
 8. 捨てて(sutete)

22. 1. カラオケバーで歌ったことはありません。(Karaoke baa (bar) de utatta koto wa arimasen.)
 2. 妹に切符をあげなくてはいけません。(Imooto ni kippu wo agenakute wa ikemsen.)
 3. まどを閉めた方がいいです。(Mado wo shimeta hoo ga ii desu.)
 4. 明日は宿題を持って来なくてもいいです。(Ashita wa shukudai wo motte konakute mo ii desu.)
 5. 日本語のクラスは大きかったり小さかったりします。(Nihon-go no kurasu wa ookikattari chiisakattari shimasu.)
 6. 友達と話しながらお茶を飲んだり昼ご飯を食べたりしました。(Tomodachi to hanashi nagara ocha wo nondari hiru-gohan wo tabetari shimashita.)
 7. 夜遅く一人で出かけない方がいいです。(Yoru osoku hitori de dekakenai hoo ga ii desu.)
 8. 車がなかったら私のを使ってもいいです。(Kuruma ga nakattara watashi no wo tsukatte mo ii desu.)

Index

CPSIA information can be obtained
at www.ICGtesting.com
Printed in the USA
LVHW061316080523
746271LV00004B/7

9 780071 7560